SUPERVISION

Charles M. Ray
Western Kentucky University
Charles L. Eison
Western Kentucky University

SUPERVISION

The Dryden Press
Chicago New York Philadelphia San Francisco Montreal Toronto London Sydney Tokyo
Mexico City Rio de Janeiro Madrid

Acquisitions Editor: Anne E. Smith
Project Editor: Ruta S. Graff
Design Director: Alan Wendt
Managing Editor: Jane Perkins
Production Manager: Mary Jarvis

Text and cover design by Barbara Gibson
Copy editing by Laurette Hupman
Indexing by Holley Goar and Nancy Madison

Address orders to:
383 Madison Avenue
New York, New York 10017

Address editorial correspondence to:
One Salt Creek Lane
Hinsdale, Illinois 60521

Library of Congress Catalog Card Number: 82-72180
ISBN 0-03-054556-0
Printed in the United States of America
345-016-987654321

CBS College Publishing
The Dryden Press
Holt, Rinehart and Winston
Saunders College Publishing

Huseman, Lahiff, and Hatfield
Business Communication:
Strategies and Skills

Huseman, Lahiff, and Hatfield
Readings in Business Communication

Jauch, Coltrin, Bedeian and Glueck
The Managerial Experience:
Cases, Exercises, and Readings, Third Edition

Karmel
Point and Counterpoint in Organizational Behavior

Lee
Introduction to Management Science

Lindauer
Communicating in Business, Second Edition

McFarlan, Nolan, and Norton
Information Systems Administration

Mayerson
Shoptalk: Foundations of Managerial Communication

Miner
Theories of Organizational Behavior

Miner
Theories of Organizational Structure and Process

Paine and Anderson
Strategic Management

Paine and Naumes
Organizational Strategy and Policy:
Text and Cases, Third Edition

Penrose
Applications in Business Communication

Ray and Eison
Supervision

Robinson
International Business Management,
Second Edition

Smith
Management System:
Analysis and Applications

PREFACE

For Those it Was Meant to Serve

This text was developed with a specific population in mind. Our target groups are those first- or second-year associate degree students, the newly-appointed working supervisors, and the employer-identified participants of in-house training programs. Many students in junior colleges, community colleges, associate degree programs in four-year institutions, and post-secondary technical schools are required to take a general course in supervision. Others elect training in this area because they foresee the supervision of others as a part of a technical or professional occupation. **Supervision** *is an effort to provide preparation in areas such as the functions of organizations, communication, personnel management, leadership, motivational factors, employee appraisal, productivity, and career paths for supervisors. These topics relate directly to the general problems of managers at the first level and those areas that contribute to production outcomes in any work setting.*

In addition to the younger student who is working toward a degree, growing numbers of older employees are moving into supervisory jobs and studying supervision in formal courses. These individuals not only seek job advancement, but they are developing their skills to meet a changing social order—one that is demanding greater communication and interpersonal skills. In concert with this trend are the in-house training programs to develop first-level management expertise for persons in larger corporations who have the potential for supervisory jobs. With these three target groups in mind, **Supervision** *has been developed in a simple and direct* *approach, based on organizational research and theory, with implications for applying practical models. We have attempted to keep all three groups in mind as we developed the materials.*

Major Themes

Any text that suggests approaches to solving problems in social systems will have underlying assumptions about how those systems function. We have developed this text on five themes that consistently arise in the literature of business, business education, and organizational psychology. These five themes are:

1. *Organizations (business, government, and other formal institutions) are complex organism-like systems that provide rewards for a wide variety of internal and external participants. In addition, those in control of the system must provide for appropriate reward processes for everyone involved—the employer, the employee, and the consumer. Reinforcement systems (rewards, benefits), therefore, become extremely important to the welfare of the total organization.*

2. *The managers, supervisors included, are the major information processors within any complex system. Therefore, effective communication skills are necessary ingredients for an effective supervisor.*

3. *Organizations in our society are not likely to be static; rather they are buffeted by complex change factors which come from both inside and outside the institution.*

    International instability contributes to the continually changing nature of organizations throughout the world. With a range from countries just entering an industrial state to countries with fully developed production systems, all organizations must provide for planned change to survive.

4. *The underlying value systems of our institutions and organizations are the basic fabric around which all activities revolve. An organization can exist for a short period of time with no value commitment other than the bottom line of profit. However, for that system to survive for an extended period of time, basic value questions must be addressed and the participants must accept basic ethical norms.*

5. *Virtually all of the variables and topics discussed in this text are of such a nature that supervisors can improve their skills in those specific areas. Skill improvement will come from learning*

about the topics, from experimenting with the suggestions, from additional reading, and from practical applications. Supervision is not an art; rather it is a function of learning, trial and success, and hard work. In addition, it requires individual effort to find that middle-ground among theory, research, and experience that works.

With these themes in mind, we hope this text will assist you in three major areas. One is the development of a general understanding of formal organizations and their limitations, structures, functions, and impact upon participants. Another is the development of managerial skills in the areas of interpersonal relationships, reinforcement systems, and leadership. A third is the development of communication skills that will enhance your speaking, writing, observing, and listening so that you can effectively convey information to those within your organizational setting.
Good practice to you!

ACKNOWLEDGMENTS

To Those Who Made it Possible

It goes without saying that without the support and cooperation of our families, this book would be much different if completed at all. For their patience and understanding we can only say thanks. Many projects were postponed because of this endeavor.

Others who stopped to listen and to make suggestions were Jim Craig, Glenn Crumb, Betty Seitz, and Robert Lancaster. Many individuals provided technical assistance: Susan Perkins, Janet McDowell, Janet Gentry, and Pam Lyons. We are especially grateful to Alan Baker for his photographs and to Ralph Bergmann for his illustrations. These business firms cooperated by sharing photographs or allowing us to photograph supervisors and workers in their organizations: The Lord Company, FMC Corporation, American National Bank, Citizens National Bank, Bowling Green Bank and Trust, Speakman Electric, and the Bowling Green Board of Realtors. Reviewers Maryann Albrecht, University of Illinois at Chicago; O. M. Oakland, Henry Ford Community College; Robert L. Trosper, Trosper & Associates; Richard Howe, Orange Coast Community College; Michael Dougherty, Milwaukee Area Technical College; Theresa Bushner, Waukesha County Technical Institute, have provided valuable reactions to the original manuscript.

Finally, a big thank you to the Dryden staff. Although many of them worked behind the scenes, Anne Smith and Ruta Graff deserve special laurels for their patience and cooperation with two fledgling authors.

Charles M. Ray
Charles L. Eison

TABLE OF CONTENTS

CHAPTER 3/SUPERVISORS AS MANAGERS   42

PART TWO/UNDERLYING INFLUENCES ON BEHAVIOR

CHAPTER 4/THE MOTIVATION FACTOR   70

PART THREE/TOOLS OF THE SUPERVISORY TRADE

PART FOUR/PERSONNEL MANAGEMENT FUNCTIONS FOR SUPERVISORS

CHAPTER 11/EMPLOYEE SELECTION 224

CHAPTER 12/EMPLOYEE TRAINING 246

PART ONE

THE NATURE OF SUPERVISION

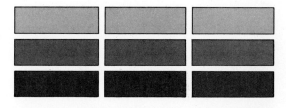

1

INTRODUCTION TO SUPERVISION

VOCABULARY TO MASTER

Supervisor
First-line supervisor
Operative
Entrepreneur
Professional manager
Bureaucrat
Supervisory management
Technical/Professional skill
Interpersonal skill
Managerial/Administrative skill
Ergonomics
Open system
Closed system

LEARNING OBJECTIVES

Upon completion of this chapter and the related assignments, you should be able to:

1. Describe seven possible role dimensions of the supervisor in organizations.
2. Discuss the history of the development of supervision and other professional management areas.
3. Contrast the concept of supervision in private organizations with supervision in other organizations.
4. Enumerate some of the problems faced by supervisors.
5. Identify some of the changes which have taken place and which continue to change the job of the supervisor.

CHAPTER OUTLINE

PROBLEM STATEMENT
WHAT IS SUPERVISION ALL ABOUT, ANYWAY?

BACKGROUND AND THEORY
THE SUPERVISOR DEFINED
    History of Supervision
    Development of Professional Managers

RESEARCH AND PRACTICE
THE ROLE OF SUPERVISION
    Workers' Views of Supervisors' Role
    What Is Supervisory Management, Then?
    Supervision in Different Organizations
        Service and Financial Organizations
        Manufacturing
        Government Agencies
    Physical Environmental Influences
    Supervising Union Employees

IMPLICATIONS AND APPLICATIONS
PREPARING TO SUPERVISE TODAY'S WORKERS
    The Move from Worker to Supervisor
    Supervising within Evolving Organizations
A PREVIEW OF REMAINING CHAPTERS

QUESTIONS FOR FURTHER THOUGHT

WHAT IS SUPERVISION ALL ABOUT, ANYWAY?

Supervision is a vital and unique managerial function in modern organizations. Throughout the free world, organizations depend upon people to make them function. Even with all the modern technology at the disposal of management, the single most important component in any organization is people. This applies to private enterprises, government agencies, public institutions, and professional organizations. People must be supervised. Supervision is a function which has common elements in all organizations, regardless of the nature of the organization or the work being done by its employees. An understanding of these common elements is essential for anyone who works as a supervisor. Such understandings are increasingly critical as line workers make the transition to supervisory positions.

THE SUPERVISOR DEFINED

supervisor manager

The word **supervisor** means different things to different people and can have different applications. Some people consider any superior in a working environment to be a supervisor to all of his or her subordinates. Others think of their immediate superiors as supervisors. As organizations grow, several layers of management develop. To some extent managers at every level are supervisors to the people reporting directly to them. The most popular application of the term *supervisor* is to that first level of supervision—the people to whom the workers report. The term **first-line supervisor** is the most popular descriptor of these managers. *They represent the level of supervision to which this book is directed.* The role of supervision in today's organizations is one of overseer of the group frequently referred to as **operatives**, the workers, those who carry out the basic activities of the organization. Supervisors do not always perform physical, hands-on work. Rather, supervisors direct those who do perform such work. In some organizations one worker in a group may be designated the supervisor, even though that worker continues to carry out physical tasks and, at the same time, oversees the work of others in the group.

first-line supervisor *first level manager, immediately above workers*

operative *worker*

The number of people working in supervisory positions has been influenced by changes in the nature of organizations. Generally speaking, as organizations have become larger and more complex, the need for supervision has increased. In order to maintain control over the work that goes on, work forces are divided

What characteristics are expected in the ideal supervisor?

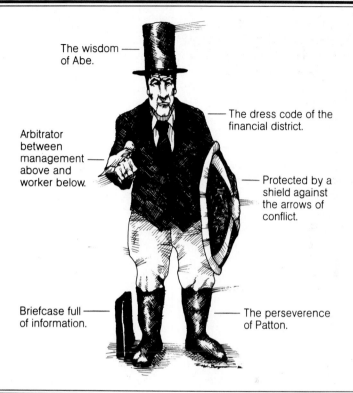

The wisdom of Abe.

The dress code of the financial district.

Arbitrator between management above and worker below.

Protected by a shield against the arrows of conflict.

Briefcase full of information.

The perseverence of Patton.

into groups with a supervisor responsible for each group. Thus, there are more supervisors than ever before.

History of Supervision

Supervision has its origins in the early days of Athens and Rome, but the orientation then was certainly not related to twentieth century views about supervision. The Greeks had slaves, as did the Romans. Loyal employees supervised the slaves, and the system of slavery was considered natural. By the fourth and fifth centuries, a feudal mold was well established where the great lords or land-owners had servants who gave allegiance to such masters in return for food, shelter, and meager wages. In time, the forces of Christianity and the medieval monks pushed forward with a new conceptualization of work. The Benedictine monks "worked out a regular system of work and prayer or meditation. . . . The original idea, though, was sound—to work is to serve God—sound not alone for Luther (who rejected many other doctrines of the Church of Rome), but later for Calvin and Wesley as well."[1]

entrepreneur *owner of private enterprise*

During the industrial revolution, production workers and business establishments were managed by owners. The **entrepreneur** made the decisions and supervised the workers. Entrepreneurs are the owners of enterprises. They risk their time and money, hoping for the reward of profit. Although small entrepreneurships still account for huge numbers of free world business ventures, the bulk of the business and productive activity (by such measures as volume of business or number of employees) is carried out by large businesses.

The factories and mills that developed during the industrial revolution required that specific roles and attributes be met; and because of the large numbers of workers involved in a single enterprise, overseers were required. "The factory system represented in one sense the triumph of the work ethic."[2] People placed in positions of supervision came from the guild system, the apprenticeship system, and trade unions. The role of those supervisors was to ensure production. And production was for production's sake. European commentators such as de Tocqueville and Grund were truly puzzled that in America there was not a class of people which devoted much time to leisure and viewed the whole country as one huge workplace or sweatshop.[3]

Out of these beginnings the productive process demanded control systems, and foremen were forced to provide such control systems. It is also from these primitive but pragmatic beginnings that the supervisor-worker relationship has developed into one of person-to-person interactions. This book is dedicated to the study of supervision. The role of supervision is still changing and people must change with it if they are to remain effective.

Development of Professional Managers

While the task of managing enterprise was growing to the point of requiring professional managers, the task of raising money (capital) for expansion of productive facilities became too great for small organizations. The corporate form of ownership was born.

---

[1] Sebastian deGrazia, *Of Time, Work, and Leisure* (New York: Twentieth-Century Fund, 1962), pp. 44–45.
[2] Daniel T. Rodgers, *The Work Ethic in Industrial America, 1850–1920* (Chicago: University of Chicago Press, 1974), p. xii.
[3] Rodgers, *Work Ethic*, p. xii.

Owners sold shares of stock to others who became part owners. For all areas except agriculture, this shift was clearly evident by the early 1920s. Those who owned large portions of the stock in a company usually controlled the company. But the increase in size brought greater and greater gaps between owner and worker. More levels of management were created and professional managers were hired. Small companies merged to form larger ones, and the levels of management grew even greater. Stockholders became less involved, and the actual direction of companies was placed in the hands of the **professional manager**. Professional managers were educated and trained to be managers. This concept replaced the idea that managers work up from operatives to management. However, some managers still got to their positions via this route. In many cases (and this is still true) influential top managers were also large stockholders in corporations. But their percentage of ownership was usually far less significant than their level of influence. Small and absentee stockholders were willing to give their proxies to corporate officials who elected the boards of directors and controlled the companies.

professional manager
salaried manager

Changes in management are not unique to the private sector. Throughout the history of the Western world, governments have also become more complex and have begun to administer their services and controls through subgroups called agencies. Agencies are subdivided into divisions or bureaus. Thus, the term **bureaucrat**. As in business, the governmental manager has become far removed from the governmental employee.

bureaucrat head of governmental unit

The elite of both business and government have come to be known as the establishment. While few individuals within the establishment have been extremely powerful, collectively this group has determined the direction of many facets of life in the Western world. They have profoundly influenced attitudes toward workers and the workers' attitudes toward their environments. Unfortunately, many of these attitudes and environments have at times been undesirable for workers. Unionization of employees resulted from such conditions, and this accelerated the clear-cut lines of distinction between worker and manager. The two groups were assumed to be economic enemies. Anything that favored one group was assumed to be detrimental for the other group. This was and is not necessarily true. *Currently there is developing a general agreement that situations which create mutual benefit and progress are the most desirable.*

Toffler points out that professional managers, "integraters" as he calls them, have been the real decision makers and movers of things during the life of industrial America.[4] While the owners of business have been blamed for failures in the system, he contends, the real shapers of the working world were the professional managers, administrators, and directors.

RESEARCH AND PRACTICE

THE ROLE OF SUPERVISION

For many years there was no clear-cut distinction between the role of the supervisor and the role of the worker, except that supervisors were loyal and capable workers who could be trusted by those in higher levels of management to share the oversight of work. Their job was to keep the workers on task. They were placed in the position of having to cross the management-labor breach. Experience as a worker was essential to becoming a supervisor. It was assumed that supervisors must have done the work before they could supervise others doing that work.

What do supervisors do? Some research conducted by Dowell and Wexley attempted to identify the primary dimensions of first-line supervisors' jobs. While their findings are slanted toward supervisors in heavy industry, their findings can be used as a foundation for explaining supervisory work of any kind.

Exhibit 1.1 shows the seven dimensions which they found to be basic.

Although these researchers found that supervisors spend varying amounts of time in each of these basic dimensions, few differences were found in the basic dimensions from one group of supervisors to another. Those who supervise workers in one functional or technical area engage in the same kinds of things as those who supervise workers in another area. No office supervisors were included in this study.

In the early days of American professional management, roughly through the 1950s, very little attention was given to preparing supervisors for their roles. They learned their management skills from the "hard knocks school." In many organizations, these practices continued until very recent years. Fortunately, this is changing. Organizations in all types of endeavors—business, government, education—are cooperating to provide training programs and formal education for supervisors and potential supervisors.

---

[4]Alvin Toffler, *The Third Wave* (New York: William Morrow & Co., Inc., 1980), p. 54.

**Exhibit 1.1
Primary Dimensions of
First-Line Supervisors'
Jobs**

Working with Subordinates
Organizing Work of Subordinates
Work Planning and Scheduling
Maintaining Efficient Quality Production
Maintaining Safe Clean Work Areas
Maintaining Equipment and Machinery
Compiling Records and Reports

Adapted from Ben E. Dowell and Kenneth N. Wexley, *Journal of Applied Psychology* (October 1978). Copyright 1978 by the American Psychological Association. Adapted by permission of the publisher and author.

Associate and bachelor's degree programs, courses in supervisory management, company training programs, workshops, seminars, and in-house training programs are evidence of a new interest in preparing supervisors for the roles they will assume and for advancement to other roles.

Supervisors who have little practical experience in the work they will supervise are not uncommon, but some areas of technical work still require extensive hands-on experience on the part of those appointed to supervision. The preparation of supervisors through formal training, rather than practical experience, is still an issue in some circles, but many organization leaders have accepted the fact that abilities in other things, such as the topics covered in this book, are probably more important to supervisory success than practical experience.

The acceptance of supervisors as leaders and as part of the management team—not as task masters—is a favorable attitude that is surfacing in progressive organizations today.

Workers' Views of Supervisors' Role

Currently practicing supervisors, students, and workers who aspire to supervisory positions need to consider the role of the supervisor as perceived by the worker. Historically, this perception has varied from one organization to another.

Many management authorities suggest that the role of supervisor has slipped to something less than a management role, at least in the eyes of the worker. They push for an environment that would put supervisors soundly back into the management camp. "Where a supervisor was 'management' to the employee only half a century ago, he or she has now, by and large, become a buffer between management, union, and worker. And like all buffers, the supervisor's main function is to take the blows."[5]

Indeed, some supervisors may be caught between workers who expect to be protected from higher management and management which holds supervisors responsible for the work that goes on in their areas. This conflict appears to be solved in organizations which place supervision firmly into the realm of management with well-defined jobs, a sense of responsibility for their workers, and a voice in the decision-making process. They are considered a part of the management team—not enforcers of management's rules and regulations.

What is Supervisory Management, Then?

supervisory management field of management; those who supervise others

Supervisory management is the basic management form—a most important managerial activity. All other management centers around assisting, coordinating, and directing the work of these managers. Supervisors are teachers, counselors, and leaders for the workers. For the organization, they are the management group closest to the activity for which the organization exists. Organizations exist to produce products and services or to meet needs of the public. If supervisors feel responsible for the quality and zeal with which workers attempt to fulfill these objectives, the organization is more likely to succeed. While much of this positive atmosphere depends upon those who control the organization from the top, the attitude and the knowledge of the supervisor plays an equally important role.

Supervisors are managers. The material in this text centers around equipping supervisors, and students of supervisory management, with necessary knowledge and attitudes about their work. The text deals with the differences between the role of workers and the role of supervisors. It attempts to supplement technical and specialized knowledge, regardless of functional specialty, with management skills which are common among all managers and which are essential for success in all supervisory positions.

Most supervisors who fail, do so because they cannot interact successfully with those they supervise. Supervisors who succeed must be people-oriented. They must recognize the role of managers and be knowledgeable about the functions of managers. They must

---

[5]Peter F. Drucker, *An Introductory View of Management* (New York: Harper's College Press, 1977), p. 251.

be able to communicate, to provide leadership, and to facilitate worker performance. They must be able to train workers, to make decisions, and to understand the complexities of the organizations that employ them. Above all else, they must develop a philosophy of management which is ethically sound and worthy of the trust of superior and subordinate alike.

Managers need special skills. Edward J. Mandt categorizes the managerial skill needs into three groups: technical and professional, interpersonal, and managerial and administrative.[6] These skills, he believes, are used in different proportions by managers at top, middle, and supervisory management levels. Exhibit 1.2 presents Mandt's estimates of the proportions of skills required.

technical/professional skill techniques and methods used by workers in a particular specialty

The **technical and professional skills** involve the techniques and methods used by the workers in a particular specialty. Mandt would include the ability to use these skills and techniques as well as the knowledge of how others should perform them. Notice the portion of the figure that is consumed by **interpersonal skills** for all management levels. Leading, directing, and understanding other people and what motivates them may be the most crucial. Also included in this area is communication skills. Communication in all forms is an essential ability for supervisors.

interpersonal skill skill in leading, directing, understanding people

managerial/administrative skill skills, activities that involve general direction of an organization

Although the **managerial and administrative skills** consume a relatively small proportion of the supervisor's skill priority, some knowledge of the organization and its goals and objectives is necessary. While the supervisor does not participate directly in critical, organization-wide decision-making and policy-making, he or she may be able to make recommendations which will influence these matters.

Supervision in Different Organizations

Service and Financial Organizations Workers in United States and Canadian business firms and organizations hold white collar or service jobs in greater numbers and greater proportions than in the past. Mechanization and automation of the productive forces have reduced the numbers of workers in heavy industry. At the same time, the nature of our society and our standard of living have created the need for more services. Many people make their living by working for organizations that provide a service. In the private sector, banks, insurance companies, and other financial

---

[6]Edward J. Mandt, "A Basic Model of Manager Development," *Personnel Journal* 58:6 (June 1979), p. 396.

Exhibit 1.2
**Skills Needed by
Managers at Different
Levels of Management**

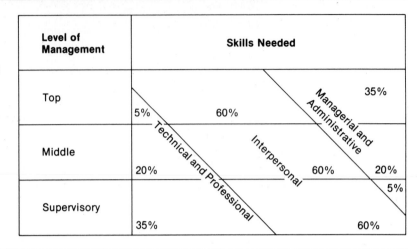

Level of Management	Skills Needed		
Top	5%	60%	35%
Middle	20%	60%	20%
Supervisory	35%	60%	5%

institutions fall into this category. In the public sector, federal, state, and local government agencies provide various kinds of services to the public. Supervisors in these organizations are concerned with supervision of either the provision of a service (for example, the local social security office) or the processing of information created by the selling of a service. A clerk in the savings department of a commercial bank works with information created because the bank "sold" its savings account services to its depositors.

It is easy for workers to lose sight of the organization's overall mission. Supervisors in service organizations are concerned about workers' accuracy in handling information, about their relationships with clients and customers, and about their working harmoniously with other employees in the organization. Both supervisors and workers must work hard at understanding overall goals of the organization. Because no tangible product is involved, this is sometimes difficult.

Since the service organization's "product" is intangible, efficiency is obvious only in the long run. That efficiency may be measured in accuracy of information processed or in the attitude of the public that has been served. Workers who deal with the recipients of public service are sometimes strained by an uncooperative public. The quality and quantity of work in service organizations is often difficult to measure.

Manufacturing Industrial supervisors deal with products that are tangible. The products can be observed, counted, tested, and evaluated for quality. While the results of supervision may be more obvious through quantity of production and quality of the product, the demands on supervisors in these facilities are great. They must supervise large numbers of people whose jobs are critical to keeping production lines moving. Production workers in manufacturing concerns must depend upon equipment which functions properly, availability of raw materials, and coordination of the labor element so that all facets of the system work in unison. Difficulties in one area frequently close down production for all workers involved in a particular assembly line. Supervisors must deal with workers who are required to perform tedious and, sometimes, repetitive tasks. The physical environment, working conditions, and physical strain required of workers complicate the jobs of supervisors.

Government Agencies Public agencies provide services for certain groups of people in society or they perform general tasks on behalf of the public. More than thirty percent of the United States labor force works for some branch of government. Budgets for government agencies are always uncertain. The absence of the profit motive removes some of the pressure for quality performance, thus complicating the task of supervisors. Many jobs are influenced by the political faction currently in office. Some government agencies are staffed by civil service employees who are immune to political changes and who are relatively secure in their jobs. At the same time, however, the number of workers assigned to do various tasks is determined almost solely by available budget, not by need. Salaries and wages frequently vary from one type of government (federal, state, local) to another—even for similar types of work. All of these factors affect morale in governmental agencies and, thus, the job of the supervisor.

Public educational institutions and other public institutions employ large numbers of workers and, consequently, large numbers of supervisors. They are subject to the same financial limitations as other government agencies. While they sometimes operate more autonomously than other units of government, they are still part of the bureaucracy; and those who supervise employees in these institutions must cope with support limitations in addition to providing the leadership and management skills expected of any supervisor. Supervisors in educational institutions must frequently deal with untrained and unmotivated student employees.

The turnover among these employees is great, and their supervision is frequently frustrating.

Physical Environmental Influences

Physical work environments often present a unique challenge to the supervisor. Workers are naturally happier and more contented in a comfortable and pleasing environment. Many supervisors in manufacturing concerns are not blessed with pleasant physical surroundings, although this situation has steadily improved during the past several decades. Many of the more progressive industrial firms are as concerned about plant cleanliness and the comfort of employees in their production facilities as they are for their central office staffs. While office environments have been generally regarded as more pleasant facilities in which to work, they too often have physical limitations. Many such offices are planned around a traditional philosophy that places little emphasis on workers and their job-imposed physical and mental strains. Fortunately, more and more office planners are following the lead of factory planners and are improving office environments. A whole science, called **ergonomics**, has grown up around the study of problems related to work environments. Ergonomics is the study of the effect of one's physical environment in a work situation. An ergonomic approach to environmental planning would look at the needs of individual workers and plan workstations and environments that would complement employee needs.

ergonomics the study of workers' physical environments

While government offices have been traditionally dull and humdrum, the 1970s brought great improvements. The public may consider it a waste of taxpayers' money to improve the aesthetics of government agency facilities, but substantial research indicates that physical surroundings affect the mental and physical health of workers. Ergonomic studies overwhelmingly support the theory that improvements in physical surroundings increase productivity.

While a large percentage of supervisors work in either an industrial or an office environment, significant numbers of supervisory jobs fit into neither of these categories. Among these exceptions are jobs in marketing, distribution, communication, scientific laboratories, building trades, and nonoffice services. Each of these presents special challenges for supervisors. Many of the workers in these areas are in direct and frequent contact with the public. Some of them do not appreciate the need for effective interpersonal relations as they deal with customers and clients. Many of them do not work under direct supervision. When supervisors are not able to observe their subordinates at work, the physical separation may complicate supervision.

Supervisors of retail sales employees have rather close and direct control over their subordinates; however, those who supervise employees who travel must depend upon a reporting system from subordinates.

It must be recognized that every supervisory job brings unique challenges and special circumstances. The supervisor who is prepared for these challenges by a sincere effort to understand people, to understand formal systems and how they function, and to make decisions based upon careful consideration of the individual circumstances will be able to deal effectively with such situations.

Supervising Union Employees

Supervisors in any of the organizations discussed in the previous sections may be working with union employees. While the basic fundamentals for dealing with people should not be any different in a union environment, the nature of the work for the supervisor will be different. Contract specifications and procedures will influence what workers do, how they handle certain procedures, and how the decision-making process is carried out. The fact that supervisors represent management in the view of the workers may create some communication barriers, if anticompany sentiments are prevalent among union members. Supervisors who are genuinely concerned about the welfare of their subordinates may feel a conflict between serving employees' needs and also reaching the organization's goals. There should be no such conflict, however. In the long run, reasonable goals of both groups should be possible. Supervisors are in a position to recognize unreasonable demands of either group and should be ready to assist in working out differences.

IMPLICATIONS AND APPLICATIONS

PREPARING TO SUPERVISE TODAY'S WORKERS

Status or prestige is sometimes measured by the number of people reporting to a supervisor. "Jim got promoted to a very important job. He supervises over twenty-six people now." Remarks like this show respect for supervisors. Some workers, however, respect the job and the authority but not the person. They think that supervisors don't work at all—that supervisors are paid to make life miserable for others. However, successful supervisors do more

New supervisors frequently find themselves inundated with demands from others. Supervision requires the management of time as well as people.

than watch other people work. They occupy the first level of management.

The Move from Worker to Supervisor

What changes when an employee moves from the role of worker to the role of supervisor? Many things will be different in the new assignment. If the change takes place within the same firm or organization, the worker must adapt to a new role and to different attitudes of fellow workers. He or she must learn to accept new responsibilities in a job that can be more mental and less physical. While decision-making is involved in most jobs, it can take on new dimensions for the supervisor. For the first time, the new supervisor assumes responsibility for the actions and progress of other people. Adjusting to this new situation is sometimes difficult. Some fail because they are not willing to let go of old roles or because they flaunt their new power and authority. It is especially difficult for the individual who must supervise those who were previously peers. A happy medium between the "one-of-the-gang" status and the aloof manager is the desirable goal.

The move to a supervisory position places one in a new dimension with respect to the organization. The supervisor will need to acquire a new perspective of the organization, whether it is a private firm, a governmental unit, a public institution, or a professional organization. Supervisors must see themselves as part of a system that is called an organization—a system that, to some extent, depends upon every person in it for smooth functioning.

Supervising Within Evolving Organizations

open system *dynamic organization, changes to fit internal and external requirements*

Supervisors are most likely to be associated with **open systems**. This categorization means that the organization can be viewed as having the characteristics of a living organism "with a life of its own." It has all the functions of an evolving being. In the process of evolving, defining its limits and boundaries, seeking new outlets and inputs, the system develops specialized functions and creates units to carry on its activities. The system not only maintains an internal balance of pressures and forces, but it also must influence and balance external forces and pressures.[7]

closed system *rigid organization, ruled from the top down*

The opposite form of this structure might be categorized as a **closed system**. A closed system is ruled from the top with communication and control levied in a vertical fashion. These organizations are viewed by their personnel as being self-contained and resist change from within and from without. Rules and regulations are considered the main source of power and authority. Change is seen as threatening. All organizations, however, must change with the times and accept the fact that decisions are made by management, not just at the top, but management throughout the organization.

One of the major influences for the supervisor is the orientation of top management. In a stiff and authoritarian system, a new supervisor may have little choice as to the approach to be taken with former peers. One may be forced to drop one's ties with friends to be a "successful" supervisor. The obvious result is that the new supervisor may be forced to do some things that are against his or her basic nature or inclination. This problem is self-defeating and the bind that it imposes is very difficult to handle. As organizations mature and grow, the closed system must change and its management must accept the role differences that are part of the positions held by individuals. Each position is only one part of a larger system and personal relationships can be maintained where worker and supervisor participate in making decisions.

One of the exciting—and perhaps also confusing—situations facing supervisors is that they face workers who appear to want

---

[7]Robert L. Katz, and Daniel Kahn, *The Social Psychology of Organizations*, 2nd ed. (New York: John Wiley & Sons, Inc., 1978), pp. 18–33.

greater challenges than yesterday's worker. They may even insist upon participating in decision making activities. Supervisors of the future must develop ". . . an ability to mediate conflicting demands, an ability to lead people with different values, and an ability to interface with other interest groups—environmentalists, minorities, government agencies—all are increasingly necessary abilities."[8] George Terry's look at the supervisor of the future warns that the supervisor must be prepared for a variety of attitudes, for workers who are very job-security conscious, and for better-educated employees. Employers are being encouraged to find places for the disadvantaged, the nonskilled, and the physically handicapped. Sex discrimination barriers are falling. While these are positive changes, they may be difficult for tradition-oriented supervisors to deal with. Working with these changing conditions will be a challenge.

A PREVIEW OF REMAINING CHAPTERS

What skills must be enhanced for the successful supervisor? This text is about the skills which will prepare people for the performance of management functions. It does not attempt to supply the nitty-gritty details of jobs. Rather, it attempts to provide a foundation in those basic "people" skills with which every supervisor must deal.

The preview of the supervisory job begins with a look at organizations. Both formal, official organizations and subtle, informal organizations are examined. The skill of organizing is necessary for smooth operation when people must work together to accomplish common goals. The concepts of authority, responsibility, and accountability are explored. These concepts are new to most supervisors.

Specific duties and responsibilities vary among jobs, but most managers—even at the supervisory level—are leading and motivating people; they are planning and organizing processes, procedures, and people. Basic management functions are performed at every level. The magnitude of the function, the number of people affected, and perhaps the consequences of error are less at the first-line supervisory level than at higher levels of management; but the nature of the function is not very different. Consideration is given to the basic management functions, to some of the

---

[8]George R. Terry, "The Supervisor of the (Near) Future," *Training and Development Journal* (January 1977), p. 41.

"schools" of management theory, and to typical supervisory tasks and responsibilities. Most people who move into supervisory roles expect to advance to even more responsible positions in the future.

Many subtle factors influence the job and the success of supervisors. Understanding and working with people is the prime ingredient for such success. Several chapters are devoted to underlying influences on behavior. These influences must be recognized by any person who works directly with people, particularly in a leadership capacity. Because supervisors directly influence workers' attitudes and feelings about the organization and about their own roles in the organization, the text includes the subject of motivation. Students of psychology would do much more extensive work in this area, but the material presented here will serve as a foundation examination of worker concerns, what they want, how they react to various stimuli, what they expect from life, and how this affects them in the work setting. Understanding workers as human beings with feelings, goals, and desires is necessary for motivating them—for making them want to contribute something to the organization. Authorities do not always agree about what people regard as rewards, so various theories and models of employee motivation are presented.

One's leadership style reflects the extent and nature of his or her participation and the participation of those who are being led. This text reviews theoretical approaches for defining the effective leader, and research studies that attempt to identify leadership traits that work. Some "do's and don'ts" are given for those who are searching for their own leadership styles.

Moral implications of supervisors' actions are explored. Supervisors must realize the existence of moral influences on what they do; they must understand that ethical considerations will create conflicts and suggest solutions for problems encountered. Interpersonal ethics and a model of moral development are presented. The new awareness of morality in business and government is explored.

Another underlying influence on the life of a supervisor is communication. The process of communication, the scope of communication involvement for supervisors, and barriers to effective communication are examined. In addition, principles of written and oral communication are considered. Popular methods of communication are explored. Particular emphasis is placed on the essential management tool of written communication and upon trends which may soon revolutionize managerial communication.

Supervisors must work with people who fill prescribed jobs and carry out defined procedures, all of which must combine into operational systems. The larger the organization, the more complex its systems. This text presents the concept of organizations and parts of organizations as systems. Particular emphasis is given to developing an inquisitiveness about procedures and how to improve them. This country's decreasing productivity can be attributed, at least in part, to people who have observed procedures and have recognized their inefficiency but have done nothing to change that condition. In some cases, they do nothing because they do not know how to tackle the problem. In other cases, organizational structure does not facilitate change. In still other cases, one or more inept but powerful persons within the structure refuse to promulgate or accommodate to change. The one central theme is efficiency and how supervisors may play a role in improving the efficiency. When productivity improves, everyone benefits. When efficiency, and thus productivity, decreases, benefits decrease.

Every manager must assume responsibility for activities that are related to the field that is called personnel management. Supervisors perform more of these functions in some organizations than in others, but they perform some of them in all organizations. The text explores the relationship of supervision and the personnel management function. This can involve assisting personnel managers in interviewing, selecting, and training. For some it can involve testing, conducting training programs, orienting new workers, and managing employee benefit programs. Others may be involved in these activities only in an advisory capacity. To some extent, the supervisor takes on the role of teacher. So the process of learning—how people learn, how much they can learn at one time, and the most effective methods of teaching new tasks— becomes an important factor.

One portion of this text is devoted to performance appraisal and attempts to equip the supervisor with the ability to evaluate other people. These evaluations can be turned into something positive and productive.

With the assumption that contemporary supervisors aspire to management careers at higher levels, career planning material is presented. Supervisors need to know what to expect in terms of additional education, added expense, and increased responsibility when promotions are offered. Many supervisors have alternative career paths mapped out or have at least considered whether or not they would want higher level jobs related to the work they are doing. The self-confidence that comes with such planning makes young supervisors more promotable and probably speeds the climb to more responsible positions. More is not necessarily better; some people need to plan a career that offers challenges without upward mobility. This additional concept is also explored.

To those who have never studied management, the subjects previewed here may still appear fuzzy and vague. That is another aspect of supervision for which the student is to be prepared. Management is not an exact science. In fact, managers everywhere argue continually about whether it is a science at all. To be sure, it is not an activity that can be carried out as a cook would follow a recipe. One does not automatically know that one has the right answer. One does not make a decision, then stand back and admire one's "right" decision. One cannot look up the answer to problems in a book of problems.

Managers are guided by personal philosophies, by principles and theories about what works and what does not, and sometimes by gut feelings. More and more, however, managers need an educational foundation to provide them with alternatives for making decisions and dealing with the people with whom they work. One book or one course in supervisory management is not sufficient to provide this depth of understanding. The materials in this text, particularly if they are read by students and supplemented by instructor experiences and class discussion, should provide a beginning.

QUESTIONS FOR FURTHER THOUGHT

1. Contrast the roles of operatives and supervisors in contemporary organizations.

2. What are the differences between an organization that is managed by its entrepreneurs and one managed by professional managers?

3. React to the following statements.
   a. Supervisors don't work
   b. Supervisors should first be operatives in the areas which they will later supervise.
   c. Supervisors are really neither manager nor operative.
   d. Workers who fail, do so because they lack technical skills.

4. Compare the level of skills needed by managers at top, middle, and supervisory management levels.

5. Contrast the nature of work and supervision among manufacturing, service, financial, and governmental organizations.

6. Discuss, from a historical perspective, the development of the need for supervisory positions.

7. Identify and describe several major dimensions of supervision

that a beginning supervisor should expect in his/her role as a supervisor.

8. What is "the establishment"? Do you react positively or negatively to this term?

9. Contrast open system organizations and closed system organizations.

2

THE
PEOPLE–ORGANIZATION
MIX

VOCABULARY
TO MASTER

Mechanistic approach
Homeostasis
Adversary climate
Production
Management
Support
Maintenance
Adaptation
Developmental phases
The third wave
Management climate
Product value
Administrative procedures
Direct supervision
Personal satisfaction
Change factor
Quality circle

LEARNING
OBJECTIVES

Upon completion of this chapter and the related assignments, you should be able to:
1. Describe four models of the people-organization mix.
2. Describe the nature of organizations as structures in transition.
3. List and describe factors that influence organizational health.
4. Describe the directions of and structures of organizations in postindustrial societies.

CHAPTER OUTLINE

PROBLEM STATEMENT
WHAT IS MEANT BY PEOPLE–ORGANIZATION MIX?

BACKGROUND AND THEORY
THEORETICAL APPROACH TO THE MIX—WHAT COMPONENTS
INFLUENCE THE INTERACTION?
  Adversary Climate

DYNAMICS OF THE MIX
  The Open Systems Model
  The Developmental Model
  A Model for the Future

RESEARCH AND PRACTICE
ANOTHER MODEL: FACTORS THAT INFLUENCE
ORGANIZATIONAL HEALTH

IMPLICATIONS AND APPLICATIONS
APPLYING THE MODEL
AN AFTERTHOUGHT:
ARE THE THIRD-WAVE ISSUES REAL?
SUMMARY

QUESTIONS FOR FURTHER THOUGHT

<table>
<tr><td>

PROBLEM
STATEMENT

</td><td>

WHAT IS MEANT BY PEOPLE–ORGANIZATION MIX?

</td></tr>
</table>

One individual working as a single unit for the purpose of achieving a goal or set of goals such as raising livestock for future sale or contracting to paint signs for business firms is obviously not an organization. But when the sign painter hires two more sign painters and a bookkeeper, rents an office building, buys delivery trucks, hires a secretary and a janitor, and contracts with a carpenter to build signs—an organization is born. All of these diverse people and their interests are now directed toward a generalized goal of creating, selling, painting, and delivering signs. In addition, general procedures or methods are established to achieve the goal of producing signs. The greater the number of workers who are needed and the greater the number of working units, the more complex that sign-painting organization becomes.

Individual needs must be meshed with organizational goals. As the number of people needed increases and the organizational structures become more complex, the difficulty of running it smoothly intensifies. Give and take among workers and structural procedures increases, even as job procedures become more formal. The answer to the question, "Who do I see to get this done?" is not always found in the formal chain of command; and it is the interplay between the formal and informal that makes organizational life so very interesting. Management consultants have found their greatest challenge is to identify these informal groups. Efforts are then made to incorporate these informal groups into the formal system. Personnel changes are invariably needed to accomplish this task, and the method used all too often by American industry to bring about this change is gross upheaval and forced change. The obvious result is resistance to change with related infighting and struggle for power by the participants.

Organizational pressures might be viewed as illustrated in Exhibit 2.1. Individuals within the organization have their own interests, needs and ways of doing things (the informal paths in the illustration). Often these do not coincide with procedures and formal operations of the organization (formal systems in the illustration). Organizations apply pressure to force workers to follow formal systems. The stress imposed upon the participants is to make the formal and informal interest and procedures the same. The problem that faces management/supervision is development of a system that makes the organizational goals coincide with the

Exhibit 2.1
**Organizational
Pressures to Follow
Formal Systems**

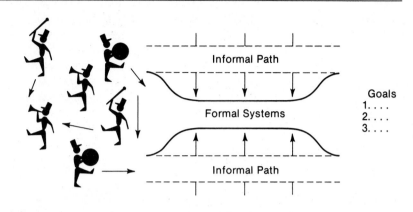

individual's goals. This is not easy, but it is an essential task of both management and supervisors.

BACKGROUND
AND
THEORY

THEORETICAL APPROACH TO THE MIX—WHAT COMPONENTS INFLUENCE THE INTERACTION?

mechanistic approach
structure and mechanics
of the system

The traditional view for looking at organizations has been what might be called the structural or **mechanistic approach**. Historically, the emphasis was on the mechanics of the system. The basic questions were as follows:

Who reports to whom?

What is the span of control?

What are the line and staff relationships?

Are the jobs simplistic and specialized?

Does everyone have but one boss?

Is the responsibility consistent with the authority?

And on and on.

The generalized model was one of viewing people as being set in motion to best serve the organization. People were used as machines to produce goods for the system, and that was accepted as

27

natural. This became known as the classical management theory and is certainly one way to look at human organization interaction. In some parts of the world (Canada, England, and the U.S. included) this approach is still the underlying scheme for management's orientation. Classical management theory, however, may not be appropriate for most organizations because it ensures an adversary climate within the organization.

Adversary Climate

homeostasis tendency for returning to a stable state

In simple terms, organizations are similar to living organisms— "they" have lives of their own, especially in the sense that systems and procedures are established to meet goals. In addition, there is a tendency for systems to seek **homeostasis** or a state of nonchange and balance. The old cliche, "don't rock the boat," is a reflection of this orientation. In the process of meeting or not meeting the individual needs of the participants (employees), organizations begin to develop squeaky wheels and the demand for lubricant in certain areas becomes great. If management fails to provide the lubricant, subsystems or subgroups develop to ensure that those demands are heard. In the Western world the major result has been the development of unionization with the unions pitted against management. Each group then competes for power within the organization and the adversary condition reaches full bloom. Not only does the total system become ill from the disease within, but considerable expenditure of energy must be directed toward solving internal problems, thereby limiting the available energy and resources for production.

adversary climate being pitted against one another

The **adversary climate** does several things to the system. First, available energy is directed inward, thus isolating the organization from other external systems in the competitive marketplace. Second, production energies become limited. Third, internal power struggles lead to organizational sabotage.[1] Finally, the total system becomes defensive, and unable to maintain flexibility to change within the marketplace. Adaptability to the outside world is lost. In a very real Darwinian sense, once the organizational unit loses its adaptability to its environment, death is at hand. One excellent example of this condition was found during the 1960s and 1970s in the United States auto industry.

---

[1]Ichak Adizes, "Organizational Passages—Diagnosing and Treating Lifecycle Problems of Organizations," *Organizational Dynamics* (Summer 1979), pp. 3–25.

Administrative support groups perform a vital service to management.

Photograph by Alan Baker, courtesy of American National Bank.

DYNAMICS OF THE MIX

The Open Systems Model

Within the last twenty years there has developed a unique literature that describes organizations in terms of open systems jargon (Katz and Kahn, 1979). The major theme is that ongoing and surviving organizations are everchanging, organism-like systems—taking in raw materials or resources, transforming those materials or resources, and producing a product or service that is offered outside the system. Energy input-output is the main activity, and there are five major functions of any surviving system. Subsystems are established to carry out these functions and the interplay among these areas is what makes the organization go. These subsystems are as follows:[2]

[2]Adapted from Daniel Katz and Robert L. Kahn, *The Social Psychology of Organizations*, 2nd ed. (New York: John Wiley & Sons, 1978), pp. 52–56.

production within open systems theory, the primary outputs

management within open systems theory, control units

support within open systems theory, units that obtain raw materials, distribute products, and provide administrative services

maintenance within open systems theory, those units concerned with reinforcement systems

adaptation within open systems theory, units concerned with research and development

1. **Production** areas concerned with organizational output or what is produced. (The assembly line, or the direct performers of a service)

2. **Management** areas concerned with controlling, coordinating, and directing other subsystems. (The bosses)

3. **Support** areas concerned with procuring and disposing of outputs, serving management, and performing administrative activities. (Purchasing, sales, administrative support groups)

4. **Maintenance** areas concerned with patterning human behavior or recruitment, indoctrination, socialization, and rewards. (Personnel)

5. **Adaptation** areas concerned with sensing change in the external world or product research, market research, and planning. (Marketing, research and development)

One way that this model might be viewed is pictured in Exhibit 2.2. This model should be seen as a delicate balancing act by management to allocate appropriate energies and resources to the various subsystems. Limited research has been conducted on describing or identifying the "correct" amount of emphasis that should be allocated to each of the subsystems, but for study purposes, it should be realized that each subsystem is important to the overall well-being of the organization. If any of the subsystems stop working (become dysfunctional), the total system is threatened by an illness from within.

The Developmental Model

An outgrowth from the general open systems approach was developed by Adizes.[3] The general idea is that all organizations tend to progress through **developmental phases** from infant to adolescent, to maturity, to old age, and death. The basic premise is that each stage of development entails a unique set of conditions and threats to the system and that appropriate adjustment to those conditions is vital for the system to survive or become revitalized. Within Adizes's model, there are four major factors that contribute to the organization's survival:

developmental phases concept that organizations mature much as a human does

1. Production. Are the results for which the system exists forthcoming?

---

[3]Ichak Adizes, "Organizational Passages—Diagnosing and Treating Lifecycle Problems of Organizations," *Organizational Dynamics* (Summer 1979), pp. 3–25.

Exhibit 2.2
Open Systems Structure

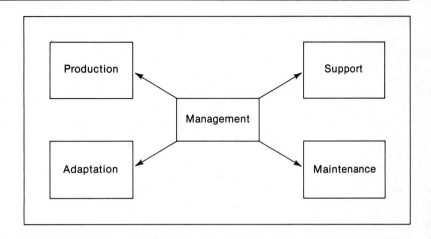

2. Administration. Are there effective decision processes?

3. Entrepreneurial. Is there effective adaptation and creative risk taking?

4. Integration. Does the team work toward similar goals effectively?

Adizes's model of passages is somewhat elaborate but easily understood, and all students of organizational behavior would find his article very interesting.

Exhibit 2.3 attempts to combine major considerations from both the open systems and passages approach. Four open systems factors are compared with organizational emphasis during different phases of life that organizations experience. This model can be used as a tool for describing the state of the organization, healthy or otherwise.

One of the interesting characteristics of Exhibit 2.3 is the way emphasis is predicted—based on stage of development. For example, during the bureaucratic stage, managerial paranoia is predicted with placement of blame on others, resignations of better people, and the development of adversary cliques.

A Model for the Future?

Any model employed to describe and predict organizational behavior is based upon the investigator's conceptualization of the

31

Exhibit 2.3
Developmental Stages and Impact on Basic Organizational Functions

Organizations' Basic Functions	Organizational Units that Perform Functions	Characteristics of Units by Growth Stage				
		Adolescent Stage	Prime Stage	Maturity Stage	Aristocratic Stage	Bureaucracy Stage
1. **Production**— A concern for: results (outcomes), output of goods and/or services	production line, program dissemination, services to customers or clients	production slowdown	*results orientation, stable systems, optimum production	*sense of urgency declines	business as usual	production falls
2. **Adaptation**— concern for: internal and external changes needed, creativity, risk taking, professional development, and planning	research and development, market research, institutional research	*long and short-run projections emphasized	*awareness of external demands is well-established	entrepreneurial risk-taking declines, market risk-taking declines, less emphasis on research and development	admiration of the past	research and development ignored

| 3. **Management**—concern for: controlling, coordinating, directing and administering the organization | boards of directors, administration, management personnel | *planning, coordinating, computer systems installation, labor policies | *high planning desired expected −1=0 (management's expectations are met) | *aspirations are held low, enjoys yesterday's fruits, procedures and policies important, formal climate develops | *ritual is important, tenure is most important, dress codes are understood, jargon phase | *managerial paranoia, infighting/blame seeking, better people leave |
| 4. **Support**—concern for: procuring and disposing of products, recruiting, indoctrinating and rewarding personnel, internal maintenance of the system | personnel services, procurement, sales/marketing | training cliques develop | support services predictable, units grow to meet needs | internal relationships are very important | *more control systems, more employee training ritual | "put it in writing," nothing gets done, the right hand doesn't know what the left is doing |

*Indicates areas which traditionally consume the greater amounts of management time and concern.

Source: Adapted from Ichak Adizes, "Organizational Passages—Diagnosing and Treating Lifecycle Problems of Organizations," *Organizational Dynamics*, Summer 1979, pp. 2–25 and Daniel Katz and Robert L. Kahn, *The Social Psychology of Organizations*, 2nd ed. (New York: John Wiley & Sons, Inc., 1979).

Free flow of communication exists in an open systems model. One mechanism to create this flow is an anonymous suggestion system. The Lord Corporation uses a rural mailbox in the plant for such a system.

Photographed by Alan Baker, courtesy of Lord Corporation.

the third wave that social order beyond the industrialized era

social order in which the system is formed. Present-day analysts view organizations as being in the industrial mode. Alvin Toffler (1981) in his book, *The Third Wave*, does an excellent job of describing the present era as the "second wave" or the industrial revolution era. As he so well depicts, the upheavals of our social order indicate that our world is now in the process of transition into another period. This transition will be even more dramatic than the change from an agricultural wave to industrial societies. According to Toffler, the nature of our work society will change because of the following pressures:[4]

1. Our physical environment will no longer allow us to arrange production systems as we have in the last 200 years. Energy supplies, pollution, and consumption habits will not allow the old systems to continue.

------

[4]Alvin Toffler, *The Third Wave* (New York: William Morrow & Co., Inc., 1980), pp. 235–240.

34

2. The social environment is far more organized and crowded, requiring acceptance of greater responsibility by the corporate systems of the world.

3. Expansion of information collecting, controlling, and disseminating systems has led to "information managers" which in turn leads to conflict over who controls the industrial systems.

4. Government has become a more important factor in the power structure of corporate entities, and power agencies have become a greater influence on the decision making process of all organizations.

5. Various moral pressures and special interest groups call into play new definitions and interpretations of appropriate institutional behavior. Ethical orientations of management are seen as important considerations in the work environment, and the regulators of the employee are more accountable.

One main theme of Toffler's book is that in the near future we will experience corporate (and other institutional) transitions where the systems are multipurpose (not just economic) with the schedules, places, and orientations of work entirely different. The work place, the nature of employment, and the skills required are now in transition. Flexibility to make the necessary transition is going to be a key factor for the organizations and participants that survive.

RESEARCH AND PRACTICE

ANOTHER MODEL: FACTORS THAT INFLUENCE ORGANIZATIONAL HEALTH

This text proposes a different model for looking at organizations—one that might be called wholistic in the sense that consideration may be given to all of the factors that play a role in the system's well-being. A diagnostic tool has been developed to analyze organizational health. The basic design is shown in Exhibit 2.4.

With this basic scheme in mind, any organization can be inspected, measured, and evaluated on these most important components or factors that make a system "go." Each of the six factors can be broken down into descriptive units that are measurable. Using this approach, organizational health is seen as the perceptions of those participants who are part of the total system.

The basic premise is that any organization must be viewed as a structure with specific functions. These functions are consistent with the open systems theory and each of these must be healthy and viable. In addition, any organization must fulfill specific reinforcement or reward expectations of the participants. Those re-

Tomorrow's supervisor may spend much of the work week at home, communicating with subordinates by electronic means.

ward expectations are factors that must be accounted for by management and given high priority.

What, then, are those factors and their components?

management climate employee perceptions of managerial style

1. **Management Climate**
   a. Ethical standards of management.
   b. Personnel perception: job security or expendability?
   c. Communication climate created by management personnel.

product value perceptions of the items produced

2. **Product Value**
   a. Value of product (whatever is produced) as perceived by personnel.
   b. Value of product as perceived by the community or any member of society with a knowledge of the organization.

administrative procedures established routines in an organization

3. **Administrative Procedures**
   a. Selection and hiring processes in terms of openness and emphasis on quality.
   b. Training programs with a career development orientation.
   c. Evaluation of personnel for growth.

36

Exhibit 2.4
Factors Affecting Organizational Health—The OQ (Organizational Quotient)

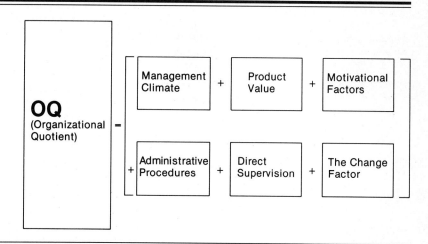

d. Maintenance of personnel within the system as a positive service (providing services for the benefit of personnel).

direct supervision fac-tors that relate to task orientation, and people orientation

4. **Direct Supervision**
   a. People orientation of leaders (a climate of trust, openness, responsibility and willingness to change).
   b. Task orientation of leaders (appropriate systems and proce-dures to accomplish tasks).

personal satisfaction individuals' perceptions of the reward systems available

5. **Personal Satisfaction**
   a. Reward systems to provide appropriate pay, promotion and career development opportunities.
   b. Personal perceptions (relationship to coworkers, family perception of one's job, and individual's job satisfaction).

change factor internal and external factors that demand change in the system

6. **The Change Factor**
   a. Organizational maturity in terms of stage and flexibility.
   b. Adaptive functions in terms of a strong research and de-velopment unit (ability to adapt).
   c. Society's need for organization's existence.
   d. External control agents that influence (external regulatory agents).

IMPLICATIONS AND APPLICATIONS

APPLYING THE MODEL

This approach to analysis of organizational health is just one of many. In a recent article by Kur three models for describing organizations are listed as being used by industrial management consultants.[5] If one continued to look for models to use in studying the organization-people mix, one would find numerous designs. Most of those available have valuable orientations, but this particular approach has been chosen simply because it tends to be more wholistic and takes into consideration a large number of variables or factors. A supervisor needs to understand that people and organizations do things to and for each other. All six of the categories affect the overall health and success (organizational quotient) of the organization. Supervisors contribute to all six categories—more to some than to others.

The remainder of this text addresses the components that supervisors influence or deal with. Supervisors often wish for simple solutions to pressing problems but there are no simple solutions; the interrelationships are too complex. Supervisors and managers who can understand the interrelationships that exist in an organization (such as the suggested six-factor model) are more likely to make appropriate judgments in solving day-to-day problems. Since the advent of the industrial revolution, there has been a steady increase in the complexity in our lives. That complexity is also found in the work place, and it will not diminish in the near future. It is here to stay, and those who best understand those complexities are more likely to also stay.

AN AFTERTHOUGHT: ARE THE THIRD–WAVE ISSUES REAL?

quality circle weekly meetings of 8–12 participants to solve problems

Rendall discusses the possibility of Quality Circles being the answer to meeting the dilemma faced by "Third Wave" workers.[6] The **quality circle** approach is one where eight to twelve workers meet during the week for the purpose of data gathering and problem solving. They are the workers' link to management. Even though this may be an old idea under a new label, it is a reflection of the emphasis being directed toward worker motivation within the organization. In addition, it is a reflection of a movement under the general topic heading of Human Resources Development (HRD) that has come from the training segment of industry and government. The basic thrust is that systems that control workers must focus upon the worker's needs as well as production.

---

[5]C. Edward Kur, "OD: Perspectives, Processes and Prospects," *Training and Development Journal* (April 1981), pp. 28–34.
[6]Elaine Rendall, "Quality Circles—A 'Third Wave' Introvention," *Training and Development Journal* (March 1981), pp. 29–31.

Rasow identified "quality of work-life issues" for the decade of the 1980s.[7] His basic theme suggests that the work-life problem will be more important during the 1980s than in recent history. Three of the issues that stand out are occupational stress, participation, and democracy in the workplace. While two of these (stress and participation) are primarily workers' perceptions, the democracy concept is one that the total organization must address. The change factor of "more democracy" is a definite reflection of worker-organizational mix issues. Even limited reflection on what the future holds leads one to believe that compromising with worker demands is a problem for the here-and-now, as well as for the future.

Third wave issues are real, but they are not new. Organizations are people and people have needs. Organizations are established to produce either a product or a service. The skillful manager is one who best facilitates both the production requirements of the organization and personal reinforcement requirements of people.

SUMMARY

Several people working together toward a common goal is an organization. Organizations have goals, and the people who make up organizations have needs. These goals and needs must be matched in order for the organization to be healthy and successful. While this appears to be a simple concept, providing this mix in large organizations becomes very complex because needs of the various groups involved usually do not coincide.

Historically, the nature of this mix has ranged from heavy organizational input (the mechanistic approach) to adversary conditions (organization versus employee) to one which equally emphasizes organizational goals and employee needs. While this condition does not exist in some organizations, social pressures are pushing organizations in this direction.

Numerous attempts to examine organizations have been made. Four models of those attempts have been presented here. The open systems model examines organizations as living organisms which are constantly changing. The developmental model looks at definite stages in the life of an organization and attempts to help people to understand the organizations by recognizing

---

[7]Jerome M. Rasow, "Quality of Work Life Issues for the 1980s," *Training and Development Journal* (March 1981), pp. 33–52.

these stages. While not a model *per se*, a currently-popular attempt to examine organizations tries to predict their future natures. This futuristic orientation predicts dramatic changes in organizations which will be made possible by technological improvements and changes in social environments.

The text model of the organization-people mix combines ideas gleaned from current literature and identifies factors which are believed to determine the health of organizations. They are: management climate, product value, administrative procedures, supervision, personal satisfaction of people, and change factor (external influences requiring changes and internal mechanisms that permit change).

QUESTIONS FOR FURTHER THOUGHT

1. Contrast an organization that is in a state of homeostasis and one that is in an adolescent stage of development.

2. List and identify the basic characteristics of three models for describing an organization.

3. Compare a closed system orientation and the open system approach for viewing organizational change.

4. List and define the five functional structures of organizations as identified by the open system approach.

5. What basic factors might one want to consider as important when considering personnel and organizational health?

3

SUPERVISORS AS MANAGERS

LEARNING OBJECTIVES

Upon completion of this chapter and the related assignments, you should be able to:

1. Contrast the role of workers and the role of supervisors in businesses and organizations.
2. Review the history of management theory and identify several influential contributors to current management practice.
3. Identify the levels of management in organizations.
4. Identify the common functions performed by managers at all levels within organizations.
5. Differentiate between functions of management and duties or routine responsibilities of managers.
6. Describe the controversy surrounding the validity of principles of management.
7. Identify factors that contribute to the development of personal philosophies of management.

CHAPTER
OUTLINE

PROBLEM STATEMENT
WHAT ARE THE FUNCTIONS OF MANAGERS?

BACKGROUND AND THEORY
SUPERVISORS AS MANAGERS
    History of Management Theory
    Levels of Management

RESEARCH AND PRACTICE
FUNCTIONS AND PRINCIPLES OF MANAGEMENT
    Planning
    Organizing
    Leading and Directing
    Controlling
    Principles of Management
        Span of Control
        Authority Commensurate with Responsibility
        Responsibility to Single Superior
        Objectives
        Open Communication
        Engendering Trust

IMPLICATIONS AND APPLICATIONS
MANAGEMENT DUTIES
    Budgeting and Financial Planning
    Reporting Production
    Selecting and Training Workers
    Routine Supervision
    Developing and Managing Procedures and Methods
    Developing Policy and Standards

MANAGEMENT PROBLEM SOLVING
    Communication Problems
    People Problems
    Routine Problem Solving

MANAGERIAL QUALIFICATIONS—
OR HOW DO I GET TO BE A MANAGER?

THE SUPERVISOR'S PHILOSOPHY OF MANAGEMENT

QUESTIONS FOR FURTHER THOUGHT

PROBLEM
STATEMENT

WHAT ARE THE FUNCTIONS OF MANAGEMENT?

Supervision is management; therefore potential and practicing supervisors should have a fundamental knowledge of management theory and philosophies. They should be exposed to basic management functions in a manner that will enable them to differentiate between the broad functions common among all management areas and specific duties and routines of a particular supervisor's job.

BACKGROUND
AND
THEORY

SUPERVISORS AS MANAGERS

Early business ventures in this country were managed, for the most part, by their owners. Institutions were managed by chief administrators, and governmental units were managed by elected officials in charge of those units. Although management theory and academic analysis techniques were available in the United States, early enterprises in this country were managed by intuition, by the exercise of good judgment, and by clever thinking. Growth in the size and complexity of business, institutions, and governments required the employment of professional managers—people who, like the workers, were employees of the organization. Owners paid managers to manage.

The bulk of business activity and most governmental and institutional management is carried out by professional managers. Most of them have experienced some type of management education—specific study of the principles, theories, and practices of managers. Small business organizations are still managed by their owners, who are both owners and managers. They make the decisions and supervise the workers. Some corporate managers are also stockholders in the company, so they have an added incentive to see the company grow and prosper.

Supervisors are managers. Every organization, whether it is a private business enterprise, a division of some government agency, or a nonprofit institution, must have leaders. Depending upon the size of the organization, the leadership role may require the work of one or two leaders or hundreds of leaders at various levels and in various capacities. Someone must bring order and direction to the organization. Others must maintain that order and direction for each segment of the organization. Every organization—from the home to football teams, from symphony orchestras to giant industries, from huge government agencies to 24-hour food markets—must be managed.

management *process of leading, directing, organizing and controlling; group of people who performs this process*

Peter Drucker has defined **management** as ". . . a function and the people who discharge it. It denotes a social position and authority, but also a discipline and field of study." He amplifies this by identifying several supplementary components: tasks, people, and delegation by ownership. He rejects the "someone who is responsible for the work of other people" definition as too narrow and, for some jobs, inaccurate. Managers have many responsibilities other than directing their immediate subordinates. They have many relationships outside their own organizational units. Management is ". . . responsibility for contribution. Function rather than power has to be the distinctive criterion and the organizing principle."[1]

Why should supervisors study management? First, supervisors perform management functions. They are part of the management team. In fact, they are the basic and most important segment of the management effort, even though they do not perform the full component of managerial functions. They have taken on a portion of the responsibility for achieving the organization's objectives. They have assumed the role of helping others to achieve—for themselves and for the organization.

Some supervisors may not consider themselves managers, and some middle managers and workers also may not consider them managers; but they are. They have moved from the role of follower and worker to the role of leader. The transition from carrying out routine job tasks and taking directions from others to the role of giving directions and assuming responsibility for others can present difficulties for new supervisors. Even more difficult may be the situation for a supervisor who has never held the position of worker. The supervisory role is further complicated by the fact that the supervisors are giving directions and exercising leadership for subordinates and, at the same time, are still followers in relationships with superiors. Almost all managers are in this situation, as are almost all college-educated workers. Very few people are in ultimate command of their employment situation; most are responsible for other people or for processes or segments of work. Supervisors are also accountable to superiors for their actions. So the supervisor is not alone in the role of managing and being managed. Only the lowest-level workers and the self-

---

[1]Peter F. Drucker, *An Introductory View of Management* (New York: Harper & Row, 1977), pp. 11, 15.

employed escape this tug of war. Even chief executive officers must satisfy boards of directors.

Good supervisors recognize the nature of their management functions and those of other managers in the organization. In some organizations the word *management* may be replaced with *administration*, but the structure for management will be similar. Good supervisors are able to view their own roles in proper perspective with other levels of management. As pointed out in Chapter One, they should not view themselves as merely buffers between subordinates and superiors.

Many supervisors progress to higher levels of management. A basic understanding of management functions and principles facilitates a grasp of the responsibilities of higher-level positions. While in supervisory management roles, individuals begin to develop their own philosophies of what management is all about. Studying the philosophies of others can simplify this process.

Certain elements of management are universal—they are essentially the same in every organization and for every manager. Even though the products of organizations differ, the processes are strangely similar. Whether the organization produces consumer products for private profit or serves citizens by producing and processing information and offering services, human beings and technical processes must be orchestrated in a planned harmony in order for the organization to accomplish its objectives.

Some managers are able to function effectively without formal study. Common sense, trial-and-error knowledge, intuition, basic intelligence, and good judgment developed through experience help in making the right decisions. Although the profit incentive is the motivation of the owner-manager of a business, the manager of any organization will more effectively accomplish the organization's goals if sound management principles guide his or her actions and management philosophy.

Supervisors are sometimes faced with special problems. Circumstances can prevent managing in the most efficient manner. Budgetary limitations and legal restrictions can hamper the supervisor in a government agency. Supervisors in private industry can be overruled by superiors who, for some reason, do not choose to follow a course appearing to the supervisor to be sound management practice. Even though these situations exist, the supervisor who is knowledgeable about the basics of management can better interpret the actions of others and provide the leadership that is expected of the position.

Management, like economics, is theoretical in nature. Students of management, particularly those with practical experience, are sometimes bothered by the fact that the assumed conditions to which management theory is applied do not exist in the working world, as they have observed it. In order to benefit from the study of theory, learners must be able to place themselves in "the big picture." They must overcome the tendency to assume that the totality of the working world is identical to that portion of it which they have observed. There is great value in "real world" practical experience, but there can also be danger in narrow, "tunnel vision" thinking. Effective supervisors attempt to understand principles and theories and to apply those which are pertinent and to resort to common sense and good judgment when that is the primary avenue open to them.

History of Management Theory

Although the work processes have been examined for improvement for centuries, there was little concentrated effort to organize a body of knowledge and principles for managing until the last half of the nineteenth century. Prior to this period attention had been directed to economic factors and to the ownership of productive resources.

Frederick W. Taylor (1865–1915) began to analyze the process of management—mostly in industrial manufacturing operations. His scientific management approach contained two elements that were new at the time: (1) breaking down the work to be done into minute parts, each performed by a different employee, and (2) relating workers' pay to the quantity produced by each worker. These ideas grew into what we now know as assembly lines and incentive pay.

classical management theory stresses functions of managers, worker's desire for wages

The work of Taylor, Max Weber, and other early writers is now referred to as **classical management theory** and has greatly influenced organizations and management throughout this century. The period of time when the classical theories were being put into practice is sometimes referred to as the *functional management era*, because it was during this period that the elements that were considered common to most management jobs were identified and labeled "the functions of management." While many of the classical approaches to management have been challenged and abandoned, their influence is still very evident. Taylor's associates, Frank and Lillian Gilbreth, pioneered time and motion studies, and laid the foundation for the practice that is now called *time study* in industrial engineering circles and *work measurement* in office administration. It identified motions used to perform tasks,

47

timed each motion, and put together the data to produce production standards expressed in quantitative terms. For example, an assembly line employee should be able to assemble a certain number of components per hour. This knowledge allowed management to plan and schedule production more accurately and, in some cases, to pay workers for above average performance.

Classical management theory emphasized the job and the worker's desire for monetary reward. The next management era, called **neoclassical management theory** and its related **human relations movement** challenged classical theory because of its lack of attention to individual worker's needs, attitudes, goals, and objectives. The neoclassical school of management thought was greatly influenced by the Hawthorne experiments (discussed in Chapter Four).

neo classical management theory emphasizes people and their role in the work setting

human relations movement era of the neo classical theory

modern management theory most recent combination of systems, behavioral approaches with theories of past eras

Recent management theory, referred to as **modern management theory,** has included ideas with such labels as *sociotechnical* (the human and the technical elements) *theory, systems approach to management,* the *behavioral science approach,* and *management science.* Elements of these theories have been combined with elements of both the classical and neoclassical theories to form a systems view of organizations. The systems approach views every organization as a system made up of numerous subsystems and even sub-subsystems, each of which must function in harmony with other subsystems, and with the human element often considered the critical element. Modern management theory regarding the structure of organizations and leadership of people has been influenced by such ideas as Abraham Maslow's hierarchy of needs, Douglas McGregor's Theory X and Theory Y approaches, and the management science movement which views business as a set of mathematical models.

This brief review identifies for the supervisor or potential supervisor the vast research and writing on the various theories and schools of thought. Those who aspire to higher-level management positions can pursue the thinking of each.

Levels of Management

For the sake of study and analysis, managers are frequently categorized into three levels of management. In large organizations, each level might be further subdivided. Those who manage the operatives, or workers are the *supervisory* or first-level managers, sometimes called first-line supervisors. **Middle management** represents those managers between the first and third

middle management management between top management and supervisory management

levels. When a unit of an organization becomes too large for two tiers of management, additional tiers of the hierarchy and additional subdivisions of the unit may become necessary. The third level of management is called **top management**. This group represents the highest level—the corporate vice presidents and those elected by boards of directors to head the various functional areas, the major directors of government bureaus, and the top-level administrators of institutions. The organization charts in Exhibit 3.1 and Exhibit 3.2 illustrate these three levels of management in private enterprises and in government agencies. There may be several levels of middle management and several levels of supervisory management in very large organizations. Notice that some of the people on the same level with first-line supervisors are not really supervisors, because no workers report to them. They are considered "staff" employees. A discussion of line and staff positions follows in a later portion of this chapter.

top management high-est level of management

RESEARCH AND PRACTICE

FUNCTIONS AND PRINCIPLES OF MANAGEMENT

The word **management function**, when used to identify what managers do, represents generalizations about the nature of the work. Identification and labeling of these functions is an attempt to depict the elements of management that are common to all management positions. While different writers and management authorities select different terms to describe these functions, they are in general agreement that the functions exist; and the terminology used here is common among most authorities. Although some of these functions are performed only on a very limited basis by supervisors, they must understand that other management personnel are performing these functions.

management function generalizations about the work of a manager

What do managers do? In varying degrees, they plan, organize, lead, direct, and control (1) people, (2) processes, and (3) physical resources. These terms are intended to identify the general functions performed—not the specific day-to-day duties performed or the routine tasks of a particular manager.

Planning

Planning *anticipating the future and stipulating necessary arrangements*

Planning is anticipating the future and stipulating necessary arrangements. Some managers must plan for the entire organization; others, for only a portion of the organization. Managers who are responsible for relatively small portions of an organization can

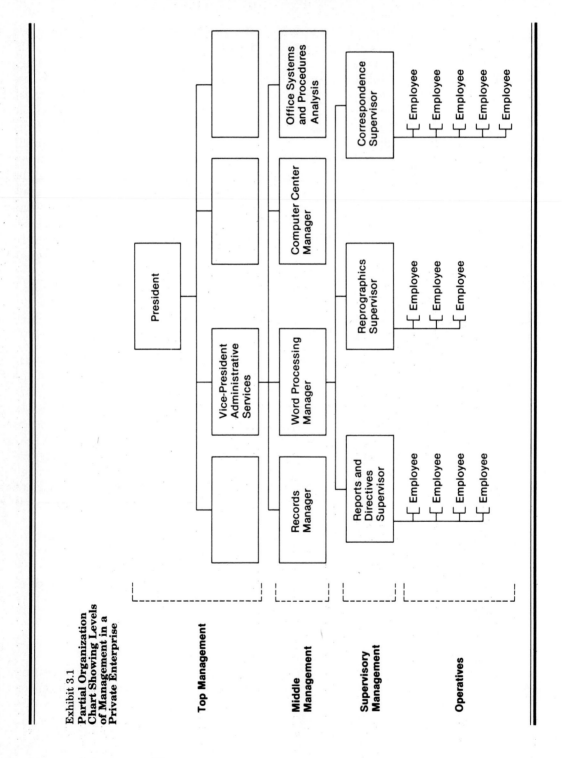

Exhibit 3.1
Partial Organization
Chart Showing Levels
of Management in a
Private Enterprise

Top Management

Middle
Management

Supervisory
Management

Operatives

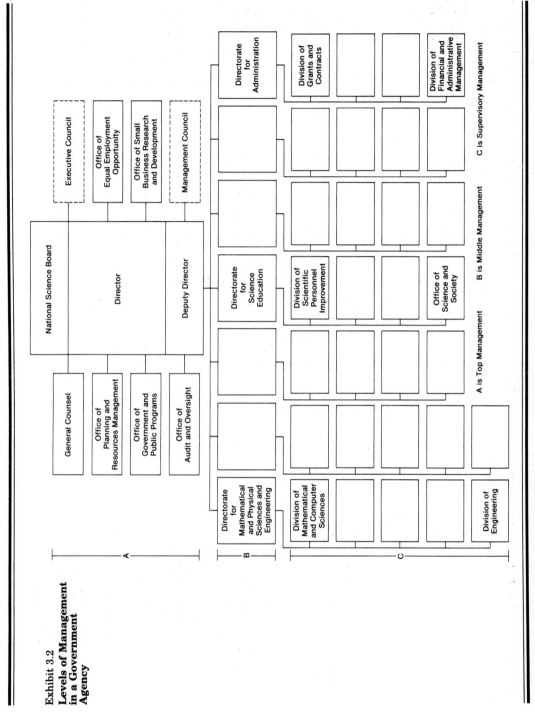

Exhibit 3.2
Levels of Management in a Government Agency

National Science Board

Executive Council

Office of Equal Employment Opportunity

Office of Small Business Research and Development

Management Council

Director

Deputy Director

General Counsel

Office of Planning and Resources Management

Office of Government and Public Programs

Office of Audit and Oversight

Directorate for Science Education

Division of Scientific Personnel Improvement

Office of Science and Society

Directorate for Administration

Division of Grants and Contracts

Division of Financial and Administrative Management

Directorate for Mathematical and Physical Sciences and Engineering

Division of Mathematical and Computer Sciences

Division of Engineering

A is Top Management   B is Middle Management   C is Supervisory Management

Source: *Organizational Directory* Washington: National Science Foundation, (Winter 1978).

participate, through advice to superiors, in planning for larger portions of the organization.

Planning is a mental activity for some supervisors; for others, it can include discussions with superiors about what will be done in the future; for still others, it can include committing plans to writing in elaborate reports. Particular targets are financial planning, personnel planning, and technical planning. Business firms must plan for the production and marketing of products or services to be offered and for financial and human resources. For all organizations, planning involves equipment and physical environments for workers, administrative systems, procedures for processing information, and communication systems.

Planning is not necessarily periodic, although many organizations require that written plans be submitted for annual review. Planning should be an ongoing, continual activity. Although top managers are thought of as the master planners for an organization, their plans are really a combination of those that have been initiated by subordinates. While planning may not consume huge quantities of time for middle- and supervisory-level managers, it is essential for orderly activity.

Organizing

organizing establishing effective relationships among people

Organizing deals with the establishment of relationships among people and with the division of activity among the various subunits. When two colleagues decide to carry out some activity together and each agrees to perform one portion of the activity, they have organized their efforts. To some extent, they have also performed the function of planning.

You are organizing when you decide to divide a company into five departments, perhaps because you realize that the work that is carried out falls into five neat categories of related activity. When one employee is appointed to the management of one of those five units, and another employee is appointed the assistant manager, and five operative-level employees are hired to carry out the work in the department, you have further organized the department. When, in a few years, the number of operative employees in that same department has grown to eighteen, and you promote two of the employees and give them the title *supervisor*, you have organized still further. These steps have added formality to the organization. Assuming that the lines of authority and the nature of jobs and responsibilities are clearly defined, the department is organized. Generally, efforts must be organized when large numbers of people and many processes must function in concert with each other. Failure to do so can result in chaos.

formal organization official hierarchy of positions

informal organization unofficial relationships among employees

This discussion has dealt with **formal organization**. Also at work or in existence in every organization is the **informal organization**. An example of such an informal organization might exist when one operative dominates activity in a section because the supervisor doesn't want to confront that employee. Another example could exist if the supervisor lives next-door to a manager in another department of the same firm. The neighbor has more influence on the supervisor over the backyard fence than the supervisor's formal superior has. Most managers recognize that informal influences exist; but they don't try to eliminate them. Instead, they attempt to work around them and to use them as effectively as possible. As discussed in Chapter Seven, the communication channels created by this informal organization can actually be used to benefit the spread of information.

organization chart paper drawing of positions

A paper drawing of an organization is called an **organization chart** (see Exhibits 3.1 and 3.2), but such charts do not necessarily depict the real relationships, authority, and hierarchy of the organization. Charts quickly become outdated; job descriptions are also sometimes inaccurate; and changes are often made without updating job descriptions. Corporate owners, business proprietors, and—for government organizations—statutory and legislative specifications create **authority** for top management. They give top management the right to make decisions for the organization. Top managers, in turn, pass authority to lower-level personnel in the organization. This passing of authority is called **delegation**. As organizations grow and as the work load becomes cumbersome for managers, the only way they can continue to progress is to share their authority with others. This necessity creates more complicated organizations, but results in organizations that function smoothly. Be sure to note carefully the distinction between authority and **responsibility** in the portion of this chapter devoted to principles of management.

authority right to act and to require action

delegating passing authority to another

responsibility obligation to act or to be accountable

line management those who receive authority from superior; responsible for subordinates

staff management those in an advisory capacity

Managers and the nature of the authority that they possess are sometimes divided into **line** and **staff**. Line managers are those who actually supervise a portion of the work force; other employees report to them. Staff managers serve in an advisory capacity. Their relationship with the work force is not as authoritative as is the line manager's authority. For example, an office procedures analyst for a firm might be assigned temporarily to the production manager to assist in the design of office space occupied by the shipping and receiving department. While his or her advice would probably be followed, there is no authority for that analyst

53

to order the production manager to arrange the offices of the shipping and receiving department according to the staff person's recommendations. The staff person is one with some special expertise who advises or serves other portions of the organization.

In real line and staff organizations, so-called "staff" people wield considerable authority because they are supported by top management which does have line authority over the recipients of advice from staff people. As the records manager, you may have line authority over the records staff only. But if company policy provides that you approve all new form designs, then you have some real authority over each department that wants to create a new form for processing information.

Some managers are line and staff managers. They have line authority over a group of workers, but they also serve in advisory capacities to other portions of the organization. The office systems specialist might be in charge of a group of employees who design information processing and handling systems, design business forms and records, and conduct analyses of office work throughout an organization. To the employees in that group, the office systems specialist is a line manager; to others, however, he or she is a staff manager.

Most organizations represent some combination of line and staff, although they are not usually as simple as textbook organization charts depict. Two alternative arrangements to line and staff are the functional organization and the committee organization. Functional organizations establish positions which are in charge of particular functions; for example, research, finances, and technical production. Workers report to the manager of a function when his or her work involves that function, but if the work changes to something related to another functional area, another manager directs the activity. Both this arrangement and the committee arrangement (committees, not individuals, manage activities) can frustrate workers because they must report to more than one superior. Professional firms (law firms, brokerage houses, and medical firms) sometimes are organized around a committee or functional basis.

leading *activating and carrying out plans with people*

directing *ordering processes; coordinating people and processes*

Leading and Directing

Another function of managers is **leading** people. Some authorities would use this term to mean the same as **directing**; others would differentiate between the two. Still others prefer to use the terms

54

motivating or *actuating*. Whatever it is called, this function involves activating and carrying out the plans of the organization. Managers who can lead and direct, who can understand people and communicate effectively with them, make the best leaders. Opinion differs with respect to the requisites for leadership—innate ability, training, age, experience, education. All are possible determinants, and no one requisite or no magic combination of characteritics enables people to lead best. However, the functions of leading people and directing processes and activities are essential functions in the management process.

Controlling

controlling evaluating and taking steps to keep organization on target

Although the functions of management have been discussed individually, managers do not perform the functions individually—one at a time or in some prescribed sequence. The functions are performed simultaneously; sometimes without thought or differentiation by the manager performing them. **Controlling** happens to be the last function to be discussed, but it should not be considered as a function that is performed after all others have been completed. Managers' functions are never completed. There are starting and ending points for major projects of fiscal periods, but controlling is an ongoing process. It is the process of evaluating and taking necessary steps to keep the organization on target. *It is the pause to compare progress with plans, accomplishment with goals, and people performance with expectations.*

Some controls are accomplished by informal, everyday observation, followed by changes as necessary. Other controls are formal, built-in checks and balances. Manufacturing concerns conduct quality control programs which involve testing and inspection of products. Variations from established standards suggest flaws in the production process. These flaws are identified and corrected.

As another means for controlling, most organizations are subjected to periodic audits of financial records. In recent years, for example, "Zero-Based Budgeting" requires agencies and departments to defend their requests for each dollar of funds annually. No appropriation is automatic just because it was in the budget last year.

While certain positions in organizations, such as the quality control supervisor, are devoted almost entirely to some aspect of control, the work of every supervisor or manager should contain some control functions. Whether the control is a formal system or the manager's watchful eye and questioning attitude, ongoing control is a necessary function.

Principles of Management

principle guide to management action

A **principle** is a guide to action and might be considered a standard which has evolved through time—a truth that has surfaced through careful study and analysis or trial and error. Dictionary definitions of *principle* include such descriptors as fundamental truth, law, and integrity. Principles of management represent standard guidelines which, when followed by managers, usually accomplish favorable results. Of course, a result that is favorable to one person may be interpreted as unfavorable by another.

Followers of classical management theory support the existence and validity of certain management principles; behavioral scientists usually prefer to discount or ignore these traditional principles and attempt to prove scientifically one approach or another. If it cannot be scientifically proven, they would prefer to avoid identifying it as a standard for action.

A few selected principles, most of which deal with either the organizing or the leading functions, are discussed in the following pages. Many of these have been carried over from the functional era of management philosophy and are criticized as oversimplifications of managerial responsibility. Nevertheless, they identify a basis for management action and topics for further study. They should not be considered recipes for success; nor should they be followed blindly.

span of control number of people that one supervisor can effectively direct

Span of Control The principle of **span of control** states that there is a limit to the number of people that one supervisor or manager can effectively direct. In other words, the number of people reporting to a single supervisor can be expanded to a point that hampers effective supervision. There is no magic number for this principle, although some people would want to suggest such a number. If the work involved and the nature of the day-to-day contacts required between superior and subordinate is great, one supervisor may wish to restrict the number of subordinates to five or six people, while another supervisor might effectively manage twenty subordinates. The nature of the oversight required and the relationships among those supervised greatly affect the number. Coordinating the work of five people who must work together in

The span of control can be extensive if the supervisor is not required to constantly oversee employee activity. In this case, the supervisor is hardly visible at the back of the office suite. Each employee is able to work independently with little direct supervision.

Photograph by Alan Baker, courtesy of American National Bank.

order for the system to function can be more complicated than coordinating the work of fifteen people who work independently of each other and merely make routine progress reports to their supervisor.

The principle suggests that it merely be recognized that there is a limit. If this limit is surpassed, either the organization or the nature of the supervision must be altered. If the limit is exceeded, the effectiveness of the supervisor will be diminished.

Authority Commensurate with Responsibility As we mentioned earlier, authority is the right to act or to make decisions. Authority can be delegated—literally, given—to another person. Responsibility, on the other hand, is an obligation. When you give someone else part of your authority by giving them the right to make decisions and to exercise judgment regarding a particular aspect of work for which you are responsible, you retain responsibility for that activity. You are responsible for your subordinates; you are accountable to your superior for their actions as well as your own. So you can pass authority—the right to act—to others, but you cannot pass your responsibility.

Because of the accountability factor, some managers refrain from delegating. Or they go through the motions of delegating, but withhold actual authority. "I'm going to turn over this job to you, Jacobs, but check with me before you make any decisions regarding it." Jacobs knows that he has no real authority. The principle involved here, then, is that one should delegate authority to act which is commensurate with (equal to or in the same proportion as) the responsibility with which a subordinate is charged. In other words, you don't say to a subordinate that you are making him or her responsible for a particular activity but refuse to allow the subordinate to make decisions regarding that activity.

Because supervisors are responsible for subordinates to whom they delegate authority, they must select and/or train subordinates carefully. Managers who have responsible, trustworthy subordinates can delegate with ease. Those who have weak subordinates probably should refrain from delegating and hope for a chance to replace the subordinates.

Responsibility to a Single Superior This principle suggests that every employee should report directly to one superior. Some forms of organization place employees in positions requiring that they report to multiple superiors. In other situations, the informal organization is so strong that an employee may feel compelled to report to more than one person. Neither of these situations is good. If the organization chart represents the true organization, each employee should be accountable to the person who occupies the position immediately above that employee on the chart. Otherwise, the employee will be confused and frustrated. When circumstances necessitate certain employee's working with multiple superiors, some system of priority should be worked out.

In reality many employees answer to more than one superior. In no case, however, should an employee who follows the direction of his immediate and official superior be disciplined or reprimanded for following those directions—even when they represent poor judgment on the part of the superior. This destroys the morale of the employee and diminishes the effectiveness of the superior. A supervisor or manager who poorly advises or directs a subordinate must answer to his or her superior and accept the related responsibility, but it is unfair to hold the employee responsible for his superior's poor judgment.

Objectives That every organization and every unit within that organization should have specific objectives is a principle that may appear to be a restatement of the obvious. However, many organizations and the individuals who comprise them flounder without specific objectives. Successful organizations and successful people can state specifically what they expect to accomplish in their work. Objectives can be associated with time periods—the immediate future, the next six months, or the next year—or they can be standards of accomplishment against which work can be measured in a generalized way. Objectives should be committed to writing. If objectives cannot be verbalized, they are too vague to be of value. Many managers cannot verbalize their own objectives or the specific objectives of their employees.

Of course, the ultimate objective of every private enterprise is profit, and managers realize that. Beyond this, however, many managers have a difficult time in identifying specific objectives which, when accomplished, will result in a profit. Progressive firms identify objectives such as the best product available for the price, fair and equitable working conditions and salaries for employees, and service to customers. Every manager should know the organization's specific objectives and be able to relate his or her own work to the accomplishment of these goals.

management by objective (MBO) system stressing formal objectives for each manager and frequent review of progress

Some firms believe so strongly in the practice of writing specific objectives and periodically reviewing progress toward their accomplishment that they have developed a system of management which is called **Management by Objectives (MBO)**. Every member of the managerial staff is required to prepare specific objectives in cooperation with immediate supervisors, and to report and evaluate progress toward accomplishing them.

Open Communication Although frequently omitted from lists of management principles, the value of free and open communication is supported by most experienced managers and by communication research. All managers should maintain an atmosphere that is conducive to a free flow of communication between the manager and superiors and between the manager and subordinates. In both directions—and horizontally among colleagues—the ideal is that parties to the communication process should be free to say what they are thinking without fear of reprisal or chastisement from the other parties involved. The technique and the timing of such communication are very important. Chapter Seven discusses the communication process and the barriers which can prevent free and open communication.

Engendering Trust Considerable investigation continues in an effort to identify those factors that contribute to the success of Japanese industry. One factor or "principle" appears to be the idea of trust. While the social complexity of the Japanese system is immense, a major finding is that teamwork with a view to long-term gains is based on a climate of worker-management trust.[2] In addition, it has been the experience in Western organizations that units that demonstrate a great deal of trust among the workers and supervisors are more stable and productive over the long term. The term "trust" (which is defined differently by the Japanese) for our purposes is the development of clear and concise understandings of expectations, roles, and objectives within the work setting. This provides all employees with a sense of security in knowing who will do what and when. This sense should include the idea that "I can trust you to do the best job possible for the welfare of the total group." "I know you will be responsible not only for your own actions but for the welfare of the team." This sense of responsibility and trust applies to all levels of employment and is an integral part of an open communication system. The supervisor cannot develop this climate of trust overnight. As a matter of fact, it may take months or even years before people come to accept a trust climate as a reality, but that principle objective will pay off tenfold in the future quality-of-work-life for both employer and employees.

Numerous additional principles guide the thinking and decision making of men and women in leadership capacities. Some avoid the word *principle* and use "implications," "propositions," and "hypotheses." While eschewed by some modern management theorists, principles can be especially helpful for new supervisors. Every supervisor is likely to modify standard principles in application, which is why some prefer to call management a set of practices, not a science or a profession.

IMPLICATIONS AND APPLICATIONS

MANAGEMENT DUTIES

To illustrate the difference between managerial functions and managerial duties, the following specimen duties are presented and discussed. These represent the more routine tasks. Not every manager would be involved in all of these activities; however, they are typical.

---

[2]William G. Ouchi, *Theory Z: How American Business Can Meet the Japanese Challenge* (New York: Avon Books, 1982).

Reporting to superiors consumes large portions of the supervisor's time. New supervisors sometimes resent the volume of "paperwork" in their jobs.

Photograph by Alan Baker, courtesy of American National Bank.

Budgeting and Financial Planning

Many managers would prefer to avoid responsibilities for financial matters, but such responsibilities are necessary. Managers must anticipate expenditures for human resources, materials, supplies, equipment, buildings, and raw materials for their particular areas of the organization.

Accountants keep track of spending and financial data, but managers must periodically justify what they have spent and what they want to spend in future periods. When expenditures exceed what has been budgeted (planned) for a particular item, decisions must be made regarding the source of additional funds or cutbacks in expenditures.

Reporting Production

Every unit of an organization must produce something in order to justify its existence. Production departments of manufacturing firms produce products; personnel departments produce processed applications for employment, fill vacant positions, and provide employee services; accounting departments produce financial rec-

61

ords and interpretations of financial data; and other departments produce information regarding services provided to clients. Managers must account for production to superiors, usually in writing. This consumes large portions of their time.

Supervisors who must complete daily and weekly production reports or fill out forms which document the work of their subordinates sometimes question the value of such information. They treat the task as cruel and unnecessary punishment. As a result, their reporting is frequently inaccurate. In an investigation conducted by the authors, production line supervisors in a small manufacturing plant were asked how much time they spend filling out the required daily production reports for their lines. One supervisor estimated that he spends three to five minutes a day on the activity; another estimated one hour and fifteen minutes; and a third supervisor estimated that she spends fifteen to twenty minutes. The production manager believed the third estimate to be the closest to the time which should be devoted to the task. Obviously, one of the supervisors is spending too much time on the task, and another is spending too little.

Management should require only reports that are necessary and contain valuable information, and the value of accurate reporting should be emphasized.

Selecting and Training Workers

This responsibility is explored more fully in Chapters Eleven and Twelve. Managers at all levels spend some time interviewing prospective employees, advising those who make the final decisions regarding hiring, orienting, and training new employees. Operatives may make some contributions to the training of new employees, but the supervisor and other management personnel should direct this activity.

Routine Supervision

A large portion of managerial time is spent in observation, evaluation, and direction of the routine activities. Some employees are prone to think that managers do nothing—that they are paid for watching others work. It must be understood, however, that managers handle unexpected problems and make decisions that keep the productivity of the unit going.

Developing and Managing Procedures and Methods

Managers are continually looking for new ways to do things. Someone must decide the sequence of activities that is best to get the job done. When many employees participate in the performance of a procedure, someone must decide who performs each portion and the sequence of performance. Most routine activities are carried out more smoothly if a standard procedure is followed each time the task is performed. Chapter Nine presents a description of formal procedures analysis and design.

Developing Policy and Standards

policy guideline for decision making

Managers create **policy** and set standards of performance for employees and standards of quality for goods and services. Higher levels of management have greater responsibility for these tasks than middle and supervisory level management. Policy is a guideline for decision making. It is a permanent decision for a particular set of circumstances. If the firm has a policy that states that employees who have been with the firm for five years or more are entitled to three weeks of vacation, then no discussion of the length of a particular employee's vacation period is necessary. When his tenure reaches five years, he automatically gets an extra week of vacation.

Standards are set to guide workers in evaluating themselves and to guide management in evaluating production—whether that production is a tangible product, a service, or information. Supervisors are more likely to recommend policy than to set it. They will be more involved with applying standards than with setting standards.

The job description for some managers may contain long lists of specific duties. At the first-line supervisor's level, the list may be relatively short. Managers should continually evaluate their own duties and those of the managerial staff members for whom they are responsible. Duties which are no longer necessary should be eliminated; activities which would improve the productivity of the organization should be added. Continual questioning and evaluating can result in improvements. On the other hand, frequent changes for the sake of change can be detrimental to productivity. Skillful managers should strive for the right combination of inquisitiveness and acceptance of proven procedures. They accept new responsibilities and relinquish those that are no longer necessary or that could be better managed by another person.

MANAGEMENT PROBLEM SOLVING

Managers are problem solvers. The problems they must solve fall into three categories: technical problems, communication problems, and people problems. Of course, many of the problems with which managers deal are of a technical nature and are related to the basic work being managed. People who are employed as managers usually have the technical skills to handle these problems. Technical knowledge and experience are easy to quantify and evaluate when candidates for management positions are being considered. These problems are time consuming, but managers usually deal with them routinely.

The other two problem-solving areas are common to most management positions and their scope reaches outside the technical expertise of managers. These problems deal with communication and interaction skills required for managing the people.

Communication Problems

Although skillful managers are able to avoid many communication problems through careful study and development of their own skills, communication problems are unavoidable. Managers must communicate with multiple groups of people, each of which may have separate interests and goals. Among these groups are subordinates, superiors, customers or patrons, outside organizations, and governments. When breakdowns in communication with individuals who represent these groups occur, the most successful managers recognize the crucial nature of the problem and they attempt to keep lines of communication open and to handle problems which develop because of failure to communicate. Two chapters of this text are devoted to the vital communication process and techniques for improving managerial communication skills.

People Problems

Society has advanced to a state that makes solution of technical problems relatively easy, but technical advances have not provided solutions to people problems. Managers must deal with the problems that are created as subordinates interact with each other and with those outside the work unit. Personal problems of employees often create work interference.

New directions in management thinking represent changing attitudes and philosophies regarding employee problems. In the past, traditional approaches suggested that employers should get rid of problems by ridding themselves of the people who created the problems. This is still necessary in some cases; but increasingly, organizations are making attempts to help employees to rid themselves of problems. This is evidenced by the number of organizations who employ professional counselors and who participate in rehabilitation programs for employees with such problems as alcoholism, drug-related difficulties, and emotional disorders. Through policy, instruction, and training programs, managers are taught to assist in these problem-solving activities. In most cases, the supervisor or other manager is expected only to recognize the existence of problems and to seek professional assistance for the employee. Managers are not expected to assume the role of psychologist. In fact, most supervisors are not equipped to assume that role.

The more informed a manager becomes regarding people, their needs, and motivational considerations, the better that manager will be able to deal with the problems that arise.

Routine Problem Solving

Every supervisory or managerial job involves continuous survey of activities within the unit for which the manager is responsible. Routine troubleshooting and problem solving becomes a way of life for supervisors. Although good planning and organization keeps problems to a minimum, any management position involves on-the-spot problem solving.

MANAGERIAL QUALIFICATIONS— OR HOW DO I GET TO BE A MANAGER?

Specific qualifications for managerial positions must be developed for each organization. Certain general personal, educational, and professional qualifications, however, can be identified for practically any management position. Exhibit 3.3 outlines such qualifications. The educational qualifications might be gained through formal education, independent study, or employer-sponsored educational activities such as institutes, seminars, and training programs. More and more organizations are requiring at least an associate degree from a college or university for persons who enter management positions at any level.

Additional managerial qualifications are discussed in Chapter Twelve under "Career Paths for Supervisors."

Exhibit 3.3
General Qualifications for Management Positions

Desirable Personal Qualifications

Understands people—their needs and desires—and is able to motivate them

Makes decisions easily and systematically

Understands the organization—its objectives, products or services, role in the community, and relationship to the economy

Positive attitude about job, effective leadership techniques, appropriate balance of task and people orientation

Communication skills—both oral and written—which will permit free exchange of information with all individuals or groups with whom the manager must communicate, directly or indirectly

Honesty in all relationships

People interaction style (open, trustworthy, responsible for own actions, willing to change)

Educational Qualifications

General education sufficient for understanding people and for communicating and problem solving

Technical knowledge and skills necessary for directing the work managed

Minimum formal education and/or training program required by employer

Professional Qualifications

Professional management knowledge and skills (principles, functions, and philosophies of management)

Membership and participation in professional development organizations and learned societies appropriate for the field of work being managed

Ability to select subordinates and develop them into productive employees

Plans for continued self-development and renewal of technical knowledge and skills

THE SUPERVISOR'S PHILOSOPHY OF MANAGEMENT

Every supervisor should study the various theories of organization and management, the thinking of past and present leaders, and the functions and objectives of management which are thought to be common. Such study and analysis should be related and compared to the work in one's current position and to the work anticipated in future positions. Serious thinking and analysis of this type enables supervisors to evolve a personal philosophy of management. From other philosophies, one should borrow the precepts in which one can believe. One should analyze, interpret, and expand one's own ideas and experiences.

A philosophy of management should reflect a supervisor's thinking with regard to (1) people, (2) the organization, (3) the quality of one's own contribution, (4) the evaluation of performance, and (5) the ethical implications of the job. This philosophy is reflected in one's performance; it is a general guide to action—not a set of self-imposed or externally imposed rules and regulations. Philosophies of individual managers are changed and molded by experiences and events through time. A carefully devised philosophy of management will enable managers at any level to make decisions with which they can live comfortably when the buck must stop with them. The supervisor who has a full understanding of his or her own management philosophy can make a difference.

Some employers restrict managers' actions or push them beyond limits which they can tolerate. Job requirements which seriously conflict with one's philosophy and personal goals and standards may become the basis for conflict and frustration.

SUMMARY

Private enterprise is managed by its owners or by professional salaried managers. Public organizations and nonprofit institutions are also managed by professional managers. Supervisors represent the first-level of managers above the operative or worker level. Even though supervisors believe that middle- and top-level managers make the major decisions, they should consider themselves managers and should be as knowledgeable as possible about the history, theory, and functions of management and organizations.

Management is a young discipline, having passed through several schools of thought identified as classical, neoclassical, and modern management theories. Numerous other distinguishable schools of thought have been associated with various time periods and philosophies. The management functions include planning, organizing, leading, directing, and controlling. These functions are applied to managing people, processes, and physical facilities in varying degrees from one manager to another. Planning for the future, organizing the people and processes necessary to carry out the objectives of the organization, and providing leadership for employees consume large portions of managerial time. Control involves evaluation of what is happening and making appropriate changes to keep things on target.

Although many disagree on the validity of some management principles, they represent guidelines for action and decision making. Principles involving authority and responsibility of subordinates, the number of subordinates supervised, and the importance of objectives are examples of these guidelines. Routine but significant duties consume another large portion of managers' time and include budgeting, financial planning, oral and written reporting, selecting and training workers, developing procedures for doing work, and handling routine problems. These "duties" are more specific identifications of what managers do, while "functions" are broad generalizations regarding their work.

Experience has enabled the identification of certain managerial qualifications which appear necessary for most management jobs. Personal, educational, and professional accomplishments and activities prepare individuals for work as managers.

Every supervisor should begin to develop his or her own philosophy of management which becomes a background for action in the current position and for career development in the future.

QUESTIONS FOR FURTHER THOUGHT

1. Defend the statement that supervisors are managers.
2. What are the major differences between working at an operative-level job and working as a supervisor?
3. What was the major focus of classical management theory?
4. Identify the three popular levels of managers in modern organizations and differentiate among the three.
5. What are common functions of managers?
6. Contrast the probable planning and organizing functions for managers in several of the following organizations:
   a. a bank
   b. a heavy-industry manufacturing plant
   c. a community college
   d. an engineering firm
   e. a small firm that manufactures craft kits for sale to retail craft stores
   f. an insurance agency
   g. a retail department store
   h. an agricultural equipment dealership
   i. a small advertising agency
   j. the local state employment agency
   k. the regional social security office
7. List and define the major management duties of first-level supervisors.

PART TWO

UNDERLYING INFLUENCES ON BEHAVIOR

4

THE MOTIVATION FACTOR

LEARNING OBJECTIVES

Upon completion of this chapter and related assignments, you should be able to:
1. Describe the difference between employee motivation and environmental reinforcement systems.
2. List and understand several approaches for describing worker motivational factors.
3. Describe the difference between primary and secondary motivations.
4. Develop your own list of motive-reinforcement factors that are important for a successful supervisor to consider when dealing with the organization-people mix.

CHAPTER OUTLINE

PROBLEM STATEMENT
MOTIVATION: A FUNCTION OF REWARD SYSTEMS

BACKGROUND AND THEORY
WORKER MOTIVATION—WHAT IS IT?
    The Classic View of Motivation
    Is There a hierarchy of Needs?
REINFORCEMENT—THE OTHER SIDE OF MOTIVATION
WHAT IS THE HAWTHORNE EFFECT?
JOB SATISFACTION OR SATISFIERS VS. DISSATISFIERS

RESEARCH AND PRACTICE
RECENT EFFORTS IN JOB MOTIVATION
CONSIDER JAPAN—WHERE LIES THE MOTIVE?

IMPLICATIONS AND APPLICATIONS
SOME ADDITIONAL CONSIDERATIONS
IMPLICATIONS FOR THE SUPERVISOR
CHAPTER SUMMARY

QUESTIONS FOR FURTHER THOUGHT

PROBLEM
STATEMENT

MOTIVATION: A
FUNCTION OF REWARD SYSTEMS

Hundreds of articles and books have been written on the subject of worker motivation. The few listed below will provide a feeling for the variety of approaches to the topic of motivation.

A major problem that arises with this topic is that management people frequently do not understand the nature of worker motivation, cannot define the term, and know little about reward systems. This chapter reviews several of the major events in employee motivation research in an effort to draw some general principles about the limitations and possibilities for motivating people.

BACKGROUND
AND
THEORY

WORKER MOTIVATION—WHAT IS IT?

Worker motivation is one of the most misunderstood, misused and abused conceptualizations in the world's industrial sphere. Motivation is seen by the business world as something you give to your employees and then your troubles are over. Motivation is the corporation's answer to all ills. Motivation is like the apple-a-day system. The employee eats the apple of motives, it is ingested, and thereafter the employee is driven by the inherent properties contained within that apple. Nothing could be farther from the truth. Motivation comes from within, and is not something that can be fed in. There are external rewards and internal motivations, and it makes little sense to think in terms of external motivation.

Leonard Ackerman, "Let's Put Motivation Where It Belongs Within the Individual," *Personnel Journal*, July 1970.

Bruce M. Broad, "Not by Bread Alone," *Personnel Journal*, November 1970, pp. 913–917.

Fredrick Herzberg, "One More Time: How Do You Motivate Employees?" *Harvard Business Review*, January–February 1968.

Lucien Karpik, "Expectation and Satisfactions in Work," *Human Relations*, July 1968, pp. 327–349.

David C. McClelland, *Motivational Trends in Society* (New York: General Learning Press, 1971).

William J. Paul, Jr., Keith B. Robertson and Fredrick Herzberg, "Job Enrichment Pays Off," *Harvard Business Review*, March–April 1969, pp. 61–78.

William J. Roche and Neil L. Mackinnov, "Motivating People with Meaningful Work," *Harvard Business Review*, May–June 1970.

Thomas C. Rodney, "Can Money Motivate Better Job Performance?" *Personnel Administration*, March–April 1967.

Irwin Ross, "The Booming Benefits of Profit Sharing," *Reader's Digest*, August 1969, pp. 111–114.

Melvin Sorcher and Herbert H. Meyer, "Motivation and Job Performance," *Personnel Administration*, July–August 1968.

One possible internal motivator is pride in the product quality. In addition, people have a need for belonging; and team work provides a setting for satisfying this need.

Photograph by Alan Baker, courtesy of FMC Corporation.

motivation *individual internal and directional energizer system*

Motivation can be thought of as an internal energizer with built-in directional properties.

If that is the case—that motivation is within the individual—the only thing that management can do is provide the most rewarding environment possible so as to encourage the individual to seek to satisfy those motives. There is of course another approach and that is the use of punishment or the threat of punishment. The general topic, therefore, can be viewed as having two basic components. The first is the motivation that *exists* within the employee, and the second is the environmental influences in the form of external reinforcements. As can be seen by this phrasing, motivation exists only within the individual, and all else one talks about is external. The employee comes to the workplace with a set of given motivations; management will continue to try to create the impossible, which is external motivations. The only things external to the individual are various forms of rewards or reinforcements. For our purposes **reward** is defined as a stimulus that increases the probability that designated future behavior will occur. Supervisors can use rewards or lack of rewards or even discipline to entice the employee into certain work behavior. If

reward *condition that increases the likelihood that a specific future behavior will occur*

supervisors think that rewards—like pay—are of most concern to all employees, the supervisor loses sight of a greater concept. That concept is that an individual must expect more than pay. After all, any organization offers a wage. Motivation springs from within and the range of external conditions that can "motivate" individuals suggests that individuals must have some freedom in selecting the rewards and some freedom in achieving those rewards.

The Classic View of Motivation

need perceived deficit that should be changed

Motivation has generally been considered to be made up of several components. Any identifiable motive is thought to be a result of some **need** (a deficit, a desire for more) as well as learned response patterns that have worked in the past to reduce need, and provide a tendency for action. Exhibit 4.1 expresses this approach. What this picture should suggest is that everything is internal except for the objects that are identified as drive reducers.

Is There a Hierarchy of Needs?

hierarchy of needs an ordering of human needs
self-actualize tendency to fulfill potential capabilities

Abraham Maslow developed a need system that has essentially been accepted by a large number of practicing industrial managers.[1] His main theme is that people have five basic needs and that these needs are arranged in order so that the first must be satisfied before one will try to satisfy the second—and so on up the ladder. This ladder is termed a **hierarchy of needs**. In addition, people in some degree have a tendency to **self-actualize** or to fulfill their potential. Exhibit 4.2 describes Maslow's basic approach.

Many of the studies done to test Maslow's model have not been very supportive; but, be that as it may, for this purpose it should be understood that if the safety and physical needs are not taken care of there is a tendency to return to those needs until they are fulfilled. Another way to say that is that if my biological needs aren't satisfied, how could I be concerned about creativity or beauty or self-actualization?

Hersey and Blanchard present an excellent discussion of the concept of motivation that is similar to Maslow's.[2] Adapting sev-

---

[1] Abraham H. Maslow, *Motivation and Personality* (New York: Harper & Row, 1970).
[2] Paul Hersey and Kenneth H. Blanchard, *Management of Organizational Behavior: Utilizing Human Resources* (Englewood Cliffs, N.J.: Prentice-Hall, 1977).

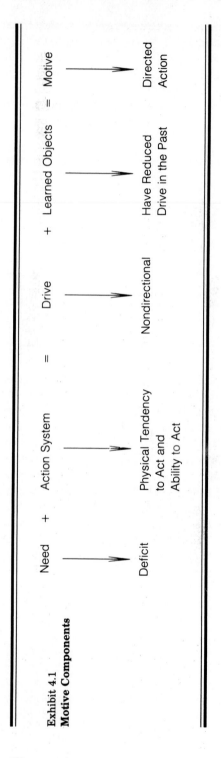

Exhibit 4.1
Motive Components

Need + Action System = Drive + Learned Objects = Motive

Deficit → Physical Tendency to Act and Ability to Act → Nondirectional → Have Reduced Drive in the Past → Directed Action

Exhibit 4
Maslow'
Hierarch

primary (
physical or
basic requi

secondary
dividual lea
ments

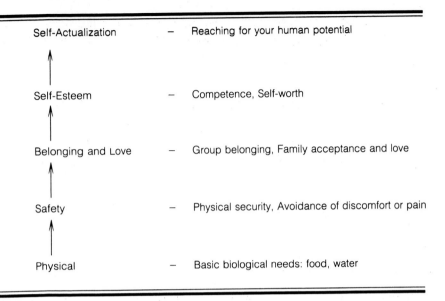

Self-Actualization — Reaching for your human potential

Self-Esteem — Competence, Self-worth

Belonging and Love — Group belonging, Family acceptance and love

Safety — Physical security, Avoidance of discomfort or pain

Physical — Basic biological needs: food, water

eral ideas (expectancies and goal behavior) from Hersey and Blanchard and combining them with the ideas in Exhibit 4.1, the model in Exhibit 4.3 is presented to describe a complex set of relationships among needs, motives, goals, and expectations.

As depicted in Exhibit 4.3, the individual's internal system is composed of the motives to act for the purpose of changing a condition both in quantitative and qualitative terms. The external rewards available will influence one's level of expectation, but that is primarily a function of the individual and the perceived likelihood of the rewards being available.

It may also help to understand that there are two broad types of motives. The **primary motives** can be thought of as being physical or biological in origin. Motives that fit into that category are hunger, thirst, survival, sex, stimulation, physical safety, and others that are due to physical deficits or changes. **Secondary** or **learned motives** are acquired through the learning process, very much like habits are developed. There are probably as many learned motives as there are reasonable descriptions of directional behavior. Such ideas as achievement, affiliation, power, self-esteem, aggressiveness, gregariousness fit into this category. Because the secondary motives are acquired through a learning process, the role of reinforcements is an important factor in influencing which motives are chosen and by whom. People, as they mature, find certain activities rewarding and satisfying; and as

ives)
logical
ents

otives) in-
d require-

Exhibit 4.3
**Motivational Factors
in Terms of Internal
and External Systems**

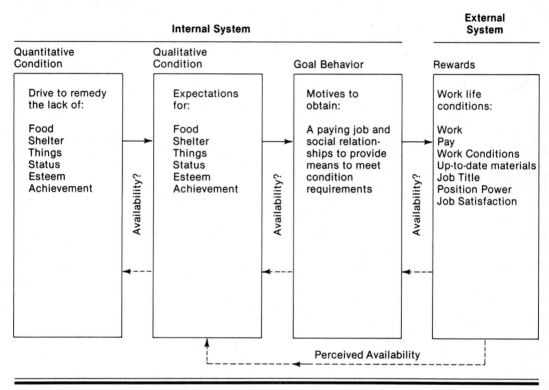

	Internal System		External System
Quantitative Condition	Qualitative Condition	Goal Behavior	Rewards
Drive to remedy the lack of: Food Shelter Things Status Esteem Achievement	Expectations for: Food Shelter Things Status Esteem Achievement	Motives to obtain: A paying job and social relation-ships to provide means to meet condition requirements	Work life conditions: Work Pay Work Conditions Up-to-date materials Job Title Position Power Job Satisfaction

Availability?   Availability?   Availability?

Perceived Availability

they grow further, past successes accrue, and increasingly in-fluence future behavior. As behaviorist B. F. Skinner suggested as early as 1939, learning is not a trial and error process, but rather a trial and success process. Those successes take on motivational characteristics for future activities.

REINFORCEMENT— THE OTHER SIDE OF MOTIVATION

reinforcements rewards

The work done by Skinner and other behavior or learning psychol-ogists points up the importance of **reinforcements** for getting people to operate on their world. These reward psychologists developed the concept of differing schedules of reinforcements and the subsequent behavior change or nonchange as the case may be. Everyone learns to do certain things to receive certain things in return. Wages fall into this category and are a function of an individual's own perceived needs. In addition, people become comfortable with certain work routines for obtaining money or work rewards. In determining the kinds of rewards that are available in the work place, a study by Blum and Russ concluded that five motives are directly affected on the job.[3] They are advancement, security, salary, supervision, and hours of work. Stagner found that employees are not concerned about pay as such but respond to other rewards like prestige, power, recognition and security.[4]

If one analyzes the source of these rewards, they appear to be external. And indeed the way one responds is a function of the probability of the reward or expectation and the value placed on achieving that reward. Therefore, there are two factors in learned motives: one is *how often* will a person be rewarded or reinforced; and the other is *how much* does the individual want it, like it, or need it.

The research done by behavior theorists indicates that there are several schedules of reinforcement and that we react differently to those schedules. One specific schedule of reinforcement has the worker receiving a paycheck after a predictable period of time (at the end of the month). This is the least productive form of pay system in terms of sustained work behavior. It is, however, very difficult to pay someone on a random and unpredictable schedule. Therefore, for those rewards such as praise, bonuses, or promotions, one might provide a variable reward system and thus achieve higher levels of productivity from the employees. One might conclude that predictable praise is not as meaningful as not-so-predictable praise; however, it should be remembered unpredictable and sporadic praise in whatever form may generate its own confusions, strains, and anxieties. The employee may interpret such behavior as the supervisor's uncertainty about the employee.

The truly superior manager must not only understand all the types of reinforcements at work but the total system in which the employee can achieve those reinforcements. The magnitude of the

---

[3]M. Blum and J. Russ, "A Study of Employee Attitudes towards Various Incentives," *Personnel* (1942), 19: 438–444.
[4]R. Stagner, "Psychological Aspects of Industrial Conflict: II, Motivation," *Personnel Psychology* (1950), 3: 1–16.

One external reinforcement that can be easily provided is an employee-of-the-month program that recognizes excellent performance.

Photograph by Alan Baker, courtesy of American National Bank.

reward (the how much) is a function of the individual and the organizational setting. For example, in a union situation, wage is closely tied to length of employment or seniority. In a sales environment, workers accept the association of earnings and individual effort.

WHAT IS THE HAWTHORNE EFFECT?

Hawthorne studies
productivity studies at a
Western Electric Plant

One of the most interesting series of worker productivity studies ever undertaken is the **Hawthorne studies**. These studies were initiated at the Western Electric plant in Illinois during the early 1920s. The basic concern at that time was the effect of various working conditions on performance or output. The working conditions of most interest were physical in nature such as lighting, temperature, and food. Over a number of years thousands of pieces of information were collected and evaluated. In one project, teams of five women worked in a telephone relay assembly room. As physical and other conditions were systematically changed, productivity levels were measured. The general outcome was that as conditions changed production increased. The interpretations that were forthcoming were varied and interesting and were as follows:

1. It was a process whereby the group could recreate a tribunal society that was highly meaningful and led to greater productivity.

2. Job autonomy and challenge were key factors.

3. Management was paying attention to the individual worker who, therefore, felt important.

4. Because of a sense of group identification, the workers' morale increased, thereby leading to improved production.

5. The workers were responding to what Douglas McGregor later called a Theory Y situation, where workers were allowed to integrate their own motives with those of the organization and provide direction to the everyday operation. (Theory Y is discussed in Chapter Five.)

In 1975, an article was published in *Organizational Dynamics* titled "Hawthorne Revisited." It compiled the results of a symposium held by Western Electric Company and the Harvard Business School. Fifty years later, the Hawthorne studies interpretation is different.

The women received more power to control work-a-day events. They were part of the decision-making process that made work event changes. As Robert L. Kahn stated at the symposium, "There was . . . a genuine transfer of power in specific degree and for no trivial period of time."[5] Chalk one up for worker participation in management decisions.

---

[5]"Hawthorne Revisited: The Legend and the Legacy." A Symposium: *Organizational Dynamics* (Winter 1975), pp. 66–80.

JOB SATISFACTION OR SATISFIERS VS. DISSATISFIERS

job satisfiers job content elements that contribute to motivation

job dissatisfiers environmental conditions that contribute to motivation

Frederick Herzberg made a plea to industry, not only in this country but also in European and Soviet countries, to realize that today's workers respond to two different types of motivation.[6] Theoretically his two motivational factors are distinct, relatively uncorrelated, and have differential impact upon individual workers. Factor number one is **job satisfiers**: those elements of work "which essentially describe the relationship of the worker to what he does, his task, or job content as opposed to job context." Factor number two is **job dissatisfiers**: "those aspects of work which essentially describe the environment or surroundings within which one performs his work tasks."

The two-factor approach initially rested on one major study conducted by Herzberg, Mausner and Snyderman which was set in book form in 1959.[7] Sampling from nine heavy industry plants around Pittsburgh, the researchers chose to use engineers and accountants as their subjects. Interviews were then conducted asking for "any kind of story you like—either a time when you felt exceptionally good or bad about your job." These experiences were called incidents. With 228 high (good) job-attitude sequences, five factors were mentioned at least 20 percent of the time. Conversely those low-attitude (bad) sequences seemed to load percentage-wise on other types of factors as indicated below:

Factors Mentioned	Impact Areas High	Low
achievement	X	
recognition	X	
work itself	X	
responsibility	X	
advancement	X	
salary		
possibility of growth		
status		
subordinate relations		
superior relations		XX
peer relations		XX
supervision-technical		XX
company policy		XX

---

[6]Frederick Herzburg, "The New Industrial Psychology," *Industrial and Labor Relations Review* (April 1965), pp. 364–376.
[7]F. Herzberg, B. Mausner, and B. Snyderman, *The Motivation to Work* (New York: John Wiley & Sons, 1959).

Factors (continued)

Factors Mentioned	Impact Areas High	Low
working conditions		XX
personal life		XX
job security		XX

X = satisfier   XX = dissatisfier

From this basic information the general model was developed and it suggests that those experiences (feelings) that are good (high) were associated with one kind of factor or dimension. Those bad experiences are associated with a different kind of dimension or factor.

Herzberg quite eloquently described the historical development of industrial psychology (achievement psychology might be more appropriate in this context) using Maslow's motivational scheme as a starting point. His theme is that as industry has become more able to meet the lower order needs, progressive managerial approaches have sequentially been addressing the higher needs. This all started with scientific management (addressing the basic needs), progressing to the human relations era which was prodded by the Hawthorne studies (addressing the belonging/social needs), and then progressing to the organizational behavior era (addressing the self-actualizing needs).[8] In an attempt to keep the approach simple and to identify major components influencing job satisfaction, the two-factor theory is suggested by Herzberg to be applicable to all types of workers.

The dissatisfiers (hygiene factors) and the satisfiers (motivator factors) model has come under considerable attack in recent years (Blum and Naylor, 1968) but related research testing the model's functionality continues to be conducted.

RESEARCH
AND
PRACTICE

RECENT EFFORTS IN JOB MOTIVATION

Considerable work has been done in the area of job satisfaction, organizational climate, and personnel training programs. Much of management's efforts is hidden under the guise of being a benefit for the employee and aiding in job satisfaction. The bottom line has been and probably will continue to be a concern for production increase, and the job satisfaction rhetoric is of secondary interest—except to the employee. The whole area of personnel train-

---

[8]Not Herzberg's term, rather one that is more appropriate for today.

82

human resource development *management specialists that deal in personnel training and development*

ing has undergone considerable change in the last ten years especially with a group of practitioners that call themselves **Human Resource Development** (HRD) specialists.[9]

Exhibit 4.4 lists several recent efforts to improve worker satisfaction. Even a quick glance at those efforts leads one to speculate on the motives of management in its attempts to make jobs more satisfying. Many of the financial incentive programs feed money back into the organization with the primary beneficiary being the corporate unit.

CONSIDER JAPAN— WHERE LIES THE MOTIVE?

The major question that is being asked is, what are the factors that make the Japanese system go? What makes the worker of Japan so very productive? One finding is that Japan's management has been studying the American industrial models and has improved on the system to such an extent that the United States can no longer compete. Exhibit 4.5 is a representation of those factors which are then compared to the approach used in the West.

One must ask an additional question: What are the motivations that are at play with this orientation? From those six factors listed in Exhibit 4.5, the most obvious internal motivations at work are:

1. Pride in quality product; there is worth in producing a fine and functional item because it is a reflection of the individual.
2. The corporate whole (any organization) is greater than the parts and reflects a family orientation.
3. Security within the organization is traditional so that individual effort rewards both the organization and the individual. Each makes a long-term commitment to the other.
4. Individual achievement is engendered as personnel are promoted from within.
5. Achievement is given an added dimension because it is corporate achievement rather than individual. Because peers work together to compete with other groups there is an additive motivation for group effort.
6. Self-esteem is developed because consensus management is practiced and most opinions are considered valuable.

---

[9]For further information on this topic, consult 5 or 6 past issues of *Personnel Development Journal* (published monthly.)

Name of Program	Reward Factor	System
1. Profit Sharing and Other Financial Incentives	Future money gain Ownership in organization	Employer and employee may contribute to various savings programs—stock options, forced savings, tax exempt annuity, etc.
2. Job Enlargement	Reduced boredom Increased responsibility	Increase range of job complexity or expand job tasks to reduce frustration
3. Employee recognition programs	Competition and status/money receipts Playing the game to win	Any one of various systems whereby the worker is rewarded for performance or longevity.
4. Quality Circles	Worker as important input agent Self-esteem and competence Decision power at work	Small groups make suggestion to management for improvements on the job.
5. Professional Development	Long-range career rewards Personal worth Self-esteem and importance	Any of a number of approaches to train staff for professional growth, either in-house or at external sites

Exhibit 4.4
**Examples of Worker
Motivation Programs
used by Industry**

**Exhibit 4.5
Comparison of Work
Factors in Japan and
Western Counterparts**

Work Factor	Factor Defined	Japanese	Western Counterparts
1. **Imitation**	Use the best from the rest	Highly-organized adaptation functions to find out what the competition is doing	Limited adaptation function, mostly inward looking
2. **Group Agreement**	Membership seeks to arrive at agreements	Accepted systems to compromise for achieving common purposes, participatory management	Unionized interaction system or adversary within system, competition and limited trust within
3. **Futuristic Approach**	Long-term commitment to corporate improvement	Fast payoff and short-term benefits are not all as banking system demands long-term savings program; management is permanent, promoted from within	Sales programs geared to short-term profits and personnel promoted on basis of quick success—not long-term planning; management transitory, high rate of mobility among employees
4. **Product Quality**	Explicit concern for high quality control on products	Individual pride and competition to produce quality items with low reject rates	Sales effort emphasizes numbers at the expense of quality
5. **Quality Testing**	Products are tested on a do or die basis	Before exporting, products are intensively tested in domestic market	Marketing "medium" more important than product; limited testing before major production (1970s autos), subsidized major industry
6. **Commitment**	Whole is greater than sum of parts	Individual makes lifelong commitment to organization and country	Individual's right to "do own thing" emphasized; self-enhancement takes precedence over group welfare

Is the Japanese system perfect? Of course not, but there are some components that are worthy of consideration. It is likely that managers in the Western world could adopt several of these basic orientations and make improvements in their industrial/organizational management systems.

IMPLICATIONS AND APPLICATIONS

SOME ADDITIONAL CONSIDERATIONS

Again consider Exhibit 4.5 which compares two different orientations toward worker well-being and organizational style. A number of easily identifiable motives are satisfied by the Japanese model. The United States model, on the other hand, appears to frustrate those motives of security, group cohesiveness, and pride in a quality product.

One of the most discussed problems in the management sphere is the lack of increases in productivity in the Western industrial complexes. Gross National Product cannot keep pace with inflation. The question that industry asks is why? But before an answer can be forthcoming, industry spokesmen declare: "We must increase sales and improve our marketing support." As an answer, this not only is wrong but it is the antithesis of a complex but much more reasonable answer. That answer is the development of a quality-product oriented work force. This can be achieved only if a set of conditions is established to reinforce certain behaviors in the work force of the organization. Those conditions must provide an atmosphere which shows the worker that a quality product is a valued end result, in and of itself. For this to happen, management must understand the motivational and reinforcement variables involved. These variables can be described as those six factors identified in Chapter Two and in Exhibit 4.6. The importance of each factor can be considered in terms of the contribution of specific organizational units in facilitating a quality work-life for the employees.

Exhibit 4.6 provides a picture of the organizational structure versus the motivational factors that play a role in the overall health of an organization. This relationship might be termed the *Functions-Factors Matrix* for identifying the reinforcement factors that should be emphasized by various functional units within the organization.

The checked boxes represent areas of primary interest in reinforcements needed to engender a productive and healthy organization. For example, the reward factor of organizational climate logically falls under the purview of the management function.

Exhibit 4.6
Functions = Factors Matrix for Organizations

Organizational Functions	Reinforcement Factors					
✓ – Area of Emphasis	Climate	Product Value	Administrative Procedure	Supervision Style	Personal Satisfaction	Change Factors (Internal and External)
Management (The Bosses)	✓	✓	✓	✓	✓	✓
Maintenance (Personnel Systems)		✓	✓		✓	
Support (Input-Output Systems)		✓				✓
Production		✓				
Adaptation (Research and Development)		✓				✓

Product value, on the other hand, is a motivational consideration that needs to be emphasized by all functional units in an organization.

IMPLICATIONS FOR THE SUPERVISOR

The Functions-Factors Matrix is derived from a combination of research in organizational development, program evaluation, and motivational theory. It has not been tested empirically as a total system. It is, however, rationally based on research and theory and it provides a useful description for reviewing an organization's approach to meeting worker reinforcement requirements.

In addition, it provides supervisors with an easy checklist for testing their own orientation toward the supervisor-subordinate relationship. Exhibit 4.6 shows three main interactions that can be of most importance:

1. Management functions have the greatest potential impact upon the motivator-reinforcement factors.
2. Product value should be the most potent motivator-reinforcement factor upon the organization.
3. Change factors should be the second most important variable in influencing the organization.

This factor matrix is not a simplistic solution to all of supervision's problems. It is, however, one approach to categorizing areas that require supervisors' consideration. Concern for these areas should improve a supervisor's skill in dealing with problems in organization reinforcement systems. The more concise your understanding of these factors, the more skilled you will be as a supervisor.

SUMMARY

Concepts about motivation have evolved from the discredited view of motives as something implanted in the individual to the realization that motives are internal and can only be dealt with indirectly by arranging external reinforcements.

The classic view of motivation which entails the need-deficit concept plus past successes, along with Maslow's needs-hierarchy system, was considered. In light of the extensive Hawthorne studies, the facilitative nature of altering reinforcement systems was also considered. One of the major efforts to identify job satisfaction factors (studied by Frederick Herzberg) was suggested as one way to identify reinforcement factors.

Based on recent efforts to find reward components that are working, several approaches were suggested. One is the idea that organizational goals and individual motives need to be matched as much as possible. A second is that management and workers need to return to the basic value premise that a quality product is at the heart of any healthy organization. And finally, consideration is given to viewing organizational health as an interplay of six reinforcement or reward factors as supported by the basic functions of any corporate entity. Motivation is not something that management imparts to its workers, rather it comprises a number of factors which must be nurtured by the organization's reward systems. In addition, the nature of those reward systems is at the center of management's tasks for keeping the organization running.

QUESTIONS FOR FURTHER THOUGHT

1. Contrast the concepts of internal motivation and organizational reinforcement.

2. Contrast Herzberg's satisfiers and dissatisfiers.

3. How would Maslow's need hierarchy logically suggest that management should structure its worker-motivation system?

4. List and describe two or three characteristics that are basic to Japan's industrial management style.

5. In your opinion, what is the most reasonable implication of the Hawthorne studies?

5

LEADERSHIP

**LEARNING
OBJECTIVES**

Upon completion of this chapter and related
assignments, you should be able to:
1. Identify the basic factors that influence
    success of leaders.
2. Describe three models or approaches that
    have been used to evaluate leadership
    styles.
3. List several do's and don'ts of successful
    leaders.

CHAPTER OUTLINE

PROBLEM STATEMENT
HOW DO I GET THEM TO DO THE JOB?

BACKGROUND AND THEORY
VARIABLES THAT MAY INFLUENCE LEADERSHIP SKILLS
EFFECTIVE LEADER MODELS
    Type Model
    Theory X and Y
    Behavioral Model

RESEARCH AND PRACTICE
RECENT FINDINGS AND IMPLICATIONS

IMPLICATIONS AND APPLICATIONS
WHAT SHOULD YOUR STYLE BE?
SOME DO'S AND DON'TS FOR LEADERS
CHAPTER SUMMARY

QUESTIONS FOR FURTHER THOUGHT

PROBLEM STATEMENT

leadership *getting others to do required tasks and believing those tasks are worth doing*

HOW DO I GET THEM TO DO THE JOB?

The term **leadership** causes different people to see different pictures of individuals who were "great" leaders—frequently a great soldier, a champion of justice, or some outstanding political figure. However, for supervisors, effective leadership should be thought of as the process of getting others to complete required tasks in the belief that those tasks are of some value. Many feel that effective leadership qualities are not very important at the lower managerial levels. In reality, however, lower level supervisory decisions reflect upper management, have ethical implications, and provide a general atmosphere that defines the organization's total personnel orientation.

A prevailing assumption surrounding the study of leadership behavior is the idea that leaders are born and not made. However, there are many factors that contribute to being a successful leader. One major factor is learning. To think that one's genetic or physical makeup supersedes the other factors is too simplistic. A major emphasis of this chapter, then, is the identification of those factors that play a consistent role in predicting successful leadership behavior.

BACKGROUND AND THEORY

VARIABLES THAT MAY INFLUENCE LEADERSHIP SKILLS

Like most psychological behaviors, leadership can be measured on a scale or continuum from one to ten or poor to excellent. Any scale one could devise to measure another person would entail behavioral descriptions of leadership skills. In addition, there are environmental conditions that appear to influence one's overall leadership style. Exhibit 5.1 identifies several factors that should be considered when thinking about one's leadership skills. Those factors not only include individual characteristics but organizational components that influence leadership style.

Numerous investigations on leadersip have found that several of the variables listed in Exhibit 5.1 do indeed influence how managers are rated. Because those variables are controlled by the individuals involved and are subject to modification by experience (learning), it is a safe bet that any supervisor can improve his or her leadership skills.

Exhibit 5.1
**Variance Factors that
may Influence
Leadership Style**

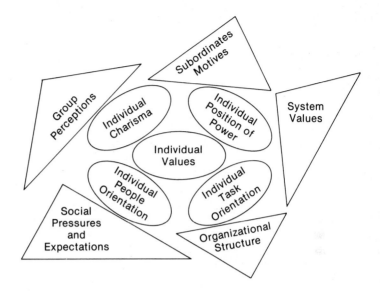

A study by Schneider sought to identify situational characteristics that influence worker performance levels.[1] Three factors
found to influence or moderate performance levels were: (1) incentive system, (2) job characteristics, and (3) supervisory leadership
styles. Keller and Szelogyi found that there was a relationship
between leader style and employee satisfaction and promotion.[2]
Numerous other projects have related leader behavior and organizational functioning and the general indications are that a supervisor's operational style has a direct effect on employee behavior.

It should be understood that the leadership style of a first-line
supervisor is one of the greatest influences on the employees'
overall relationship with and feeling toward the organization. The
leadership style of first-line supervisors becomes an influential
part of the organization and the skills that contribute to that style
can be modified and/or improved.

[1]Benjamin Schneider, "Person-Situation Selection: A Review of Some Ability-Situation Interaction Research," *Personnel Psychology* (1978), pp. 281–297.
[2]R. T. Keller and A. D. Szelogyi, "A Longitudinal Study of Leader Reward Behavior, Subordinate Expectancies, and Satisfaction," *Personnel Psychology* (1978), pp.119–129.

EFFECTIVE LEADER MODELS

There are a number of ways to approach the question of what makes an effective leader. Several methods can set the stage for arriving at a useful model of what the effective leader possesses, is, does, or looks like.

Type Model

type model to classify leaders based on personality descriptions

As early as the forties, Bradford and Lippit described a four **type model** of supervision.[3] With each of these types was an array of personality descriptions, behaviors, and outcomes that might be expected. The four types were as follows:

Type	Personal Approach
Hard-boiled autocrat	Total disciplinarian
Benevolent autocrat	Source of all standards
Laissez faire leader	Paper work and no decisions
Democratic leader	Planning and group decisions

A more recent type model was suggested by Michael Maccoby in *The Gamesman*.[4] Selecting 250 managers from twelve industrial companies, Maccoby used a psychoanalytic interview process to classify individuals into emotional attitude types. Four basic types were described as follows:

Type[5]	Personal Approach
The Craftsman	Conservative work ethic and pride in job
The Jungle Fighter	Entrepreneur, ruthless manipulator, seeks power—not cooperation
The Company Man	Fearing insignificance, they become functionaries accepting bureaucratic roles
The Gamesman	Detached but drives to compete, makes play of work but must win by using imaginative gambles

creative gamesman imaginative, flexible, and internally motivated manager

Maccoby goes on to describe a fifth evolving type of manager that he defines as the **creative gamesman**. This individual has both the flexibility and imagination to motivate others to go the last

---

[3]L. P. Bradford and R. Lippit, "Building a Democratic Work Group," *Personnel Journal* (1954), pp. 1–12, 22.
[4]Michael Maccoby, *The Gamesman* (New York: Simon and Schuster, 1976).
[5]These labels for leader types come directly from the book *The Gamesman* and are not the author's terms.

Theory X managers assume that workers need to be controlled and do not want to work—that they work only out of necessity.

Photograph by Alan Baker, courtesy of FMC Corporation.

mile and the depth of character to retain an internal directional system apart from that established by the organization.

Theory X and Theory Y

One of the classic approaches to discussing leadership has developed from Douglas McGregor's *Theory X* and *Theory Y* concepts.[6] He suggested that management could treat employees in one of two ways. The first assumes that workers need to be controlled and directed because they do not want to work and do so only out of necessity. The resultant managerial style would be rigid, authoritarian, and distrusting. This management type McGregor labeled the Theory X manager.

The second approach assumes that the worker wants to work, will accept responsibility, strives to produce good things, and can in general be trusted to participate in producing goods. The manager who possesses these assumptions and beliefs uses a Theory Y

---

[6]Douglas McGregor, *The Human Side of Enterprise* (New York: McGraw-Hill, 1960).

approach. This approach entails a humanitarian, equitable system for allowing workers to be involved in production efforts. Obviously these assumptions are different from Theory X.

Behavioral Model

critical incidents
unique experiences as re-
membered by the
individual

Evaluation of the psychological outcomes of what one does has become a popular method for looking at supervisors. The basic system used is to: (1) collect what are called **critical incidents** or outstanding and/or unique experiences that come to the mind of the employee. This is done by interviewing employees. (2) Scale the critical behavior as to how good or bad each item is considered to be. (3) Develop a checklist questionnaire and arrive at scores for individual supervisors.

behavioral approach
the method of studying
(leaders) in terms of what
is done

This **behavioral approach** has led to some complicated statistical data analysis to develop factors that appear over and over in the studies. Examples of projects using this approach are Fleishman and Harris in the Ohio State studies,[7] and Katz, Maccoby, and Morse in the Michigan studies.[8] From these and others, two behavioral factors seem to emerge. (1) Employee-centered behavior (or consideration for others or **concern for people**). These terms come from several of the studies with a basic underlying theme of the supervisor being highly interested in maintaining a supportive environment for the employees. (2) Production-centered behavior (or task structured **concern for production**) with the basic theme being a high interest for the output from the employee.

concern for people
being employee-centered

concern for production
being task oriented

During the early 1960s several different approaches emerged that can be classified in the category of behavioral studies. One model that received considerable acclaim was the **Managerial Grid** by R. R. Blake.[9]

managerial grid a
two-dimensional chart:
concern for production
and concern for people

The idea that a manager could be categorized on two different factors was not unlike the Ohio State and Michigan studies. The two components that Blake described were concern for people and concern for production, and any individual could be classified on a scale of 1 to 9 for each of those two components. Exhibit 5.2 is a description of Blake's model.

---

[7]E. A. Fleishman and E. F. Harris, "Patterns of Leadership Behavior Related to Employee Grievances and Turnover," *Personnel Psychology* (1962), pp. 45–46.
[8]D. N. Katz, N. Maccoby and N. Morse, *Productivity, Supervision and Morale in an Office Situation* (Survey Research Center, University of Michigan, Ann Arbor, 1950).
[9]Robert R. Blake and Jane S. Mouton, Louis B. Barnes and Larry E. Greiner, "Breakthrough in Organizational Development," *Harvard Business Review* (November–December 1964), pp. 133–155.

Theory Y managers consult with subordinates, assuming that the worker wants to work, will strive to produce quality, and can be trusted to carry out responsibilities.

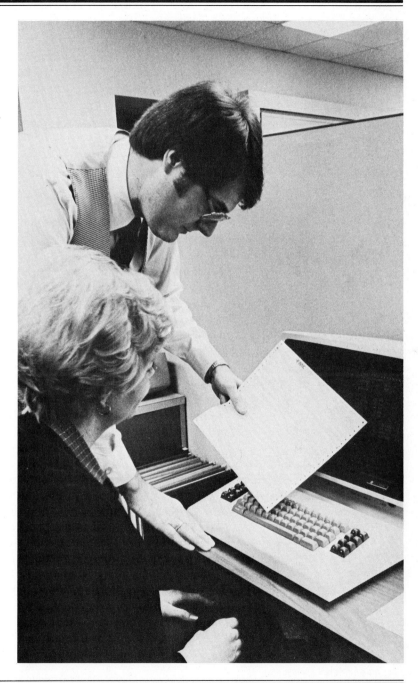

Photograph by Alan Baker, courtesy of FMC Corporation.

Exhibit 5.2
Blake's
Managerial Grid

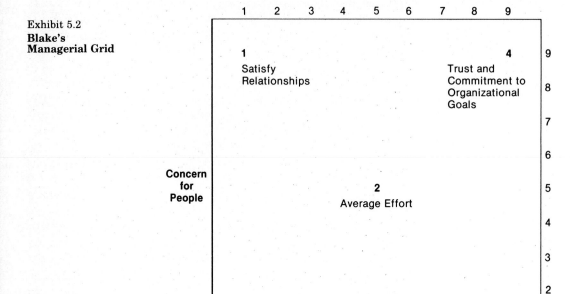

Interpretations:
1 (1,9) – Comfortable Manager
2 (5,5) – Adequate
3 (9,1) – Efficiency Orientation
4 (9,9) – Optimal

(Adapted from Robert R. Blake and Jane S. Mouton, *Harvard Business Review*, (November-December, 1964), p. 136.

The second approach that came along during the 1960s was one by Fred Fiedler in an article called "A Contingency Model for Leadership Effectiveness."[10] Fiedler's approach was a forerunner of a fairly popular current approach to leadership that suggests that a leader's ability cannot be considered outside the context of the group or social organization with which that leader works. The **contingency model** suggests the following three basic factors:

contingency model
leader's concern for
people, concern for pro-
duction and supervisor
power position

[10] Fred E. Fiedler, "A Contingency Model of Leadership Effectiveness," in *Advances in Experimental Social Psychology*, ed. Leonard Berkowitz (New York: Academic Press, 1964), pp. 150–190.

position power *perceptions of power held by leader*

task structure, the individual's **position power**, and leader-member relations. The last, leader-member relations, is closely related to a concern for people. The major thing to remember is that not only are there individual factors that are important to leadership, but there is another factor that has to do with the nature of the social organization and the power that is available to the supervisor within the organization. Before any prediction can be made as to how good the person will be as a leader, that organization factor needs to be considered. What this really means is that almost anyone can be an effective leader or a good supervisor in some situations and that, likewise, almost anyone can be an ineffective leader when the situation does not match the individual's orientation.

The contingency model suggests that one can only talk about a supervisor's being effective in one situation or ineffective in another situation. The implications for improving an individual's supervisory ability are that (1) the individual can learn to adopt a different kind of leadership style, (2) the situation in which the individual works can be modified or changed, or (3) specific supervisors can be matched with the environments in which they would be most productive.

RESEARCH AND PRACTICE

RECENT FINDINGS AND IMPLICATIONS

At least three major factors appear to influence supervisors' ability to deal with their people and can be recapped as follows: (1) the way they treat people, (2) the intensity and motivation with which they attack a task and set the stage for others to work on a problem, and (3) the organizational climate in which individuals work in terms of their power. Before dealing with the first two factors, supervisors need to understand the organizational constraints which affect them.

Most of the organizations that supervisors work in are moving toward an open systems kind of structure. This is an organization in which there is a relatively free flow of information, both up and down the chain of command. Employee and employer actions are relatively open to inspection and observation by others and criticism is easily forthcoming, both from within and from without. Three pieces of information will exemplify this point. Two pieces show how not to lead and one example shows what appears to be working very well in leadership style.

The first is a description of the Jonestown incident by Elliot

Aronson.[11] His article chronologically describes what set the stage and what took place for the final mass suicide of 900 people in Guyana. The Reverend Jim Jones was the leader of the People's Temple Settlement in Guyana and presided over the final chapter of the People's Temple. Jones used three major techniques in the process of leading his flock. *First,* he used every form of persuasion possible, from conducting miracles to logical arguments to physical punishment. *Second,* he demanded complete conformity to the rules he had established, and *third,* he used a form of self-justification to insure that each one was satisfied with the cause that he proposed. His form of leadership worked quite well up to the point of self-destruction. Obviously, that form of leadership did not create an organization that would endure over time, and it is not the kind of leadership that anyone would advocate in today's social organizations and institutions.

The second piece of information comes from a series of studies done by Irving Janis that describes the victims of group think.[12] His research dealt with the basic dynamics of different kinds of groups that have been successful and unsuccessful. He has classified a number of activities within groups that are closed in what he calls a **group think syndrome**. Contained in that group syndrome are eight basic characteristics that indicate the group is in trouble. Groups always have some kind of leader or leaders, and Exhibit 5.3 lists those eight characteristics that good leaders will minimize in leading any organizational unit.

group think syndrome
members begin to believe
everything they say

One of the major contributions that Janis makes is that in circumstances where the group does not employ these techniques, group success is positive. If that is the case, the implications for supervisors (leaders) is quite clear—employ these characteristics in reverse. These factors are redefined in Exhibit 5.4 and, while further research needs to be done to verify the utility of these factors, experimenting with the concepts is suggested.

The third piece of evidence, first identified in Chapter Four (see Exhibit 4.4) is the substantial literature dealing with Japan and its management orientation, compared to that of the United States.

Several factors stand out in the Japanese approach. Their management approaches the production of materials from the

---

[11]Elliot Aronson, ed., "Making Sense of the Nonsensical: An Analysis of Jonestown," in *The Social Animal,* 3rd ed. (San Francisco: W. H. Freeman and Company, 1981), pp. 69–71.
[12]Irving L. Janis, *Victims of Group Think—A Psychological Study of Foreign Policy Decisions and Fiascos* (Boston: Houghton Mifflin Company, 1972).

Exhibit 5.3
**Group Think
Syndrome**

Characteristic	Result
1. Illusion of Invulnerability	Group feels secure in approach which leads to taking extreme risks
2. Rationalization	Uses several methods to discount negative concerns which lead to answering a question with a question
3. Morality is Unquestioned	Group ethics appear greater than all others and lead to a holier-than-thou approach
4. Stereotyped Views of Others	Leads to a we-they approach in that if you aren't for us, you are against us—others are the enemy
5. Direct Pressure	When contrary opinions arise, everyone knows each others' weaknesses and will use that knowledge to belittle others' divergent comments
6. Self-censorship	Because each participant wants to remain a member in good standing, they will minimize self doubts
7. Unanimity	One for all and all for one means that silence is consent
8. Mindguarding	Some members take on the role of protecting the group and the leader from adverse information

Source: Adapted by permission from Janis, Irving L., *Victims of Group Think—A Psychological Study of Foreign Policy Decisions and Fiascos* (Boston: Houghton Mifflin, 1972).

standpoint that what has worked in the past does not need to be reinvented. They take what works and improve upon it.

Management consensus is important. The Japanese operate from the standpoint of using all the information available and having the members of the organization decide what direction they should go and how it should be done.

Diametrically opposite to the Western industry approach of making everything work (profitably) immediately is the Japanese concern for the long term gain. They emphasize quality of product, pride in workmanship, and lifetime employment and job security with the organization. Japanese workers know that their employment is secure.

The Japanese style is to put a large percentage of profits back into research and development. In 1980, this percentage was six times greater than that of the United States.

A Japanese cultural heritage that influences their work climate is the belief and acceptance that the organization is greater than the individual. Individuals are willing to work for the organization because they know that the institution will provide for

Exhibit 5.4
Reverse Group Think Behavior

Factors or Behaviors	Behaviors Defined	Leader Approach
1. Vulnerability	Consider decisions from all angles	Be open to criticism and seek internal discussion
2. Reality checking	Consider negative concerns as appropriate for discussion	Ask for clarification of input
3. Value checking	Review directions of decisions in terms of organizational goals and welfare of others	Ask for impact implications from decisions made and place responsibility on the group
4. Not all outsiders enemies	Consider views of outsiders as important information	Reward input from all sources
5. Belittle none	Accept opinions from group and treat all information as having some value	Allow all thoughts in brainstorming phase even though for a limited period
6. Trust factor	Participants must not fear for loss of group support just because views held individually	Insure that all are secure within group by team rewards
7. Dissent factor	Those in disagreement may shed light on the subject	Press for verbal responses from group; seek divergent thoughts; silence not acceptable
8. Adaptive function	Seek all available information on subject	Consider long-range protection for group more important than leader image in short term

their needs. One Western plant supervisor said, "The Japanese do not realize that many of us live for the week-end, while the Japanese live for the week."[13]

IMPLICATIONS AND APPLICATIONS

WHAT SHOULD YOUR STYLE BE?

It is fairly clear from the studies and the approaches suggested that an individual must assess the flexibility that exists within the organization for which he or she works. If one sees that the position one holds allows considerable flexibility in terms of decisions and power, the approach taken should be task oriented. If, however, the position is moderately favorable to the leader, the orientation should facilitate member-leader relationships. In other words, the supervisor should be more concerned for people.

---

[13]"How Japan Does It—The World's Toughest Competitor Stirs a U. S. Trade Storm," *Time*, March 30, 1981, p. 58.

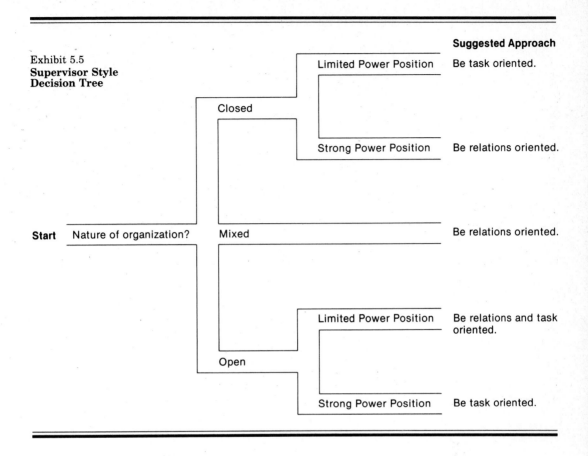

Exhibit 5.5
**Supervisor Style
Decision Tree**

One way to consider the outcomes of this chapter's orientation is to look at a decision "tree," a chart based upon information available. Exhibit 5.5 is a decision tree showing recommended approaches that a supervisor should take to increase the likelihood of success in various organizational settings.

This scheme suggests that, given a "closed" or authoritarian type of organization where decisions are made at the top and little information flows up and down the institution, the approach should be personnel relations oriented. At least, the likelihood of success is greater if this particular strategy is employed. If, on the other hand, the organization is an open system where information flows freely up and down the units and there is an atmosphere of participatory management, then the supervisor can concentrate on getting the job done or the "task structure."

An inquiry into the subject of leadership cannot be reasonably considered without a discussion of those who are being led. There are some very obvious considerations that will affect the leader's role.

Recall the legacy or arguments that have continued since the 1940s (Chapter Four, the Hawthorne studies). They concern the real cause of increased employee production and morale. A 1975 article in *Organizational Dynamics*, titled "Hawthorne Revisited: The Legend and the Legacy," represents a more recent interpretation. This interpretation suggests that workers participated in work-related decisions and that there was a certain amount of power gained by those employees in establishing work-a-day activities.

If we can accept this interpretation of the Hawthorne studies, it suggests that part of a leader's responsibility is to appropriately place organizational power within the worker's position. That is, the employee requires a sense of control over his own activities, at least to the degree that his input is received and considered by the supervisors.

SOME DO'S AND DON'TS FOR LEADERS

There is no simple formula for identifying leader behaviors which will work in all settings; however, some overriding values or principles are likely to appear repeatedly.

Do
1. Evaluate subordinates' work fairly.
2. Be available to subordinates.
3. Delegate sufficient authority.
4. Encourage open communication flow.
5. Be both people and task concerned.
6. Reward appropriate behavior.

Don't
1. Give public reprimands.
2. Depend upon superior position.
3. Simulate great knowledge.
4. Limit divergent thinking.
5. Stereotype others as the enemies.
6. Play favorites.

These principles are neither complete nor are they checklists. They should be used for study as one's own skills are being developed.

SUMMARY

Within the context of this chapter, a number of variables that influence leadership skills have been considered. A case has been made for the idea that leadership and supervision represent the organization and are major influences on workers' perceptions of the organization.

Some of the models of the past have been used to look at leadership and leadership styles; one is the type model, another is the trait model, and the last one is the behavioral contingency orientation. That is, not only are the behaviors of the supervisor or leader important, but the organizational context and climate are also important. In addition, one is cautioned about group-think behavior. Once a person becomes a part of a group, the group tends to adopt self-sustaining approaches to insure that the organization continues without criticism from outside.

Finally, a decision tree has been presented. Its branches can be helpful in learning how to be better supervisors.

One last caution should be made. The process of supervision and the process of learning to be a good supervisor are processes that do not end with the attainment of some specific characteristic such as being task structure-oriented or simply being concerned about the relations that one has with employees. The process requires change and adjustment as the environment and organization change.

QUESTIONS FOR FURTHER THOUGHT

1. In your own words, describe what is meant by a contingency approach to leadership.
2. Contrast the differences between analyzing leadership from a trait or types approach with a behavioral approach.
3. What components make up the group think syndrome?
4. As indicated from the group think syndrome, describe the reverse approach which might enhance leadership success.

6

SUPERVISION ETHICS

**VOCABULARY
TO MASTER**

Moral
Ethics
Scientific Management Era
Therblig
Human Relations Era
Interpersonal Relations Era
Pre-conventional stage
Conventional stage
Post-conventional stage
Code of ethics
General precepts code
Specific code
Negative reward
Positive reward

**LEARNING
OBJECTIVES**

Upon completion of the chapter and related
assignments, you should be able to:
1. Recount the historical development of
   business ethics.
2. Identify reward systems employed by
   organizations.
3. Identify and explain three stages or
   levels of moral development.
4. Summarize empirical research studies
   about the subject of business ethics.
5. Relate the ethics of decision making to
   the job of a supervisor.
6. Identify two broad categories of codes of
   ethics and express an opinion regarding
   the value of such codes.

CHAPTER
OUTLINE

PROBLEM STATEMENT
THE VALUE QUESTION

BACKGROUND AND THEORY
ORGANIZATIONAL ETHICS DEFINED
    What is Business Ethics?
    Public Interest in Ethics
HISTORICAL DEVELOPMENT OF ETHICAL CONCERNS
    Scientific Management Era
    Human Relations Era
    Interpersonal Relations Era
PSYCHOLOGY OF ETHICAL DECISION MAKING

RESEARCH AND PRACTICE
EMPIRICAL RESEARCH ON MANAGERIAL ETHICS

IMPLICATIONS AND APPLICATIONS
THE SUPERVISOR AND ETHICS
    Codes of Ethics
    Reward Systems and Ethical Questions
    A Model for Evaluating the Ethics of Supervisory Decisions

QUESTIONS FOR FURTHER THOUGHT

PROBLEM STATEMENT

THE VALUE QUESTION

Supervisors' actions usually have moral and ethical content which implies organizational concurrence. Discrepancies between the ethical interpretations of individuals who work for organizations and organizational policy and practice will lead to conflict.

The level of concern exhibited by various organizations is quite divergent; and even within the same institution, various concerns are present. The ever-changing social order causes additional interest in the nature of positions taken by industry and government alike. The values and ethics exhibited by the supervisor, in the context of organizational settings, make interesting study and are a subject that will have increasing importance in the future.

BACKGROUND AND THEORY

moral judgmental basis as to right and wrong

ORGANIZATIONAL ETHICS DEFINED

Supervisors in all organizations make **moral** decisions. Decisions which are reflected in their actions (or failure to act) not only affect their own careers, status, and future, but also the lives of subordinates, superiors, peers, customers, clients, and to some extent, the general public. Everyday supervisory responsibilities may at times present conflicts between superior and subordinate, between a request or a directive and what the supervisor feels is "right."

What is Business Ethics?

ethics standards of conduct

Ethics may sound purely moralistic, but fundamentally, it just means the kind of behavior that enables people to live together in a free society.[1]

People in all walks of life appear to understand what the word ethics means. In research conducted by the Ethics Resource Center among a wide cross section of ages, economic levels, and ethnic backgrounds, "more than 86 percent of all people interviewed associated ethics with standards and rules of conduct, morals, right and wrong, value, and honesty."[2]

---

[1]With permission, from Marvin Stone, "Ethics—Making a Comeback?" *U.S. News and World Report*, December 8, 1980, p. 84.
[2]"Ethics in America," *Leadership* (September 1980), p. 10.

108

Although the question of moral influences on supervisory and managerial personnel is not limited to those who hold such positions in the private sector, much of the literature that is reviewed here comes from the field most frequently referred to as "business ethics," and is devoted to managerial ethics in general or ethics at high corporate levels where major decisions are made. Few attempts have been made to apply these principles to the supervisory level, however. Supervisors are continually engaged in activity requiring moral judgments or having moral implications and examination of these will enable the supervisor to function more effectively.

Like most institutions, the business community in the mid-1970s revived corporate soul searching to examine the ethical implications of standards, practices, and everyday routines. This activity was prompted by frequent media reference to morally questionable, if not illegal, acts within the private sector and between private business and certain government and quasi-government officials.

The press and the broadcast media have emphasized top-level business management when examining some of the greatest concerns of the 1970s. Additional concerns and issues have implications for supervisory personnel at all levels and are also applicable to management in government, institutions, and the professions.

Most supervisors probably consider themselves far removed from influence buying, conflicts of interest in government contracts, and illegal political campaign contributions. Recent attention to these practices has brought to the surface some more basic issues which *do* reach almost all employed persons.

Public Interest in Ethics

Since the early 1970s a growing literature and interest within the business community and government have dealt directly with ethics and organizations and the moral implications of management decisions. Numerous journals and publications featured articles dealing directly with values, ethics, and the ethics of management actions. One overriding result of this general concern was the development of various regulatory bodies within the government concerned with the treatment of people in such areas as affirmative action, employment procedures, and employee complaints. The federal government has, for example, authorized the expenditure of money on a very large scale to oversee activities in industry and government. The Office of Civil Rights, for example, as recently as 1978, was willing to pay over $16 million for the employment of investigators to review complaints filed by employees or prospective employees in governmental and industrial organizations. That expenditure of money involved somewhere in the neighborhood of 4,000 individual complaints by individuals who believed they had been wronged by the organizations in which they worked or for whom they wished to work. Many of these complaints were filed by minority persons who, in the context of the total employed population, constitute a very small percentage of employees in the United States. Nonetheless, society is willing to pay the price, at least on paper, to right some of those perceived wrongs. The attention devoted to such activities varies from one administration to another and reflects the cyclical nature of value concerns. But we can be assured that, to some degree, current and future generations will need to address this issue.

The Equal Employment Opportunity Commission has established vast regulatory procedures for overseeing the employers of this country relative to employment procedures, affirmative action, and nondiscrimination. The crux of this approach is that managerial decisions and supervisory decisions do have ethical or moral content related to the decision-making process and the outcomes of those decisions. Whether these concerns are a reflection of society's sophistication in dealing with people in the work place or simply a proliferation of agencies that now have funds is immaterial. Although enforcement efforts have decreased in the 80s, the fact is that in the 60s and 70s people were concerned enough about appropriate and humane treatment of employees to permit the mechanism for attempting to right the wrongs.

HISTORICAL DEVELOPMENT OF ETHICAL CONCERNS

Scientific Management Era

Prior to 1930 and during much of the industrial revolution in the United States, the major approach by managers within industry and production organizations was what might be termed *machine theory* or *Taylorism*. Another term that has been used in the literature is **scientific management**. Within this orientation work was considered the basic function of man. The major concern for industrial firms was the idea that maximum possible productivity was the function and most important activity of the organization.

Scientific Management Era *time when scientific engineering techniques were used to obtain maximum productivity*

110

Frederick W. Taylor pioneered what today is known as the time and motion study process for analyzing task performance and that process, in a sense, is still a primary feature of industrial planning. Time and motion concepts dealt with identifying how much movement and time were required to produce a single unit of output. Another early investigator was Frank Gilbreth who coined the term **therblig**, which described basic movement units of any specific task, for example, reach and grasp. During the infancy of industrial management there was considerable variation in movements for simple tasks, and Gilbreth tried to systematize those movements so that the smallest amount of energy could be expended for the greatest productivity. In general terms, scientific management did not work. The workers revolted at being treated like machines, unions developed, and the workers organized so they would have some way of throwing off managers' impersonal treatment of the employees.

therblig basic time and motion unit

Human Relations Era

By the 1930s the motives and personalities of workers were recognized as being important. What followed was a period that might be called the **human relations era**. The basic thought was that a happy ship is an efficient ship; and as can be seen, the pendulum of attitudes began to swing from the extreme of the "machine" to the extreme of the "happy." Personnel managers within industrial firms became helpers for workers, and during this period many of the family-owned firms in the United States developed a very paternalistic approach. One of the major emphases for this turnabout came from a group of studies that were initiated in 1924 called the Hawthorne studies at Western Electric in Chicago, Illinois (see Chapter Four). Implications of these studies were that motivational and personality transactions were equally as important as the physical environments. Improvement in productivity which initially appeared to result from an improved environment were later attributed to the employees' perception that someone cared about their welfare.

Human Relations Era time when management took a paternalistic approach toward the worker

Interpersonal Relations Era

A third orientation began to develop during the 1950s and 1960s. This era in organizational management sought ways to facilitate the matching of organizational goals with employees' goals. This point of view contains three basic ideas. First, focus on the rela-

Interpersonal Relations Era time when management sought to match the individual's goals with the organization's goals

111

tionship of the individual to the group in which he or she works. Second, use more sophisticated and rigorous research methods to seek ways of improving personnel-management relationships. Third, use innovative models of transaction as proposed by social scientists in the industrial complexes throughout the world. Examples of some of the latter are the scientific training approaches, various executive selection techniques, game theory, management training, job enrichment, and participatory management techniques.

Some influences which affected research and experimentation during this era were not entirely in tune with the new orientations. But the major push was toward improving employee-employer relations and matching the goals of each. One of the obvious outcomes, if indeed there was an honest intent to match these goals, was that management and workers needed an open exchange of information. Open communication requires that decisions be defensible, and this is where the ethical concerns become most important. "Management by secrecy" allows for a considerable amount of dishonesty, but open communication allows for the questioning of the decision-making process and the questioning of the moral bases for those decisions.

PSYCHOLOGY OF ETHICAL DECISION MAKING

Within recent years a number of approaches have been proposed for meeting management's problems within the realm of interpersonal relationships. Whether the approach has been process consultation,[3] organizational development, or the experiential approach, the major emphasis has been upon honest, open communications within the organization. By the very nature of these approaches the assumption is that decisions are open to evaluation, not only by management and supervisors but by the employees who work down the chain of command. If indeed decisions are open for scrutiny, the only way those decisions can stand on their own merit is that there be a general agreement by those involved that decisions have a generally acceptable ethical basis.

The assumptions surrounding a decision must fall within an acceptable group morality as to what is right and wrong. One additional assumption that must be made is that those making the

---

[3]Edgar H. Schein, *Process Consultation: Its Role in Organizational Development* (Reading: Addison-Wesley, 1969).

decisions do so under a "helping relationship" climate. A helping relationship is one in which at least one of the parties has the intent of promoting growth, development, and improved functioning in the life of another. One of the more difficult areas within this total discussion has to do with one's concepts of levels of ethical or moral development. That is, what is the basis for much of the moral decision making.

One system of levels of moral development comes from Lawrence Kohlberg's differential stages of moral development.[4] Kohlberg's research, and the research that has been done on his model by others, have led to a consistent and interesting description, not only in this culture but in other cultures throughout the world. Three basic stages seem to identify man's behavior when it comes to moral or ethical decisions. The first level is called the **pre-conventional stage** whereby the individual is concerned primarily with punishment and personal gratification as reasons for doing something or not doing something. While there may be some element of fairness and reciprocity, there is very little conscious concern for that which serves the individual's own needs or the needs of friends. Children start at this level and gradually progress to other levels.

pre-conventional stage moral judgments based on punishment and personal gratification

The second stage is called the **conventional stage** where there is a "good boy" or "good girl" orientation, or the idea of law and order. Society's norms are not questioned. As an example, supervisors would always be considered right. This orientation stresses hard and fast rules with a major concern for authority and the active maintenance of the existing social order. Right behavior is doing one's duty.

conventional stage moral judgment based on law and order norms for behavior

A third level is called the **post-conventional stage** where an individual's behavior is due to his or her conceptualization of either a social contract or an orientation toward self-chosen ethical principles. The social contract is the idea that the right action is defined in terms of standards agreed upon by the whole society. The more well-defined the post-conventional stage, the more likely individuals' decisions will be based upon universal principles. Right resides in abstract concepts, such as justice, equality, and freedom—rather than in concrete moral or legal rules as might be experienced in the conventional stage.

post-conventional stage moral judgment based on social contract or universal principles

Exhibit 6.1 graphically presents the levels of moral development. The pre-conventional stage is at Level I and is most in-

---

[4]Lawrence Kohlberg, "Moral Development and Identification" in *Yearbook of the National Society for the Study of Education* H. W. Stevenson, ed. (Chicago: University of Chicago Press, 1963).

113

Exhibit 6.1
**Implication
Matrix—Levels of
Moral Development
and Organizational
Reward Style**

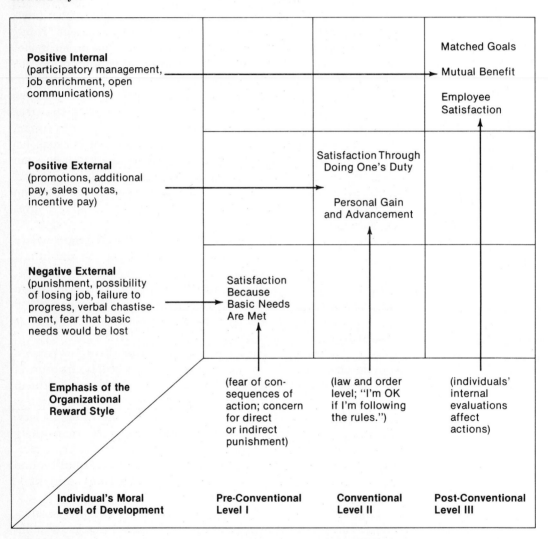

fluenced by negative external (outside the individual) rewards. The fear of what might happen if these negative rewards materialize is the major influence. The rewards are not necessarily immoral, but they are controlled by others.

Level II moral development is the conventional stage, and at this level the individual is most influenced by positive external rewards. Satisfaction, for these individuals, is forthcoming because rewards have materialized and support their comfort in having done the right things. The organization still retains the option to use negative reinforcements, but emphasis is placed on positive reinforcers.

Workers who are rewarded by positive internal feelings have advanced to the third level of development and are in the post-conventional stage. Organizational policy can greatly influence the climate for developing this stage. When workers at all levels are able to participate in decision making in an environment of free and open communication, the atmosphere for this stage has been created. This does not guarantee, however, that individuals will advance to the higher level of the post-conventional stage or that negative and positive external rewards will be eliminated. To the contrary, organizations must continue to use appropriate positive external reinforcers.

Attempts to make jobs more interesting for people (managers as well as operatives) and to provide for their individual needs enhance Level III behavior. A post-conventional/participatory management atmosphere engenders mutual trust, matched goals of organization and employee, and job-satisfied employees.

Any decision that is made within an organizational setting can be evaluated in terms of these three levels of moral development. The lower the level of development in this model, the more capricious, variable, unpredictable, and corrupt the decisions *can* be. Kohlberg and his associates would maintain that as few as ten percent of the population ever achieve a high level of post-conventional moral development. The individual, who operates solely on the basis of what the boss says, does so most likely because the individual is operating at a pre-conventional level. One who questions the establishment may also be operating at that level; however, she or he most likely is operating at a post-conventional level. In this case, one's own personal gyroscope (conscience) identifies universal principles as being more important and demanding on personal decisions.

RESEARCH
AND
PRACTICE

EMPIRICAL RESEARCH ON MANAGERIAL ETHICS

At least two attempts at compiling empirical research data about ethics in business have been published by the *Harvard Business Review*.[5] Both studies examined conflicts between personal values and employer practices, factors influencing ethics, and ethical codes of conduct. The 1977 study attempted to identify changes and trends in business ethics since the first study in 1961. The earlier study involved essentially the same questions. While respondents were predominantly corporate managers, eight percent of the 1,277 participants in the 1977 study were represented by the professions, government managers, and other noncorporate managers.

Definitive conclusions on such a controversial issue are difficult, but the following interpretations of the data by Brenner and Molander offer some insight. People perceive themselves to be more ethical than others in similar positions. While almost three-fourths of the respondents cite unethical industry practices, they consider their departments more ethical than other departments within the company and their companies more ethical than other companies. This point is also prevalent in two surveys reported by *Business Week* magazine.[6] Among executives surveyed in one firm, sixty-one percent agree that "most managers would not refuse orders to market off-standard and possibly dangerous items." At the same time eighty-three percent of the same group said "I personally would refuse . . ." to do the same thing. Apparently many of us consider ourselves more ethical than our peers.

An alarming number of the respondents in the Brenner and Molander study believe that others (in a specific situation) would engage in activity they believe to be unethical (specifically, payment of a bribe to land a foreign contract). "And more than one-third of the respondents who themselves see payments as unethical admit a willingness to pay them anyway."[7]

Even though some of the results of ethics studies are discouraging to some observers, comparison of recent data to data gathered fifteen years earlier suggests an improvement in business ethics. Statistical evidence pointing to improved standards

---

[5]Raymond C. Baumhart, "How Ethical Are Businessmen?" *Harvard Business Review* (July–August 1961), p. 6, and Steven N. Brenner and Earl A. Molander, "Is the Ethics of Business Changing?" *Harvard Business Review* (January–February 1977), pp. 55–71.

[6]Reprinted from the January 31, 1977 issue of *Business Week* by special permission, © 1977 by McGraw-Hill, Inc., New York, N.Y. 10020. All rights reserved.

[7]Brenner and Molander, "Is Ethics of Business Changing?" p. 65.

and practices, however, are themselves questionable. Have ethics improved or have standards deteriorated so that things are accepted which formerly would have been rejected or criticized? One business executive has suggested that there may be no un-ethical conduct involved in bribing public officials in some foreign countries because of customs which exist in those countries. He compares it to our commonly accepted practice of tipping for special attention in restaurants. "Would anyone think it unethical to tip the maitre d' in order to get a table in a crowded restaurant?" he asked. It should be noted that in some countries to not practice economic profit sharing is seen as unethical.

Most surveys of business ethics reveal that business people think that their ethics are as good as the ethics of society as a whole and that business ethics are, in fact, a reflection of society's ethical standards and practices.

Some businesses are conducting specific campaigns to analyze ethics among their employees and to identify pressures for managers and others to compromise their personal standards. Results of these efforts include "conflict-of-interest" programs, codes of conduct, and guidelines for decision-making.

IMPLICATIONS AND APPLICATIONS

THE SUPERVISOR AND ETHICS

Any decision in a working environment can have ethical implications. While the supervisor's solution to a moral problem may not carry consequences as far-reaching as the decisions of high-level officials, the problems exist and must be resolved. Young supervisors face the task of continual re-examination of personal standards. "Should I continue to think this way even though my career here might be damaged, or have I been unreasonable in my interpretation of this situation?" they must ask themselves. Individuals' interpretations of issues change, but in the final analysis every individual's own interpretation of what is "right" should prevail. A general guide to those who have doubts about a decision they are about to make is frequently offered by those who deal with ethics of decision making: "Would I want my family, friends, subordinates, and employers to see me make this decision and view its implications on television?" One who has doubts about having these groups "tune in" on his or her activity should probably reconsider.

Ethical questions facing supervisors may involve specific incidents requiring decisions or definite action. Others, however, are more subtle. An ethical violation may come about when a super-

visor ignores a situation or fails to act at all. The following suggestions are attempts to identify areas of potential moral conflict. No
attempts will be made to solve the problems. They are offered to
stimulate the thinking of supervisors and potential supervisors.
Having considered the possibility of facing them, one should be
better able to deal with them as they arise.

Conflict between superiors' directives and personal standards
of conduct, the possibility for dishonesty in reporting information
and keeping records, and prejudice toward and treatment of subordinates represent areas where specific incidents may arise. For
some, additional incidents in this category will involve interaction
and honesty with customers, clients, or others outside the organization and with other employees within the organization. What
does a supervisor do when the boss asks him or her to "forget" to
record something when this conflicts with the supervisor's personal standards, knowing that subordinates will suffer as a result?
Does the fact that one's following a superior's directions free one
from any personal guilt? How about telling a customer that something cannot be done because responding to his or her request will
require more personal effort? Does this constitute a breach of
professional ethics?

Should one direct an employee to sell a defective product to a
customer because one knows that the customer will not recognize
the defect? Should one pad an expense account because one knows
that sufficient funds have been budgeted? What about the sup-
plier's representative who agrees to split his commission with one
who will influence the purchase of his product? These have been
rather specific examples, about which most people could make a
decision rather quickly. Some moral issues are not so obvious,
however.

More subtle issues may reflect a person's ethical standards,
sometimes without one being specifically aware that moral issues
are involved. Is the evaluation of a subordinate influenced by the
fact that he or she may have caused trouble in the past—even
though the trouble-making may have been justified? How objective is a recommendation for promotion of a person from one's own
group? Is it wrong to prevent a subordinate's promotion because
one does not want to lose him or her from the department? Is it
acceptable for a supervisor to reject applicants for employment
because they represent a group whose performance in the supervisor's department "has never worked," (women or racial minorities, for example). Is it right to discourage the placement of
women/men or minorities in the department because one does not
want to disturb the "happy family" image in the department?

A large portion of the decisions made by supervisors will have ethical content. The more defensible decisions are founded upon universal principles of ethics, such as "the golden rule."

What about the young employee who is so energetic and efficient that he or she may pose a threat to one's own position? What about the subordinate with a physical handicap? Which ethical standards are your own, based on thorough analysis and careful thought, and which are those of your superior or your peers?

Supervisors must perform in situations which may cause them to face a conflict between company policy or a superior's instruction and their own standards of personal integrity. Keep in mind, however, that complete information is not always available to lower-level supervisors. So what appears to be unethical compromise may be justified when all of the facts are known. One authority sees three choices in conflict situations:

119

1. Ignore conscience and follow corporate policy out of blind loyalty;
2. Make a determined effort to change the policy, or
3. If the policy continues to be unacceptable and cannot be changed—resign.[8]

Although the third alternative seems severe, we concur. If a situation involves a genuine moral compromise and if thorough thought and careful analysis (after one gets accurate and complete information about the situation) still results in the same decision, there seems to be no alternative but to seek employment elsewhere. This recommendation does not suggest an uncompromising stand on every issue. Many claims of moral conflict are nothing more than rationalization for stubbornness. One must recognize and acknowledge the difference.

Conflicts in moral issues for the supervisor are not limited to those between supervisors and superiors or company policy. Open conflicts of opinion may arise between supervisor and subordinate, particularly if the age span between the two is great. These conflicts may involve direct conflict regarding the handling of routine, job-oriented activities. For example, an employee may object to telling a customer that the firm will not refund money, because he or she feels that the firm should make the refund under the particular set of circumstances. These conflicts can be worked out if both parties (employee and employer) are objective and look at all facets of the conflict. On the other hand, supervisor-subordinate conflict in basic values may cause communication difficulties between the two. Supervisors must guard against "turning off and tuning out" employees merely because they hold different values, particularly when the value differences do not involve work related conflicts.

Open communication will reveal subordinates' values. Some firms may formally test values of supervisors and employees. In the process, there is hope that those involved will become more aware of their values—perhaps changing some of them. Attempts may be made to match employee groups with supervisors holding similar values. For most firms, however, this is not possible; and it does not appear necessary. Instead, a conscious effort at open-mindedness and understanding among supervisors offers opportunity for less strained relationships.

---

[8]Dik Warren Twedt, "Society and Management: Where Do We Go From Here?" *Administrative Management* (January 1975), p. 23.

code of ethics standards
of conduct that are for-
malized

Codes of Ethics

Professions have adopted codes of conduct for centuries. So rigorous is the adherence to codes of ethical conduct in some professions
that violators are punished or ejected from the profession. Some
are even tied to legally required licenses to engage in particular
functions. Others are less rigid. Most people know someone who
has violated such a code—perhaps someone who was not "caught"
or punished. Because detection is sometimes difficult and proof of
guilt is even more difficult, codes of ethical conduct are frequently
dismissed as ineffective. Activities of the past fifteen years, coupled with growing public cynicism regarding business, have renewed efforts to develop and/or enforce codes among many groups,
including business managers and government employees.

Because of the adverse publicity created by those found guilty
of violations of public standards in the 1970s, business firms are
being exhorted from many directions to engage in house-cleaning
chores to identify and eliminate corrupt practices. Among actions
taken by business firms to accomplish these things have been the
use of codes of conflict of interest programs. Participants in the
development and implementation of such programs have ranged
from chief executives all the way down to operative employees.

general precepts code
conduct which is to be
avoided
specific code *specific*
practices to be avoided

Two broad categories of codes are employed: (1) **general precepts codes**, which offer guidelines for behavior and identify
conduct which is to be avoided and (2) **specific codes**, which
identify practices (accepting a gift worth more than $10 from a
potential client) which are to be avoided. The desirability of establishing codes, their specific nature, and their effectiveness are all
unsettled questions. However, three apparent interpretations
from current literature address these factors:

1. Most employees desire ethical codes, but they prefer the type
   described as general precept codes.

2. Based on personal experiences, managers do not believe that
   ethical codes are likely to improve business conduct.

3. Ethical codes offer little help in controlling outside influences
   and solving basic ethical problems.[9]

Codes do not represent the final answer. At best they cannot cover
all facets of moral conflicts. Specific practice codes are difficult to
deal with unless violations fit the described practice exactly. Any

---

[9]Brenner and Molander, "Is Ethics of Business Changing?" pp. 59, 68.

121

Codes of ethics are
often displayed
prominently within the
offices of members of
professional associa-
tions.

Photograph by Alan Baker, courtesy of Bowling Green Board of REALTORS.

code provides enforcement difficulty. Their existence, however, provides support for managers to exercise their own judgments in questionable situations. In other words, the code can be an excuse for doing what one's conscience would have dictated without the code. Superiors cannot complain too much when employees act within a code previously endorsed by superiors.

Reward Systems and Ethical Questions

negative reward
reinforcement that is
punishing in nature
positive reward
reinforcement that is
positive in nature

As discussed in the chapter on motivation, there are basically two types of reward systems that are employed in organizational settings. The first system is a **negative reward system**; it employs punishment or fear of reprisal or concern for personal welfare. The second system is a **positive reward system** that uses methods of encouragement leading to financial or personal gain. The two systems represent the classic "kick in the behind" versus the carrot on the stick. I may or may not wish to produce the best mechanical part on a machine or an automobile, depending upon my interest in doing that; but I can be induced to do just that—whether or not I am interested—if the rewards are great enough. If I am an assembly-line worker at an automobile plant and if the rewards are great enough, I will produce parts for an automobile regardless of my feelings about whether or not an automobile ought to be produced.

A third alternative to this bipolar arrangement of rewards facilitates individuals to draw from their own interests and values the internal motivation to accomplish organizational tasks. This implies the matching of organizational goals and individual motives. This latter concept is one that industry and organizations rarely tap because of the complexity of individual differences.

The problem is in achieving agreement among the firm's participants that there is inherent value to everyone's work effort. There must be a general consensus among the employees and employers that, for example, the automobile is a valuable product, produced by workers with pride in their output and a company interested in the consumers' welfare. Organizations which continue to show a major interest in consumer welfare are the ones which survive in the long term.

The question of whether more and bigger automobiles should be produced is an ethical question, and it may play a role in whether or not I produce parts for an automobile. If my convictions are that that large automobiles ought not be produced for the sake of society, I may still produce parts for automobiles because personal gains are great. If, however, I am producing parts that lead to a more economical and functional automobile, my own personal interest may induce me to produce more efficient parts. The decision as to whether or not I will participate in the manufacturing of parts for automobiles, then, is a three-part question.

1. Am I doing it because I am afraid I might lose my job?
2. Am I doing it because the pay is so great that I cannot afford to do otherwise?
3. Am I doing it because there is some apparent value in producing a better part leading to a more efficient product?

Dealing with the third area has been and continues to be a major concern for decision makers. Without question, the literature indicates that if the individual's personal interests coincide with the organization's interests and the reward system is positive in nature, productivity will reach an optimum level.

A Model for Evaluating the Ethics of Supervisory Decisions

Exhibit 6.2 presents a model of the defensibility of ethical decisions. This model suggests that there are at least three distinct categories of ethical decision making that are based upon underlying moral principles and existing influences. Category I coincides with Kohlberg's Level I of Moral Development and implies that decisions are made due to fear of external consequences. The resultant behavior is often difficult to defend. Category II suggests that individual decisions are made because of adherence to rules, laws, and regulations with some concern for others. The outcomes are often mediocre. Category III decision making is based on overriding universal concepts of right and wrong and the general welfare of mankind. This style of ethical thinking fosters superior and defensible decisions.

SUMMARY

Supervisors' jobs are affected by moral and ethical influences. Although people disagree on specifics, most agree that ethics should and does enter into decision making and that it involves individual interpretations of what is right and wrong.

Exhibit 6.2
**Bases for
Decisions**

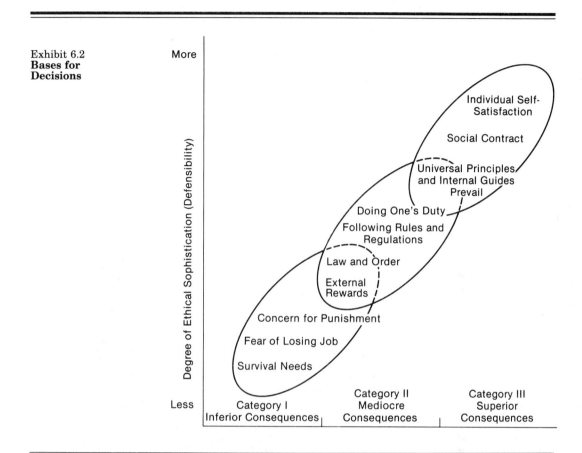

Public interest in ethics has grown in the years following widespread publicity about government and business acts which raised doubts about ethics. Concern for ethics has moved through three discernible eras—the scientific management era, the human relations era, and the interpersonal relations era. The outcome appears to be genuine attempts to match employee and employer goals and interpretations.

Moral development seems to move through stages, identified by one researcher as the pre-conventional, conventional, and post-conventional stages. Negative forces outside the individual (parents, employers, the state) and fear of punishment operate at the first level. Positive forces, perhaps from the same sources, outside the individual influence the second stage; and positive internal (self) forces influence the third stage.

Research suggests that workers consider themselves and their own work groups to be more ethical than other workers and other groups (other departments, or other companies). Supervisors must deal with the ethical elements in their everyday activities. Some ethical decisions are specific, easy to recognize, and can be made easily. Others are more subtle and take considerable thought. When conflicts arise, individuals have the choice of violating their own personal codes, attempting to change situations which cause them concern or removing themselves from a situation (requesting a transfer or resigning).

While many organizations use codes of ethics as guides for conduct, other approaches to improvement of the ethical climate appear to work better. Open communication, appreciation for employees' internal motivations, and a sincere effort to deal straightforwardly and honestly with employees create the most positive climate. In this climate, all parties have some concern for and interest in other parties involved.

QUESTIONS FOR FURTHER THOUGHT

1. How would you define *morals* or *ethics*? Do you see any difference between the two terms?

2. To what extent is ethics involved in the life of the supervisor?

3. Discuss the presence of governmental regulatory bodies and legislation which attempt to regulate ethical behavior. To what extent do you believe that these are effective?

4. Contrast the ethical implications of the three "eras" of ethical concerns discussed in this chapter.

5. Do you believe that something which was ethical for a manager in 1930 could be unethical today?

6. Is it possible that a practice in one country is ethical and, in another country, unethical?

7. What determines the degree of ethical sophistication of the decisions of individual supervisors? (See Figure 6.2.)

8. What are the moral implications of each of the following statements?
   a. "Will that company repair the defective equipment here or pick it up and take it back to the company?"
   b. "This is an excellent report, John."
   c. "I had to pay from $200 to $500 to each of three French officials in order to land the contract for this job."
   d. "If our purchasing agent accepted a color television set from the firm that got our contract, fire him."

e. "If that equipment needs repairing in order to make our workers safe, repair it."

f. "I don't think the public will pay the price we would need to charge if this safety device is added."

g. "Our objective is profit."

7

SUPERVISION AND THE COMMUNICATION PROCESS

LEARNING OBJECTIVES

After completion of this chapter and the related assignments, you should be able to:

1. Identify and explain the directions of communication flow for supervisors within organizations.
2. Illustrate typical situations which require communication skills.
3. Identify the sender's role in the communication process and the factors which influence the message and the medium.
4. Recognize potential mechanical and climatic barriers to communication and review some of the models which researchers have developed to explain communication environments.
5. Differentiate among the various receiving functions in the communication process and identify influences on the decoding process.

CHAPTER OUTLINE

PROBLEM STATEMENT
TO SUPERVISE IS TO COMMUNICATE

BACKGROUND AND THEORY
THE FLOW OF COMMUNICATION
    Attitude
    Abilities
THE COMMUNICATION PROCESS
COMMUNICATION SITUATIONS
COMMUNICATION CLIMATE

RESEARCH AND PRACTICE
COMMUNICATION INFLUENCES
ENCODING AND MEDIA SELECTION
BARRIERS TO INTERPERSONAL COMMUNICATION
    Mechanical Barriers
    Climate Barriers
COMMUNICATION IS ALSO RECEIVING

IMPLICATIONS AND APPLICATIONS
PRECAUTIONS FOR DEALING WITH MODELS
LISTENING IS ALSO COMMUNICATION
SUMMARY

QUESTIONS FOR FURTHER THOUGHT

PROBLEM STATEMENT

communication the process of sharing information, ideas

TO SUPERVISE IS TO COMMUNICATE

Supervision is basically a **communication** process. It involves conveying information, feelings, and understandings to individuals and groups; and it also involves receiving and interpreting communications from others. The core of supervisory success is understanding these processes and the climates within which they take place.

BACKGROUND AND THEORY

upward communication communicating to a superior

downward communication communicating to subordinates

horizontal communication communicating on the same level

THE FLOW OF COMMUNICATION

Conveying information to another person or to a group and receiving and interpreting information from individuals and groups is one of the most important tasks that any supervisor performs. Responsibility for the actions of others and accountability to superiors for these actions require communication in three directions: upward to superiors **upward communication**, downward to subordinates **downward communication**, and horizontally to fellow supervisors **horizontal communication**. Some communication flows to and from individuals with whom there is no official relationship. All are examples of internal communication flow. While many supervisors do not become involved in external communication to any great extent, some can have contact with customers, suppliers, service employees, and others outside the organization. These external communication contacts can take on special significance because of their public relations and image-creating effects.

Upward communication involves anticipating information needs, understanding the limitations on the time of superiors, honesty in reporting information, and attempts to communicate thoroughly and accurately. Horizontal or "staff" communication, like external communication, may involve the supervisor with people he or she does not know very well—people whose special problems are not always obvious. Downward communication involves the people supervisors know best; but because of this close contact, there is a tendency to disregard subordinates' feelings, problems, and needs.

Attitude

Whatever the direction of flow, communication flow is affected by communicators' attitudes and abilities. Communication is effec-

130

tive when "senders" understand "receivers." The more one knows about others, the better one is able to communicate with them.

A conscious effort to involve the receiver's interests ahead of one's own interests is frequently referred to as the **you attitude** or *you approach* in business communication. However, the real spirit of this attitude is just as frequently misunderstood and inappropriately used.

Attitude is a state of mind; it is more than using the pronoun *you* when communicating with others—more than asking people questions about their wants and desires and telling people that they are important. Unless these practices are supported by a genuine interest in the people with whom one works, the "you attitude" is a false front through which anyone can see—eventually, if not from the beginning. The described practices may actually hamper communication if they are contrived or represent selfish attitudes.

Supervisors must develop an empathy for those with whom they work and communicate. Empathy is the ability to feel what others are feeling. Of course, empathy in an extreme interpretation is impossible, but conscious efforts to put oneself in the place of those with whom one communicates and to overcome any selfish inclinations improves communication.

you attitude *effort to involve receivers' interests in communications*

Abilities

The very core of supervisory success may depend upon the ability of the supervisor to communicate in a variety of forms: face-to-face, on the telephone, and in writing. Whether in small groups or on a one-to-one basis, communication quality is an important ingredient. All members of the management team influence the communication process. Any member of the team may be responsible for communication breakdown. However, the supervisor cannot use the weaknesses of another as an excuse.

THE COMMUNICATION PROCESS

Communication is a process that must be learned, practiced, and refined. It is a skill that will develop with experience. It is not a skill that is inborn. Nor does it appear automatically with the promotion to a management-level job. Supervisory communication may range from informal interpersonal communication to more formal interviews with prospective employees to the creation of written messages and reports. Supervisors spend most of their

Internal management meetings represent the beginning of the downward flow of communication.

Photograph courtesy of Citizens National Bank.

time communicating. Working supervisors, those who perform operative tasks as well as supervising others, may spend less than half of their time communicating, but full-time supervisors spend ninety percent of their time communicating in some form. Thus, supervision, to a great extent, is a communication process.

What is *communication*? What happens when people communicate? How do I know that I have communicated? What prevents communication from taking place? How do I get through to people in "difficult communication situations"? How do I relate to those I supervise? How do I write what I'm thinking? These are questions faced by supervisors in all business firms, governmental agencies, and institutions. This chapter and Chapter Eight explore these questions. Specifically, they attempt to assist the supervisor in becoming a better communicator by 1) presenting and explaining the components of the communication process through some simple models, 2) identifying and examining some barriers to interpersonal communication, and 3) presenting basic principles and mechanics of written and oral communication which will assist in the development of productive communication skills.

There is no formula for instant success in communication. Neither is there one "right" answer to any communication problem, nor one "right" thing to say or way in which to say it for a particular situation. The discussions are intended to stimulate thinking about the process and about the need for developing skill in this area. The application of these suggestions will provide a foundation which will grow with practice into a comfortable, effective communication atmosphere for supervisors and those with whom they communicate.

Two of the questions raised earlier are: What is communication? What happens when people communicate? Communication involves the transfer of information and the mutual understanding of those participating in the transfer. This understanding is affected by both **message content** and **intent**. If the information (message) involves instruction, for example, the content of the message is what is to be done; the intent involves all past planning and hoped-for outcomes—the reasons for the instruction. Combined with content and intent are two other components that might be called the "flavor" of the message and the "mode of expression." Additional considerations include the message, the sender, the receiver and the direction of communication flow.

Communication takes place when messages transpire among individuals. The center of communication is the message, but messages do not move by themselves. They are created, transmitted, received, interpreted, and reacted upon in atmospheres that influence their effectiveness. Although no model adequately identifies and amplifies all the facets of supervisory communication, the graphic presentations which follow attempt to clarify the discussion in these two chapters.

message content the literal message
message intent the expected outcome of a message

COMMUNICATION SITUATIONS

Almost everything a supervisor does involves communication. As pointed out in Exhibit 7.1, supervisors must communicate with new employees during formal and informal training activities. Training usually involves a combination of oral communication, written communication, and demonstration. Written training materials usually represent messages which have been created by someone other than the supervisor or trainer, perhaps someone who is not even an employee of the organization. Manufacturers frequently provide training materials for operators of equipment. Some firms provide standard procedures manuals for use as reference tools and as training devices. Some are well written; others are difficult to understand. The role of the supervisor, then, becomes one of interpretation of others' messages.

Instruction in new processes, special procedures, or equipment operation requires communication. Explanation of the organization's policies is also a task of the supervisor. Instruction and

Exhibit 7.1
**Communication
Situations for
Supervisors**

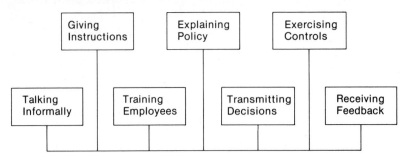

A variety of situations create communication demands for supervisors.

policy explanations are difficult to communicate orally. Therefore, a combination of written message and oral interpretation may be desirable.

Supervisors communicate when they receive messages from their superiors and pass these along to subordinates. They communicate during informal conversation with subordinates. Feedback from employees provides an indication of potential problem areas. A keen awareness of employee satisfaction is essential for complete communication.

Although these are merely examples of communication situations, they are offered to point out the vast number of communication possibilities for supervisors. The list could be expanded easily.

COMMUNICATION CLIMATE

*communication climate
perceived honesty and
attitudes within the organization*

One important ingredient in the communication process is virtually impossible to depict in a model. That ingredient is the **communication climate**. The climate permeates every facet of the process and is influenced by most of the other factors discussed in this text. The rapport among communicators, the attitudes of the communicators, the environment created by the organization's management, and the honesty with which people deal with each other are some of the things that influence this climate. "Climate barriers" are discussed later in this chapter.

**RESEARCH
AND
PRACTICE**

COMMUNICATION INFLUENCES

Supervisors are influenced by numerous factors as they send messages and interpret messages being sent to them by others. Exhibit 7.2 depicts some of these influences and the other components that

134

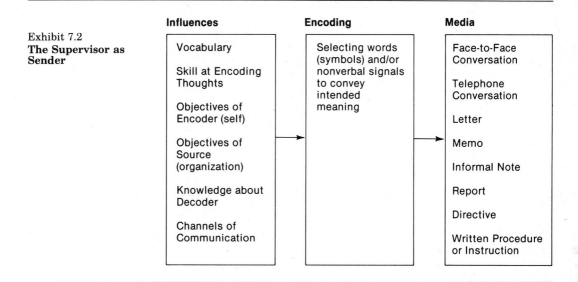

Exhibit 7.2
The Supervisor as Sender

Influences	Encoding	Media
Vocabulary	Selecting words (symbols) and/or nonverbal signals to convey intended meaning	Face-to-Face Conversation
Skill at Encoding Thoughts		Telephone Conversation
Objectives of Encoder (self)		Letter
Objectives of Source (organization)		Memo
Knowledge about Decoder		Informal Note
Channels of Communication		Report
		Directive
		Written Procedure or Instruction

affect the creation of messages. The communicator's own vocabulary and skill at pulling from that vocabulary the best words (symbols) greatly determine the effectiveness of messages.

Communication takes place when the thought patterns of the decoder of a message are identical to those of the encoder. For the purpose of discussion, the supervisor is initiating messages, but remember that most supervisors are equally involved (if not more involved) in receiving. This model differentiates between sender and encoder and between **destination** and **decoder**, because supervisors are professional managers who communicate on behalf of their employers, whether a private or public organization. As used here, **encoder** represents the person who creates a message—the person who speaks or writes a message. **Source** represents the organization (company, professional firm, institution, government, governmental agency, or a unit within one of these, such as a department, production line, or work group). In some cases one person, a shopkeeper operating as a sole proprietor, for example, may be both the source and the encoder. Frequently, however, supervisors or managers speak for something larger than themselves when communicating with others. What a manager or supervisor says represents the organization; it may even legally obligate the organization.

destination organization receiver in a communication process
decoder person assigning meaning to message
encoder person who selects symbols to represent a message
source organizational sender of a message

135

Supervisors communicate through various media: conversation, telephone, reports, electronic data transmissions, letters, and memos. Ease and speed of transmission and the need for documentation influence the selection of media.

ENCODING AND MEDIA SELECTION

The message originator is influenced by his or her own vocabulary and language skills. One encodes a message by selecting the vehicles—words, phrases, sentences, terms—to convey thoughts. Sometimes communicators are 1) careless in this process, 2) their language skills are limited, and 3) their vocabularies are significantly different from the people with whom they communicate.

136

These factors affect the quality of communication. Media selection also affects quality. Some messages are brief and simple and easily transmitted through conversation or by telephone. Others, by policy, may require written media. Messages containing quantitative data or specific instructions are more effectively communicated in writing. Written messages may be very expensive to create (more than $6 for the average business letter, according to an annual Dartnell survey). A phone call may be more appropriate. Written messages to a group may create fewer difficulties than trying to get the group together or to see each person individually. Uniformity of messages going to multiple receivers may be critical, so distribution of a written document which duplicates what has been presented orally in a group meeting may help prevent misunderstandings because some people may misinterpret or may not remember what they have heard.

medium the means of conveying a message

Medium indicates the means of conveying messages. Conversation, letter, memorandum, report, telephone call, mailgram, and data terminal transmission are examples of media. Using these media, communicators write or speak messages; but they are *flavored* or punctuated by style, tone of voice, gestures, physical appearance of written messages, and choice of words. These factors significantly alter or enhance the effectiveness of messages, depending upon how skillfully they are used.

BARRIERS TO INTERPERSONAL COMMUNICATION

barrier interference with the communication process

noise barrier in the communication process

Supervisors must recognize the existence of **barriers** to effective communication. Exhibit 7.3 identifies some of these barriers. Some are mechanical; others relate to the communication climate identified earlier. Barriers are sometimes referred to as **noise**.

Mechanical Barriers

What is the greatest problem for new supervisors? This may well be the difficulty in the use of language—choosing words which convey precise meaning. Jargon, use of slang, vague message content, grammatical errors, and spelling errors further contribute to communication difficulty.

Because new supervisors lack experience is using words, they find the use of language and choice of words difficult. A second major problem encountered is the failure to consider all the neces-

Barriers to Communication

Exhibit 7.3
**Communication
Barriers**

Mechanical Barriers   Climate Barriers

Technical Jargon	Attitudes of Communicators
Grammar	Limited Public Arena
Sentence Structure	Physical Distance between Communicators
Regional Slang	Vague Intent
Vague Content (vs. Intent)	Non-verbal Signals

Noise

sary details for adequate information that will enable receivers to understand the total content.

More extensive treatment of these barriers is given in Chapter Eight, but they are identified here because they consistently create problems for communicators.

Climate Barriers

Of even greater importance to the supervisor are the barriers relating to the communication climate. Skillful communicators can recognize the existence of these barriers and avoid them.

Recall the discussion concerning the "results" of the Hawthorne Studies. One interpretation of this situation is that the high morale and productivity came about because line workers had greater participation in the decision-making process. Open communication contributed greatly to that participation. Even within the considerable literature on job enrichment research and industry experiments an open system of communication networks is considered a vital component. These networks for open information exchange must be present, not only for peer exchange but also for communication from management to worker and from worker to management. The flow must move up, down, and across worker associations.

138

		Known to Self	**Unknown to Self**
Exhibit 7.4 **The Jo-Hari Window Communication Model**	**Known to Others**	Public Arena	Blind Area
	Unknown to Others	Private Arena	Unknown Area

Source: Joseph Luft, *Group Processes* (Palo Alto, Ca.: National Press Books, 1963), pp. 10–15.

Jo-Hari window picture window of the interaction process

Joseph Luft provided an interesting model for looking at the interaction options between or among parties interacting on an interpersonal level.[1] This model is known as the **Jo-Hari window** (see Exhibit 7.4). In general terms, when two persons are working with each other there are four loosely identifiable bodies of information surrounding the situation. Two bodies consist of information known exclusively by each of the two persons (the private arena); neither party has access to the other party's private arena. A common body of information is known by both parties (the public arena), and a fourth body of information includes information known by neither individual (the unknown area). To illustrate assume an imaginary colleague with whom you are communicating. These bodies of information affect what you say and how well you communicate:

1. Things you know and your colleague also knows. (Public arena)

2. Things you know but your colleague does not know. (Your private arena, colleague's blind area)

3. Things your colleague knows, but you do not know. (Your blind area, colleague's private arena)

4. Things that neither you nor your colleague knows. (Unknown area)

---

[1]Joseph Luft, *Group Processes* (Palo Alto, Ca.: National Press Books, 1963), pp. 10–15.

Exhibit 7.5
**Matrix of
Communication
Components**

	Known to Sender	Unknown to Sender
Known to Receiver	Public Arena	Blind Area
Unknown to Receiver	Private Arena	Unknown Area

The information known by both parties, the public arena, represents a situation where free information flow is acceptable and agreed upon. For the most useful and meaningful interpersonal relationships to exist, the public arena needs to be large. Keeping information in one's private arena prevents effective interpersonal communication. This model can be expanded to include the concept of content/intent discussed earlier in this chapter. Exhibit 7.5 presents a graphic illustration of this expanded concept. Content includes what is actually communicated; intent represents the reason for the communication. Exhibit 7.6 identifies specifics which may be included in intent or content, depending upon the nature of the message. An example will shed additional light on this idea.

Assume that as a supervisor you instruct a subordinate as follows:

"George, write up a report on your section's activities for the past six months. Include figures to describe materials processed, etc. I need the report in three days."

On the surface, looking at this simple message one would think it difficult to misunderstand what was wanted by the sender. Consider, however, some of the components of this communication situation:

1. The sender is a supervisor and the receiver is a subordinate. The expected outcome is that the subordinate will do what is

Content or Specific	Intent or Implicit
What	Why
Who	Hidden agendas
When	Importance
Where	Priority
How	For whom

Exhibit 7.6
Content and Intent Factors

requested. As this communication transpires between only two people who are located in one "shop," it is very easy to operate on a face-to-face basis—as long as each party will allow that to happen. Involved also are the likes and dislikes of each person toward the other. This whole area is what might be called the psychological mix by the communications specialist. This mix even includes the prejudices and interests of both parties. Perhaps you were at a local restaurant the previous evening and saw George working overtime on several beers. If you do not approve of beer drinking, there is a psychological mix that may lead you to impose a task too difficult for George to handle or you may write your communication in such a way as to confuse your real meaning. Withholding information, then, is a barrier to communication.

2. The content of the message is fairly straightforward: You want a report—in three days—with figures. However, the content does not include the nature of the report: how long, what style, whether rough draft or final form, treatment of data to be used, kind of figures, whether graphs or raw numbers are to be used. The content, then, is not clear; but since both of you work fairly close together, you can iron out these questions. If this message were going to someone in another department, the problems would be compounded by the separation distance, a not-too-unrealistic condition in today's organizations.

3. The intent of the communication is not clear. No specific purpose is expressed, and George has no way of knowing the main thrust or reason for the report or the major interest of the supervisor. The purpose may be to describe a specific change in the work flow in one part of your section. This biannual report may have been chosen as a method of bringing the change to the boss's attention. You may also like the use of a specific kind of graphic display of information, and in your mind's eye, the

141

report is already designed using that style to inform the intended audience.

nonverbal communication without words

More specific, but **nonverbal**, influences may also be barriers. Among these are tone of voice, facial expressions, and other "body language." These barriers will be discussed more specifically in Chapter Eight.

The main concern for the message sender, then, should be—What is the psychological mix? What is the basic intent so that the content will inform the receiver about that which is needed? And what are the hidden components that influence the content and the intent? Once these questions are answered, one is able to decide the most appropriate content for the message.

COMMUNICATION IS ALSO RECEIVING

Too much attention to sending messages, at the expense of receiving them, is a failure to get "the big picture." Even though the supervisor must make every effort to communicate in a manner that will be effective, many of the people with whom this communication takes place will not be aware of the need to communicate effectively. For them, there is no conscious effort to communicate well. Some may even strive to communicate as little as possible, or they may be too shy to express themselves fully. Their language skills may be limited. They may be easily discouraged by communication failures or difficulties. The supervisor realizes that receivers are influenced by the same variety of factors that influence the sender. (See Exhibit 7.7). The whole point of this discussion is that supervisors must work as diligently in both roles—as receivers and as senders.

For the purpose of this model, *destination* and *decoder* are considered separately, as were source and encoder. Destination represents the organization or entity to which messages are directed—the counterpart of source. *Decoder*, the counterpart of encoder, is the person who actually assigns meaning to the message. The manager of a company, agency, department, work group, or production line may decode messages directed to that unit. Even though departments are the receivers (destinations), a *person* must assign meaning to the message and interpret it for the department. The decoder is that person.

feedback information about performance returned to the individual

Feedback is a reaction to a message. Some communication requires feedback; some does not. If one communicates information to another and that information is understood and requires no response, the cycle is complete and no feedback is involved. If the

Exhibit 7.7
Receiving Messages

Influences	**Decoding**	**Followup**
Listening	Assigning meaning to words and other symbols used to relay messages	Responding
Reading Skills		Taking Action
Vocabulary		"Filing" Message for Further Reference
Objectives as Decoder		
Objectives of Destination (organization)		
Attitude toward Encoder		
Attitude toward Source		

receiver wishes to ask a question, seek an interpretation, or originate a related message, however, feedback is involved. Answering the question or providing additional information ends the cycle.

IMPLICATIONS AND APPLICATIONS

PRECAUTIONS FOR DEALING WITH MODELS

This chapter presents numerous illustrations to help one understand concepts relating to the communication process and ends with a combined model of the entire process. Don't assume that they represent complete information or depict all situations, however. Many factors, such as the time element, the physical distance between communicators, and other factors can create special sets of circumstances for particular communication situations.

The time element involved in the communication process can cover only a few seconds. Some researchers think that more may be communicated by brief nonverbal behavior than by the words used. Complete communication cycles can, on the other hand, take days or months. "Sending" in our model does not, necessarily, mean that time elapses between sending and receiving; nor does encoding necessarily imply a time-consuming, deliberate activity. The remark "It's about time you finished that job!" accompanied by

Communication is a two-way process. The receiver must also participate. Which of these two people is listening effectively? Do the nonverbal signals of their posture and facial expression communicate?

Photograph by Alan Baker, courtesy of Lord Corporation.

a harsh tone of voice and a frown and followed by a feeling of disappointment by the person to whom the remark was directed, can represent a complete communication cycle. It may take only five seconds, and there may be little or no feedback. However, most of the elements of the communication process are present.

LISTENING IS ALSO COMMUNICATION

Communication is also listening—allowing others to communicate. The person who is eager to express an opinion while another person is still "sending" is not truly communicating. In these situations the sender is not heard. "Nobody hears a word I'm saying," a line from a musical lyric that was popular a few years ago, can represent the sentiments of workers toward their supervisors. If this is the case, management can expect difficulties.

144

Like sending skills, listening and reading are receiving skills that must be developed. Particularly for the new supervisor, development of these skills requires deliberate and specific effort. Real receiving is more than remaining quiet when someone else is speaking; it is more than reading every word of a written message. In this world of electronic technology, the word *input* has taken on new significance. A twenty-year-old dictionary may not even list it as a word. Yet it describes a major factor of communication. While people generally accept and even joke about the fact that computers are limited by input, they forget that people are likewise limited. Failure to listen wipes out vast quantities of everyday communication input. One cannot possibly react effectively to messages one does not receive.

SUMMARY

In putting together all the components, a model of the communication process can be developed. While it has been presented within the context of the supervisor's role as communicator, communication in any professional environment resembles this model.

Exhibit 7.8 is a model which is made up of the combined illustrations of the various facets of the communication process. Review the discussion of the components of the process, examine the model, and view it as one big process.

Communication takes place when the thought patterns of the receiver of the message are identical to those of the sender. The process can be complicated by barriers which prevent the receiver from thinking what the sender intended. The term *sending* when applied to messages and the communication process means "transmission." One "sends" oral messages, but communication is affected by numerous other factors such as the sender's abilities and the receiver's knowledge. Recognizing these factors, the sender encodes messages, selects the medium, and realizes that nonverbal signals may accompany these messages.

Mechanical and climate barriers affect communication effectiveness. While no communicator expects to eliminate all barriers, skillful communicators remove as many as possible and avoid others. Mechanical barriers are tangible and frequently visible; barriers that involve the communication climate are intangible and theoretical.

Senders in the communication process strive to understand receivers (destination and decoder). This attempt increases the probability that the message received will be the same as the

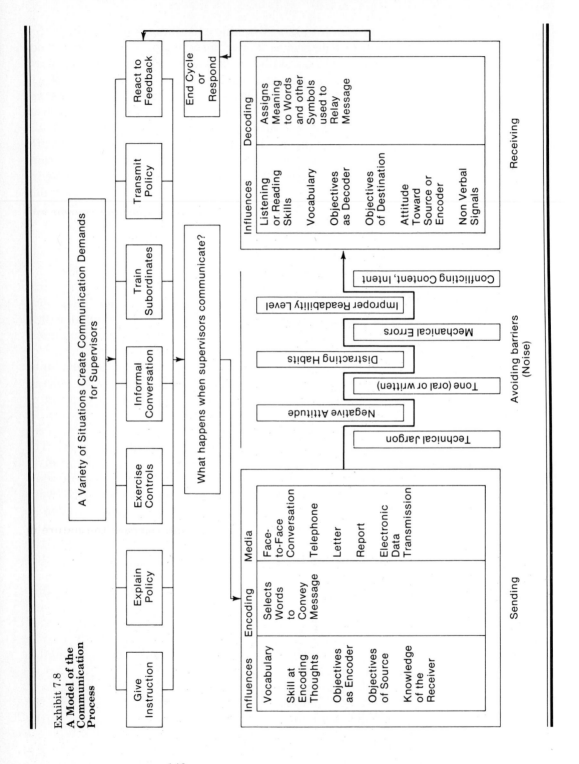

Exhibit 7.8
A Model of the Communication Process

A Variety of Situations Create Communication Demands for Supervisors

Give Instruction | Explain Policy | Exercise Controls | Informal Conversation | Train Subordinates | Transmit Policy | React to Feedback | End Cycle or Respond

What happens when supervisors communicate?

Sending

Influences | Encoding | Media

Vocabulary

Skill at Encoding Thoughts

Objectives as Encoder

Objectives of Source

Knowledge of the Receiver

Selects Words to Convey Message

Face-to-Face Conversation

Telephone

Letter

Report

Electronic Data Transmission

Avoiding barriers (Noise)

Technical Jargon

Negative Attitude

Tone (oral or written)

Distracting Habits

Mechanical Errors

Improper Readability Level

Conflicting Content, Intent

Receiving

Influences | Decoding

Listening or Reading Skills

Vocabulary

Objectives as Decoder

Objectives of Destination

Attitude Toward Source or Encoder

Non Verbal Signals

Assigns Meaning to Words and other Symbols used to Relay Message

message sent. Supervisors are receivers as well as senders, and their skill at listening, reading messages, and observing nonverbal signals may be as critical as their sending skills. Feedback is a reaction or response to a communicated message. Feedback begins the communication cycle anew. Written and oral messages, as well as nonverbal signals may be involved in feedback.

Finally, the supervisor should recognize the limitations of models and theories in explaining the communication process.

QUESTIONS FOR FURTHER THOUGHT

1. Using the materials in this chapter, formulate your own definition of communication.

2. What is the difference between *communication content* and *communication intent*?

3. Explain the roles of the following participants in communication:
   a. Source   c. Destination
   b. Encoder   d. Decoder

4. Explain the concept of "noise" or barriers to communication.

5. Identify several factors which can be barriers in oral communication situations and several others which are barriers in written communication situations.

6. What is a communication medium? Identify several possible media which supervisors might use.

7. Identify the bodies of information represented by *public arena*, *private arena*, *blind area*, and *unknown area* in the Jo-Hari Window.

8. What are some of the climate factors which affect communication but are not part of either the sending or the receiving processes?

9. Explain the concept of *feedback* and compare the nature of feedback among face-to-face oral communication, telephone communication, and written communication.

147

PART THREE

TOOLS OF THE
SUPERVISOR'S TRADE

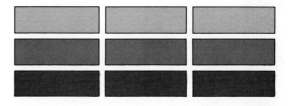

8

COMMUNICATION MECHANICS

VOCABULARY TO MASTER

Semantics
Internal communication
External communication
Formal communication
Informal communication
Kinesics
Proxemics
Passive voice
Active voice

LEARNING OBJECTIVES

Upon completion of this chapter and related assignments, you should be able to:

1. Identify four skill areas that affect the quality of supervisory communication and relate them to probable communication situations for supervisors.
2. Identify three directions of communication flow for supervisors and list two or three examples of messages which flow in each direction.
3. Demonstrate the "you" attitude in communicating with others.
4. Differentiate between concrete and abstract words, giving examples of each and recounting the problems that use of abstract words may cause.
5. Relate the importance of tone and tact in communication and demonstrate effective use.
6. Create positive sentences communicating negative information.
7. Identify four activities in which supervisors should engage prior to attempting to communicate instructions to subordinates.
8. Describe a six-step plan for giving employees instructions.
9. Identify examples of nonverbal communication.
10. Write simple business letters and reports.
11. Dictate business messages.

CHAPTER OUTLINE

PROBLEM STATEMENT
BACKGROUND AND THEORY
CHARACTERISTICS OF EFFECTIVE COMMUNICATION
THE IMPACT OF LANGUAGE
    Tone and Tact
    Positive Language (Attitude)
RESEARCH AND PRACTICE
THE NATURE OF SUPERVISORY COMMUNICATION
IMPLICATIONS AND APPLICATIONS
ORAL MECHANICS
    Giving Instructions
        Planning
        Instructional Materials
        Methods and Procedures
        Precautions
    Communicating in Small Groups
        Personal Style
        Techniques
    Nonverbal Implications
        Body Language
        Voice
        Physical Appearance
WRITTEN MECHANICS
    Writing Situations
    Characteristics of Good Written Messages
    Writing Letters and Memoranda
    Writing Business Reports
    Dictating Business Messages
SUMMARY
QUESTIONS FOR FURTHER THOUGHT

**PROBLEM
STATEMENT**

The supervisor can improve the communication climate by mastering mechanical techniques of oral and written communication. Although it may be impossible to identify all of the required communication skills here, some essential elements are word choice, tone, tact, sentence structure, message organization, accuracy of data used, recognition of nonverbal elements and media selection. Application of these skills can take the form of face-to-face conversation or written messages and can involve formal or informal situations.

**BACKGROUND
AND
THEORY**

CHARACTERISTICS OF EFFECTIVE COMMUNICATION

Because supervisors spend much of their time communicating, they must have a good understanding of the information exchange process. This knowledge must, however, be coupled with basic application techniques. Understanding the theory without also understanding some of the mechanics of practical applications may leave the supervisor short of the goal of effective communication. This chapter explores some of the techniques of applying communication theory and moves specifically into oral and written communication situations. Some of the techniques explored here are part of any supervisory job; others become more applicable as the supervisor accepts additional responsibilities or moves to more demanding supervisory or managerial positions.

Polished communication skills are essential for growth, promotion, and progress in supervisory management. The application of functional communication skills, particularly written communication, proves to be especially difficult for many new supervisors. Lack of experience in a position of responsibility and lack of working experience accounts for much of this difficulty. Fears about communicating effectively and writing well will persist until they are alleviated by knowledge and practice. Most new supervisors have had very little experience communicating in an "official" capacity. Their formal education may have placed very little emphasis on the development of communication skills, particularly writing skills. There is, however, no reason why these abilities cannot be developed with specific effort and practice.

Several basic factors affect the applications of communication skills: 1) understanding communication flow, 2) knowledge of the effect of word meaning and word choice, 3) ability to give easy-to-follow instructions, and 4) the ability to create effective written

152

messages. Even though technology has mechanized many communication processes, there still exists a critical need for every manager to be able to communicate effectively in writing. Word processing centers, the computer, and other technological advances have made written communication easier for those who are able to take advantage of these aids. The ability to dictate to a stenographer or to a mechanical recording device can greatly ease the communication burden for many supervisors. Practical, mechanical suggestions for coping with these aspects of communication are explored in this chapter.

Keep in mind that the techniques described in the remainder of this chapter are not gimmicks. Neither are they substitutes for a proper attitude of the communicator. They represent basic, common-sense application of language, speaking, and writing skills.

THE IMPACT OF LANGUAGE

I know you think you understand what you think I said, but what you don't realize is that what you heard is not what I meant to say.

Language is the vehicle for communication, but it frequently fails as one gropes for words and combinations of words to express feelings, moods, and understandings.

semantics analysis of the changing meaning of words

Business and professional supervisors should be concerned about semantics. **Semantics**, in its broadest sense, is a critical analysis of the meaning of words, particularly changes in the meanings.

Supervisors must be aware of the multiple meanings of words and expressions. One of the difficulties created by the English language is the possibility of a single word having multiple meanings. Frequently one meaning is a slang meaning and the other, a formal meaning. Exhibit 8.1 lists some words in this category. The supervisor is not expected to analyze every word he or she utters or writes for possible double meanings. However, a general awareness of multiple meanings can improve communication.

As suggested in the previous chapter, nonverbal signals supplement words. Gestures, eye contact, body movements, and tone of voice are nonverbal symbols that support and, sometimes, contradict the words. Even typewriting quality, paper quality, and company letterheads are nonverbal influences on written communication. A later section of this chapter deals with the nonverbal signals and their importance to oral communication situations.

153

The meaning of these words can vary, depending upon context:

Exhibit 8.1
Words with Multiple
Meanings

hard (difficult, firm)

skirt (piece of clothing, go around)

hooked (rug type, addicted)

simple (dumb, not difficult)

innocent (naive, not guilty)

flexible (bendable, willing to change)

fuzz (lint, police)

ignorant (lacking knowledge, illiterate)

hit (impact, kill)

grass (ground cover, drug)

cut (slice, eliminate)

pad (cushion, apartment)

gray (color, vague)

great (big, distinguished)

gas (gasoline, vapor)

gag (joke, muzzle)

game (nervy, recreation)

frame (body shape, formulate)

force (strength, coerce)

fantastic (bizarre, terrific)

Messages (oral or written) may communicate less effectively because words having vague meanings are used. Words such as *soon, substantial, most, tremendous, seldom, love, joy,* and *happiness* may fail to communicate because they do not carry specific, concrete meanings. Fad expressions such as "with it," "right-on," "point in time," "get it together," "up tight," and "the bottom line" may hamper communication for some. For others, these expressions pose no problem.

A subordinate may be discouraged or confused by a statement that appears critical, even though the supervisor intended no such criticism. "That's good enough" or "That's okay, I guess," accompanied by a hesitating voice may communicate only minimum acceptance to the subordinate, while the supervisor who used the expressions was fully satisfied with the work being appraised. Preoccupation with other concerns may have caused the hesitation. In some parts of the United States, notably in the South, words and parts of words are frequently omitted in oral communication. For example, the expression "I don't care . . ." is a positive or, at least, neutral reaction to a proposal (meaning "I don't mind doing that" or "I don't object to doing that"). When asked "Would you mind changing jobs with Jim for the remainder of the week?" the response "I don't care" means that the person is willing to change jobs. He isn't excited about it, but he is willing.

To someone in another part of the country, this might represent a purely negative reaction ("I don't care to do that").

The choice of words may be as vital to communication as the meaning of words. Messages may communicate less specifically or less precisely because of the choice of words selected to convey a thought. The sender may know exactly what she or he means by *soon, substantial, most, tremendous, seldom,* and *brief;* but the meaning of these words may be confusing or even misleading to others. "Within 10 days" is better than "soon." A request for a one-page report is better than a request for a brief report. Abstract words are acceptable when they describe generalities. When specifics are desirable, however, more concrete terms should be used. Exhibit 8.2 lists confusing, abstract words and their concrete substitutes.

Technical jargon is acceptable among those who understand the unique language. It is unacceptable for others. Acronyms (first letters of words in compound names; for example, AIM, NOW or CORE), abbreviations of technical terms, and ordinary words used for special applications are examples of potentially confusing words. To a computer operator, the terms *COM, CRT,* and *CPU* are perfectly understandable. A communications clerk would recognize *TWX* (pronounced *twix*) as a noun (a machine) or a verb (to send a message using this piece of equipment). Others, however, might not recognize these terms. The terms "pink slip" or "blue slip" (or any color) communicate special messages in firms where the blue or pink copy of a layoff notice goes to the employee to communicate immediate layoff. In another firm, this expression might identify the form on which managers record excessive employee errors. In both cases, they carry negative connotations. "Write up" is another expression. "I'm going to have to write you up," a supervisor is overheard telling a subordinate. A new employee may not understand this message, even though plain, simple words are used. Business forms and reports are frequently nicknamed by employees and management alike. These common names, rather than their actual titles, may be used when employees are instructed in procedures. This is confusing and makes an already tense situation even worse for the new employee. The correct word should be used, or the term should be defined for those who are not expected to understand. This is particularly true for external communication. Customers, clients, suppliers, service personnel, and others outside the organization may be intimidated by a choice of words that contain expressions they do not understand.

Exhibit 8.2
Concrete Words and Expressions

Instead of these abstract words	Use these concrete words
soon	by November 6
substantial	two-thirds
most	86%
tremendous	70 feet across
high	$75, 67 feet, 19%
majority	86%

Tone and Tact

Oral communication is supplemented and sometimes enhanced by tone of voice. Identical words in written messages may take on a different "tone." It's possible to "say" things that are not meant because of the tone which underlies a written message. Stiff, formal messages may project a tone of arrogance or indifference. Tone can communicate a lack of trust even though no such implication is intended.

Tact is invaluable in interpersonal communication. This quality is particularly needed by those who must refuse requests, discipline others, communicate bad news, or disagree. Tact is sometimes lost in the effort to be precise. There will always be a disappointment for the receiver of any of these messages; however, the disappointment can be lessened through tact and tone.

Oral communication probably offers the sender of negative messages a better chance to be tactful. Tact in written messages under negative circumstances is more difficult. Being tactful is not a sacrifice of honesty. Whenever one must communicate bad news, there is always a reason for it. Tact, in this situation, is communicating bad news in such a way that the receiver understands the reasons. He or she is aware of the intent of the message as well as the content. This may mean saving the "punch line" of a letter or memo until the reader has been prepared through explanation. It may mean a choice of words that enables the receiver to maintain dignity and self-respect. It may mean an expression of confidence—when it is deserved.

Some managers believe that tact is an unnecessary ingredient in communication. Business, professional and governmental environments, they believe, are cold and tactless environments where hard facts and tough skins prevail. This text does not endorse this philosophy, however. Individuals who embrace such philosophies have lost touch with the one essential ingredient in management—people. Because supervision is communication and communication is the process of transferring information among people, tact is a necessary ingredient.

Positive Language (Attitude)

Positive communication is more effective than negative communication. Most negative statements can be reversed to a positive stance. Employees experience frustrations and anxiety when they are continually bombarded with negatives. Examples are "you failed to . . ," "Don't . . ," "You didn't . . ," ". . . cannot be done" (instead of what *can* be done), and "If you had only . . ." Communicating bad news ahead of good news is equally negative.

As the discussion of tact pointed out, supervisors frequently must react negatively to subordinates' requests. However, the effect of this negative reaction can be lessened if there is some favorable reaction that can be communicated first. Avoid making others feel that a response is going to be completely negative when, in fact, it will be only partially negative. ("We can give you three days of vacation next month" instead of "We can't do without you for a week next month".) When negative responses or criticism are necessary, they will be more completely communicated if emotion-stirring negatives which may communicate hostility are avoided. Examine this paragraph and the one before it. Their essential message is "Don't use negative expressions when communicating," but they communicated that message in a positive manner. Exhibit 8.3 lists negative expressions which should be avoided.

RESEARCH AND PRACTICE

THE NATURE OF SUPERVISORY COMMUNICATION

Most supervisory management responsibilities and tasks involve communication in one way or another. Consider the following list of activities.

Planning and scheduling work

Improving work procedures and methods

Getting the work done

Maintaining a cooperative staff

Exhibit 8.3
Avoiding Negative Expressions

Replace these negatives with positive expressions:

You failed	I am sorry	You did not
I cannot	You said	Cheap
Don't	Won't	Your complaint
You claim		

Negative: Since you failed to itemize your work hours, we can't write your check.

Positive: The accounting department needs your itemized hours so they can write your check.

Negative: I am sorry to inform you that we can't provide the information until June 16.

Positive: The information for your sales report will be ready by June 16.

Selecting, training, and developing workers

Considering workers' needs

Listening to requests, comments, complaints

Reporting routine activities

Solving problems

Maintaining quality and quantity standards

Reporting to superiors

Using organization's administrative services

Maintaining physical environment

Keeping records of activities

These supervisory activities require communication—oral and written, formal and informal, internal and external. The following brief treatment of formal versus informal communication and internal versus external communication is intended to further develop awareness of the climate in which supervisors work and the nature of communication within that climate.

Most of the activities listed previously dealt with **internal communication**—within the organization. Supervisor to subordinate, supervisor to superior, and supervisor to other employees (neither superior nor subordinate) are communication flows within the organization. However, some supervisors and

internal communication inside the organization (firm, institution, agency)

158

their staffs must also communicate with others outside the organization. This constitutes **external communication**. For the employer, this is a very critical type. Organization image is determined by external communication. Private organizations' profits and public organizations' public support are affected by image. So communication with customers, clients, patrons, or any "outsider" with whom the organization deals in a direct way, as well as the general public, becomes important.

external communication from those inside the organization to those outside the organization and visa versa

Another group of outsiders with whom organizations communicate is made up of suppliers of services, equipment, and materials; governments at all levels; and organizations with which employees have professional contact.

formal communication official; that done in one's capacity as an employee

informal communication unofficial (conversation among employees—not a function of jobs)

Formal communication is official communication—that which is a routine or special function of the supervisor's (or any other employee's) job. **Informal communication** is unofficial, but not unimportant. Various informal communication flows exist. Sometimes labeled "the grapevine," the word-of-mouth channel can sometimes transmit messages very rapidly. Frequently, they also become distorted. But the astute manager recognizes that informal communication exists and uses it to whatever advantage may exist.

Grapevine communication is most prevalent when formal communication (official messages) are inadequate or when workers are anxious about something—reorganizations, shakeups, layoffs, or the effect of new technology. Those who glean tidbits of information, pass it on and each transmitter fills in the missing gaps. Those who are frequently able to uncover interesting information gain the respect of fellow workers as long as their sources are accurate. When their information turns out to be false, however, their credibility wanes.

Management can clarify or contradict rumor mills by creating formal messages (announcements, directives, policy statements) about the rumored activity. When its messages remain accurate (more likely when the news is good), the grapevine can be an effective means of communicating information.

IMPLICATIONS AND APPLICATIONS

ORAL MECHANICS

Many factors influence the outcomes of speaking and listening. In addition to the pure content of messages, oral exchanges are affected by communicators' manipulation of content, by the medium, by their mechanical limitations, and by the climate in which oral exchanges take place.

Informal communication can be productive. The good supervisor learns to use informal systems to improve the climate for communication.

Photograph by Alan Baker, courtesy of Lord Corporation.

People manipulate information in the process of communicating with others. Information is offered, accepted, rejected, or questions are asked for a variety of reasons. We ask questions to seek additional information or interpretation (about ten percent of the time), to mask rejection of information (about thirty-five percent of the time), and to mask ideas (about fifty-five percent of the time). Estimates concerning the influence of the medium on oral communication suggest that word content accounts for only ten percent of the message impact; tone of expression, thirty percent of impact; and nonverbal behavior, sixty percent of the impact.

Most of us speak at the rate of about 150 words a minute. Most of us can listen at four or five times this rate without overload. This implies that we can become bored very quickly with conversations that are not very stimulating. In addition, most listeners tend to have a high attention level for one or two minutes and then think of similar or other topics while the speaker continues. The point is that people seem to listen in peaks and valleys, then make involuntary mental excursions, and return to the topic as the headlines are emphasized.

Climate for oral communication can be viewed in terms of the win/lose probability for participants and might be viewed as follows.

160

Communication Outcomes

Person 1	Person 2	
Win	Win	Each person gets what is needed or wanted.
Win	Lose	One person benefits from the exchange; the other does not.
Lose	Lose	Neither person benefits.

Given this type of information, several generalizations can be made. First, if possible, set up conversations or other oral exchanges so that everyone benefits from the interaction. Second, include headlines and break up topics to maintain interest. Third, use direct, clear, and unaffected speech, considering the effect of body language, tone of voice, and other nonverbal signals.

Several categories of communication techniques involve oral communication situations for supervisors. Although supervisors present few formal oral presentations, they are almost continuously involved with face-to-face communication through giving instructions and explanations. Some of this is done in one-to-one situations; others, in small group situations. Both of these involve considerable opportunity for nonverbal influences to affect the outcome.

Giving Instructions

A major communications task for supervisors is giving instructions. Instruction may be simple, such as explaining routine changes in procedures. At the other extreme is the supervisors' role in formal training programs for new or transferred employees. For the supervisor, giving instruction is likely to take the form of on-the-job training instead of formal, classroom-type instruction.

The suggestions offered here are more appropriate for giving instructions that cover identifiable, recurring situations, such as training new employees. However, consideration of these points has value for giving even simple instructions of relatively short duration.

Planning Preparation for instruction is vital. Know something about the nature of the instructional task and, if possible, how long it is likely to take. Anticipating learners' questions and difficulties will enable the instructor to prepare answers. Some on-the-spot problem solving is always necessary, however.

Determine how much the employee or group already knows about the subject of the instruction, preferably during the planning stage. Knowledge of previous experience or special training will enable the instructor to start instruction at an appropriate level. Different backgrounds may necessitate dividing employees into groups for separate instruction.

Instructional Materials While some easily understood instruction can be offered orally with few or no props, complicated or lengthy instruction can be enhanced by supplementary materials. Drawings, illustrations, and photographs are examples. Written procedural instruction and standard practice manuals may also be used. Visual aids such as films, video tapes, and projection transparencies are helpful for some difficult-to-explain instructions.

Methods and Procedures A calm, planned, methodical approach to instruction is most effective. If instruction involves tasks to be performed, the task may be easier to attack if it is divided into workable units. Each unit is mastered before moving to the next.

Precautions Supervisors who instruct employees can move too rapidly. One who knows a procedure, a process, or the operation of a piece of equipment may find it difficult to slow down to the learning rate of a beginner. Introduction of new materials must be gauged by the ability of the employee to master what has already been introduced. Too much material, too rapidly presented confuses learners and may hamper learning. Attention spans of learners are very short. Even experienced, seasoned employees may have difficulty following complex instructions for more than fifteen–twenty minutes unless the activity is varied. Stopping to examine illustrations, to answer questions, or to practice something that has been introduced are examples of activities that will break up instruction into comprehendible time spans.

Instructors may need to omit shortcuts and alternative methods of performing tasks or procedures during initial instruction. Even though employees may eventually understand the procedure well enough to employ alternative methods, introduction of too many possibilities in the initial learning stage will be confusing and discouraging.

Supervisors should anticipate the question "Why?" from employees. "That's what I was told" and "that's the way we have always done this" are not sufficient answers. Before beginning instruction, possibly guided by questions previous learners have asked, the instructor should attempt to discover reasons for procedures which may seem unusual or unnecessary.

A final precaution for those who give instruction is to expect occasional uninterested or impatient learners. Some people have difficulty in listening to complicated instruction. Instruction may appear to be repetition of the obvious. Extroverted individuals may become bored with a long instructional process that forces them to listen longer than they prefer. Their restlessness causes them to appear uninterested in learning the procedure. In some cases employees are placed in job assignments against their will by someone other than the supervisor. If instruction is necessary for persons working in these assignments, the supervisor may experience considerable difficulty. Although there is no single solution to this problem, awareness of the problem may help the instructor to overcome it by altering routine procedures or discussing the situation with the individual, privately.

Communicating in Small Groups

Small group communication is becoming increasingly important for those who manage workers. Today's employees are seeking and getting more involvement in making decisions which affect them. Oral communication skills become critical for supervisors who work with groups of subordinates and participate with peers and superiors in group settings. Careful examination of the dynamics of communication reveals a variety of approaches to communicating with and influencing groups.

To some extent all persons have a personal style and philosophy of leadership as they attempt to work with groups. The thoughts presented here should be helpful to those who are still developing a style.

While every supervisor will be actively communicating in many informal (friends or acquaintances) and social group situations, our treatment deals primarily with formal groups. *Formal* means that the group is engaged in some official activity. For supervisors, this activity is job related. For simplicity, group size is considered to be four to ten people.

Group technique and approach are influenced by the participants and the leader. Even though the purpose is formal, the approach may be casual and informal. Techniques vary from lecture (not recommended for small groups) to lively group discussion to brainstorming and roleplaying.

Of the many facets of group dynamics, two seem to involve

supervisory communication with small groups. One relates to personal style and the other to application of oral communication techniques.

Personal Style Supervisors may be either leaders or participants, but they are likely to be leaders in most group situations. Communication may be affected by the choice of leadership style. Groups led by authoritarian leaders do not elicit as much communication as those that use a democratic or participative approach.

If the group purpose is problem solving or decision making, a style which encourages a permissive atmosphere, involves all members of the group, and provides opportunity for contrasting views is more effective.

Even though personal style is important, the trainer who is knowledgeable about the content of the material being communicated will be forgiven for flaws in personal style. The attitude of sincere interest in those being trained is also important. Coupled with content, the intent reflected by sincerity and attitude provides a foundation for the development of a successful personal style.

Techniques Leaders and participants in groups communicate more effectively when they recognize and practice basic communication techniques. Voice quality (projection, inflection, enunciation) is perhaps less important for small group communication than for large group presentations, but it is always important. Eisenberg divides group behavior into *cooperative* and *obstructive* categories:

> *"Cooperative behavior in a group takes in any action or reaction serving a useful purpose for either the entire group or one of its members. In contrast, obstructive behavior takes in any action or reaction not serving a useful purpose."*[1]

Exhibit 8.4 contains Eisenberg's identification of verbal, vocal, and nonverbal techniques which are cooperative and obstructive.

---

[1] Abne M. Eisenberg, *Understanding Communication in Business and the Professions* (New York: Macmillan, 1978), p. 187.

Exhibit 8.4
Communication Techniques Representing Cooperative and Obstructive Behavior

Verbal

Cooperative Behavior	Obstructive Behavior
1. Refer to others by name.	1. Cracking jokes that distract the group's attention.
2. Ask questions if you are not clear on a point.	2. Using big words to show off.
3. Do not prejudge others or their ideas.	3. Interrupting others.
4. Allow people to finish their thoughts.	4. Changing the subject for no good reason.
5. Encourage others to speak.	5. Monopolizing the conversation.
6. Use the words *we-our-us*, rather than *I-me-my*.	6. Trying to make other people look stupid or silly.
7. Be polite.	7. Repeating the same thing several times.
8. Try to build on what others say.	8. Making self-centered remarks.
9. Use simple straightforward language.	9. Using foul language that offends others.
10. Compliment others freely.	10. Ignoring what others have to say.

Vocal

1. Use a pleasant tone of voice.	1. Shouting unnecessarily.
2. Speak up so that you can be heard.	2. Speaking in a monotone.
3. Try to avoid the use of *ers, ahs*, and *uh-huhs*.	3. Talking too fast or too slow.
4. Stress all important words or ideas with your voice.	4. Using such phrases as, You know? Right? Do you see what I mean? OK?
5. Avoid mumbling.	5. Mispronouncing certain very familiar words.

Nonverbal

1. Look at people to whom you are talking.	1. Having a bored look on your face.
2. Sit as though you were interested; leaning forward.	2. Doing something else while another person is talking.
3. Move toward rather than away from other speakers.	3. Fidgeting in your seat.
4. Occasionally nod agreeably or smile at other speakers.	4. Making purposeless gestures while you are talking.
5. Wear clothes that will tell others that you care enough about the group to dress appropriately.	5. Moving your head from side to side while someone else is trying to make a point.

Source: Abne M. Eisenberg, *Understanding Communication in Business and the Professions* (New York: Macmillan, 1978), p. 189.

Nonverbal Implications

Nonverbal symbols—communicating without words—affect all communication. Particularly affected is face-to-face communication. These symbols are usually associated with body language, space and how we use it, voice-related signals, and physical appearance. Good communicators recognize these symbols coming from others and are aware that they too are sending nonverbal signals. Supervisors are sometimes unaware of the signals they transmit.

kinesics analysis of non-verbal messages communicated via the body

Body Language We communicate acceptance, rejection, disgust, surprise, and disbelief with our bodies. Combined with words or in the absence of words, our gestures, facial contortions, glances, and stance speak volumes. Sometimes our body language contradicts our verbal messages. **Kinesics** is the analysis of such symbols and the messages that they transmit. Supervisors could read too much into minute gestures, but keen observance of others' facial expressions can give a reasonable interpretation of the impact of your communication. Because the right side of the brain provides the most expressive and emotive content relative to feelings and because the left side of the face is controlled by the right side of the brain, one's expressions on the left side of the face are more likely to reveal true feelings.[2]

proxemics study of personal space

Proxemics is the study of space and how we communicate by the distance between communicators. Researchers have determined the types of communication that usually go on within various space ranges. Intimate communication (secrets, confidential information) transpires within a very close range (up to 18″). The personal range extends from 18″ out to four feet. Friendly conversation takes place within this range. Social communication takes place within the four-feet to eight-feet range. Beyond eight feet, communication is public in nature and usually involves large groups.

For supervisors and other managers, observance of workers' and peers' private spaces is important. Invading their "space" makes them uncomfortable and hampers communication. This can vary from standing too close when talking, to locating and arranging work stations. Cultural background may influence the distance at which people are comfortable in close conversation.

---

[2]Robert A. Baron, Donn Byrne, and Barry H. Kantowitz, *Psychology: Understanding Behavior*, 2d ed. (New York: Holt, Rinehart, and Winston, 1980), pp. 340–341.

Close observation of others' reactions to the distance factor may indicate that they feel their private space is being invaded.

Voice The volume of speech, the pitch of the voice, and the speed (rate) of speech either complement or negate the verbal messages. Inflection and tone of voice may carry the clues to real meaning in oral communication. Observe these clues in others for greater understanding and be aware of nonverbal voice characteristics so that the meaning intended is the meaning given.

Physical Appearance Physical characteristics—dress and grooming and the way people order their surroundings—imply personality traits. Dress, desk tops, work stations, cosmetics, and even hair care supplement communication. Even those who are "nonconformists" in their personal appearance are telling something and, to some extent, are conforming to a style of life. While stereotyping people and judging them on the basis of appearance should be avoided, one can sometimes understand them better by the clues which their appearances offer.

Most business and professional environments or those who manage them carry codes of "acceptable" personal appearance. The codes may be unwritten and unofficial in some situations, but they are very real. Some workers need help in understanding such codes. Tact and skill are necessary in dealing with problems in this area.

WRITTEN MECHANICS

Supervisors will encounter fewer situations requiring written communication than middle and top managers. However, effective writing is a necessary skill for managers at any level. There is no better ticket to promotion than the ability to communicate well, coupled with an ability to do so in writing. Technology has not replaced the need to "put it in writing." Difficulty with writing assignments is not an indictment against intelligence, ability, or education. Many otherwise well-educated individuals face fear and trembling at the thought of having to create written reports or even letters and memoranda. Many executives, with the services of stenographers to assist them, labor over writing assignments.

Some attention to basic principles and techniques of written business and professional communication should simplify the procedure and ease the worries about this very necessary task. The treatment of the subject here is not sufficient, however, to teach supervisors all they need to know about written communication. For those who have extensive and frequent assignments requiring written messages, a college, university, or adult education course or a workshop in business communication is recommended. Self study through reading and programmed (self-directed) learning materials may be helpful, but some type of writing experience, coupled with evaluation by a competent instructor is desirable. Business and professional people should not fall into the trap of substituting sample messages from books of "Sample Letters for Every Occasion" for their own communication needs. Samples serve as guides, but they usually do not fit individual situations. Observations are that as a person becomes proficient in writing messages, his/her letters and reports take on a style or "flare" that is unique to that person.

Writing Situations

Supervisory written communication may take a variety of forms: memos to subordinates and superiors, duplicated memos to subordinates and superiors, interpretations to accompany forms and formal reports and, for some, messages to customers, clients, and others outside the organization.

For the purpose of this discussion, *letter* will refer to correspondence going outside the organization; *memorandum* will mean written correspondence within the organization; and *report* will mean an individually created collection of information on a specific subject. Reports vary in physical format and formality. They may take the form of letters, memoranda or formal manuscripts. They vary in content from those which merely transmit information to those which include writer interpretations and conclusions of research, experimentation, and data gathering efforts.

Characteristics of Good Written Messages

Written messages communicate best when they are written in plain, simple, straightforward language which readers can easily understand. For some unknown reason there still persists the belief that business and professional writing should employ elaborate language. The language of business should be no different from any other language except for the necessary use of technical terms. Written messages accomplish their purpose best when they are well organized, to the point, and mechanically correct. Poor mechanics—grammar, spelling, punctuation—can spoil an otherwise well-written message. Business correspondence and reports are not written for readers' entertainment; they are written to communicate information and, in some cases, to document the fact that communication has taken place.

Essential characteristics of business writing are completeness, clarity, brevity, accuracy, and objectivity. One should say what must be said so that it can be understood, and avoid personal prejudices and opinion. While the following list is not all-inclusive, the techniques should help to improve written messages.

1. Write in *complete sentences*—a complete thought, expressed with a subject and a predicate. Don't begin a thought and leave it dangling, unfinished. Vary sentence length. Too many short, simple sentences make messages boring. Too many long, complex sentences complicate messages and can fail to communicate. Organize sentences into paragraphs which have a central theme and are not too long.

passive voice subjects (of sentences) are acted upon (opposite of active)

active voice subjects (of sentences) perform the action

2. Although both **passive** and **active voice** are grammatically correct, the active voice is generally preferred.

When the active voice is used, the subject of the sentence does the "acting" and therefore communicates essential information first, because it usually comes early in the sentence. Active voice has more "punch," and communicates more directly.

In the following example, *employees* is the subject and *produced* is the predicate. One learns immediately that the employees produced 500 units. In the second example, it is obvious that 500 units were produced, but one must wait until the end of the sentence to learn who produced them. Furthermore, the construction of the sentence emphasizes the units rather than the producer.

Example: Employees in Department A produced 500 units.
(active: employees produced)

Example: Five hundred units were produced by the employees in Department A.
(passive: units were produced by employees)

3. Collect a small set of *reference tools* (dictionary, thesaurus, English handbook, and a business communication textbook). Use them. The need to use them will lessen as writing abilities are developed.

4. *Rewrite* messages, leaving out unnecessary words, phrases, and paragraphs. Rewriting messages is one of the most productive

ways of improving writing skill. Once one becomes proficient, this won't be as necessary.

5. Write in a *conversational tone*. Say what would be said if one were communicating orally. There is no need to "dress up" written messages with cliches and obsolete grammatical structures like "Thanking you in advance for your kind attention, I remain . . ." or a legal-sounding vocabulary such as "As per your request of the 15th . . ."

6. Avoid *repetition* of words, particularly the personal pronouns *I* and *we*, and the use of identical sentence structure sentence after sentence. Mechanical faults and repetition will capture the reader's attention and distract from the real message.

Writing Letters and Memoranda

Since the subject of letters and memos is usually a single idea or a set of multiple related ideas, these messages should be relatively short and simple. They should get to the point in the beginning and follow with necessary explanations. Avoid beginnings like "This is to inform you . . ." and "I am writing to say . . ." These state the obvious. However, directness and brevity should not be carried to extremes which make the message blunt or treat a serious subject carelessly. In some cases, written messages must convey discouraging news or persuade the reader to the writer's way of thinking. In these cases explanation ahead of the main point of the message may be appropriate. But most business messages carry more punch if they are direct and state the purpose of the message early, followed by necessary support and explanation. If you want something, ask for it. If you want the reader to do something, say so; and give instructions.

Letter writers anguish over endings for messages. "How do I stop?" To compensate, they tack on trite, meaningless or apologetic closings ("Thank you in advance . . . ," "Hoping to hear from you soon . . . ," or "I hope this won't be too much trouble"). A friendly, positive closing sentence is all that is needed ("Should you have questions regarding this procedure, see Mr. Jones in the personnel office" or "Return the enclosed card to reserve your ticket").

Physical format of written messages may be spelled out by the organization's office manual. (Sample acceptable formats are illustrated in Appendix A.) Typographical accuracy of written messages is another must. Errors, sloppy corrections, and incorrect style mar the effectiveness of letters and memoranda.

Writing Business Reports

The report is the result of data gathering and interpretation activities. Reports usually flow upward in the communication channel. Supervisors report to department managers; department managers combine the results and report to their superiors, and so on. The data presented in a report may relate to a problem-solving effort, routine description of activities, or a special need for information. There are progress reports, feasibility reports, research reports, annual reports, financial reports, budget reports, production reports, sales reports; the list is endless. Some reports are written at regular intervals (daily, weekly, monthly, quarterly); others have a single purpose and are not repeated. The formality and the required format of reports affect the approach used in writing them.

Objectivity is a standard requirement in report writing. Only facts and, when required, objective interpretations of facts are included. The objective of a report may be to gather and report opinion, but the writer's personal opinion should not enter into most reports. The writer should not embark on a report writing task with an "ax to grind." This clouds the writer's objectivity, even while the data are being collected, because only those facts which support the preconceived conclusion are likely to seem important enough for use in the report.

For recurring reports, the procedure, content, and format will probably be specified by the person or department requiring the report. The person who authorizes the report-writing task may specify the format. Whether the report is in memorandum form or a formal manuscript, the following suggested guidelines for the report writing may be followed.

1. An *introduction* should identify the problem (subject) of the report, the source of the information, how the information was gathered, and any special processes used to organize and interpret the information, such as statistical analyses. If conclusions or recommendations are part of the report, these may be communicated at the very beginning to avoid suspense for the reader. Long reports may be condensed into a one-page synopsis or summary which appears at the beginning of the report.

2. *Graphic data* (tables, charts, illustrations) may improve the communication level of reports. However, these should not be haphazardly inserted. Appropriate text (narrative, sentence-form discussion) concerning the data in the graphics should be included.

3. Reports should be well organized, with data grouped together by category. *Headings* and *subheadings* (like those used

Some supervisors are fortunate enough to have stenographic assistance for originating business messages. This combination can contribute to speed and efficiency in written communication.

Photograph by Alan Baker, courtesy of Bowling Green Board of REALTORS.

in this and other books) should be used liberally in the typewritten manuscript or memorandum to guide the reader through the report, forming a verbal outline of the report's organization. The outline suggests the wording for such headings. A good outline for a report will improve organization.

4. Because long report manuscripts are frequently read by large numbers of people, the *more formal* third person (no use of "I," "we," or "you") may be employed. However, the informal tone may be used for short memorandum reports. Some report writers abandon the formal third-person approach even for long manuscripts.

5. Every report should have a *date* and a *title* and should identify the *author*. Even though this suggestion appears to restate the obvious, these essential elements of reports are frequently omitted.

Dictating Business Messages

Improved office technology through word processing centers has given many supervisors the opportunity to dictate written messages and to have them transcribed by professional word processing employees. For some supervisors this may be the only type of clerical assistance available. Taking advantage of such a service requires the ability to apply all the principles of message creation discussed in this chapter. In addition, the "client" of a word processing center must create the message orally while a centralized recording device records the message for later transcription. A variety of equipment is available. Each requires slightly different mechanical manipulation.

Recorded dictation should be no different from dictating to a stenographer who records the dictation manually. Similar instructions should be given in each case. Because so many people are reluctant to use recorded dictation as a means of speeding the preparation of written communication, the following suggestions are offered.[3]

1. Give general instruction by identifying yourself and specifying the letterhead or business form to be used, the number of copies to be made, the names of those who should receive them, and the nature of enclosures that will accompany the message.

2. Use the indicator system on recording equipment to let the transcriber know the length of the message. Some devices permit re-recording to correct or change dictation; others provide cues for the transcriber to anticipate an error correction.

3. *Dictate* clearly and *naturally*; your voice will indicate most punctuation. Some dictators prefer to say "period," "paragraph," or "comma" to indicate punctuation.

4. *Spell* proper names and places if the transcriber does not have access to them. Spell any technical or unusual words the transcriber is not likely to know.

5. *Stop* the recording device *during pauses*. Most devices permit one to back up and listen to the last few words for review.

6. Don't mumble or meander when dictating. The microphone or phoneset should be kept two to three inches from your mouth— and don't turn away from it.

7. If the system permits, provide the transcriber a copy of the correspondence being answered or any other materials related to the message.

8. Remember that someone is listening to the recording. Talk to that person just as you would talk to someone across the desk. The only difference is that the recording will not remind the listener that the directions are incomplete.

---

[3]Adapted from A. Donal Brice, *Writing Out Loud*, The Dictaphone Corporation.

SUMMARY

Supervisors can improve the communication climate in organizations by mastering mechanics of oral and written communication.

Language is the vehicle of communication and supervisors should develop a sensitivity to words, their meanings, and their uses. Choice of words to communicate a particular message may be quite critical to complete transmission of ideas. Concise, concrete words improve communication; unnecessary use of technical jargon and abstract terms hampers communication.

Careful supervisors use a positive approach in their communication and are careful to be tactful and to phrase messages in a tone that communicates the intended mood.

The communication environment for supervisors may involve communication with people outside the organization as well as with subordinates and superiors. The scope of supervisory communication includes many informal situations and others that are formal or official.

Specific communication tasks involve instructing employees, small group communication, and routine everyday conversation. Nonverbal signals enter the picture for all oral communication and most written communication situations.

Effective writing is a necessary skill for any manager who expects promotion to responsible positions. Effective communication is a skill which supervisors can acquire through formal education, experience, and hard work. Writing for managers involves a conscious effort to plan messages, write in simple language, and avoid attempts to "dress up" messages. Letters, memos, and reports usually have a single theme and work best when written in a direct, straightforward approach. Mechanics and tone of messages are important. Reports are informative, well organized, and arranged in a format that is conducive to easy digestion.

QUESTIONS FOR FURTHER THOUGHT

1. Explain the "you attitude" for supervisors in the following situations: (a.) communicating with subordinates, (b.) communicating with people from outside the organization, and (c.) communicating in writing.

2. Compile a list of words (in addition to those used in the chapter) which have one meaning in conversation and another meaning in formal communication situations.

3. What is the difference between "tone" and "tact" in communication?

4. Differentiate between internal and external communication, between formal and informal communication.

5. What precautions should be observed by those who give instructions to employees?

6. Differentiate between "autocratic" and "democratic" as styles of communication by supervisors in small group situations.

7. Identify four categories of nonverbal communication and give examples of communicators' use of each category.

8. How can written communication involve nonverbal communication?

9. Distinguish among the purposes of letters, the memoranda, and the report as written business messages.

9

IMPROVING PRODUCTIVITY IN THE WORKPLACE

VOCABULARY TO MASTER

Productivity
Production
Quality control circle
Job analysis
Job description
Job evaluation
Job specification
Written procedure
Work measurement
Time study
Methods time measurement (MTM)
Standard

LEARNING OBJECTIVES

Upon completion of this chapter and related activities, you should be able to:

1. Identify the ingredients of worker productivity.
2. Identify environmental forces which affect productivity.
3. Explain job analysis as a tool for improving worker productivity.
4. Evaluate work measurement as a tool for increasing productivity.
5. Describe the Japanese approach to productivity through quality control circles and related activities.

CHAPTER OUTLINE

PROBLEM STATEMENT
PEOPLE GENERATE PRODUCTIVITY

BACKGROUND AND THEORY
ENVIRONMENT FOR PRODUCTIVITY
THE STATUS OF PRODUCTIVITY IN THE WORKPLACE
APPROACHES TO PRODUCTIVITY IMPROVEMENT
    Quality Control Circles

IMPLICATIONS AND APPLICATIONS
INCREASING PRODUCTIVITY THROUGH JOB DESIGN
    Job Content—Flexible or Fixed?
    Tools for Defining and Clarifying Job Content
    Practical Approaches to Improving Job Content
IMPROVING PRODUCTIVITY THROUGH WORK MEASUREMENT
    The Supervisor and Work Measurement
IMPROVING PRODUCTIVITY THROUGH VALUE STRUCTURES
SUMMARY

QUESTIONS FOR FURTHER THOUGHT

<table>
<tr><td>

PROBLEM
STATEMENT

</td><td>

PEOPLE GENERATE PRODUCTIVITY

The keys to productivity are the people and the environment in which they work. Environmental factors must exist in harmony with such formal efforts to establish effective work patterns as job analysis and work measurement. The nature of the interplay among productivity factors has been of prime interest to management for decades. While the answers are not yet in, those who study these factors may be closer to the answers than the industrial community is willing to acknowledge.

</td></tr>
</table>

BACKGROUND
AND
THEORY

productivity a measure
of employee output

ENVIRONMENT FOR PRODUCTIVITY

Organizations in the United States, Canada, and other free countries have achieved great levels of employee **productivity** through systematic approaches to planning and, in more recent years, through careful attention to the people who make productive systems function. However, productivity is currently leveling off or declining.

"Productivity is a function of responsibility freely accepted. Taken to its most essential common base, it is the inspired action of qualified individuals doing their job." This is the theme of an article on productivity by Frederick W. Harvey.[1] His approach is that the environment must be right, and the supervisor substantially affects that environment.

This chapter and Chapter Ten, therefore, are developed around the idea that both the environment and the mechanisms must operate in harmony in order for desirable levels of productivity to exist. Harvey suggests that tackling the problem of low or mediocre productivity should involve, first, an analysis of environmental factors that create such conditions and, second, that specific supervisory and managerial actions can change those conditions so that an acceptable level of productivity is generated. He believes that five things create conditions which inspire mediocre or low-level productivity. Those are:

1. Suppression of emotion
2. Jobs that become spread out . . . managers promoted tend to carry along to their new positions some of the tasks from their old positions

---

[1]Frederick W. Harvey, "Allowing Productivity to Happen," *Supervisory Management*, 25 (June 1980): 21–25.

178

"**Productivity is a function of responsibility freely accepted. Taken to its most essential common base, it is the inspired action of qualified individuals doing their job.**"
—Frederick W. Harvey

Photograph by Alan Baker, courtesy of Lord Corporation.

3. Bosses who won't make jobs clear

4. Unacknowledged mistakes

5. Contributions that are not acknowledged

Most of his suggested solutions to these conditions relate to materials covered elsewhere in this book—motivation, open dialog with employees, evaluation, communication, and environment. One, however, is a particularly appropriate backdrop for this chapter:

Make clear the purpose and performance measurements for each job . . . . The key to achieving greater and consequently higher productivity is the explicit definition of the purpose of each job and the measures of quality and quantity that show how well it is succeeding.[2]

The nation's office staffs are performing at fifty–sixty-five percent of the level at which they are capable of performing. Production workers probably come out better than this, and marketing employees are probably the most productive because of a variety of incentives for high productivity in sales and marketing. No work group even comes close to 100 percent of potential, however. Even agreeing upon what is "acceptable" or "possible" productivity is a difficult task. A later discussion on work measurement in this chapter provides some insight into identification of acceptable levels of productivity.

Low productivity is generally not the fault of the employee. For the most part it is the fault of inadequate supervision, management-created climate, defective procedures, lack of coordination of effort, and restrictions imposed by outside-the-organization forces (government regulations and controls, for example). The office workers cited earlier are not unproductive because they choose to be that way. In most cases, they are unproductive because they do not know what is expected of them, because many of them have no professional supervision, or because they work with poorly designed information handling systems. Many of them are supported by bargain-basement capital investments for equipment and technology. Much waste occurs when employees must wait for something to happen, and many workers spend a lot of their time waiting for information or materials.

In general terms, improving productivity is tied to several factors:

1. Developing efficient, well-planned systems and procedures.
2. Developing a climate conducive to worker satisfaction and participation.
3. Employee and supervisor knowledge of job content.
4. Mechanisms for measuring quality and quantity of production.
5. Appropriate internal and external reward structures.

---

[2]Harvey, "Allowing Productivity to Happen," p. 21.

THE STATUS OF
PRODUCTIVITY IN THE WORKPLACE

Recent years have brought great concern among American managers over the productivity of workers. Accustomed to continual improvement and many decades of increased productivity, managers are alarmed that many organizations now show declining or steady productivity levels. These conditions exist in most every kind and size of organization.

Productivity is measured by the employees' per hour output in all nonfarm businesses. Approximately a year is needed to process actual productivity data. Data compiled in late 1981 revealed that productivity in the United States fell in 1980.[3] Even though there were gains in some industries, such as coal mining, petroleum refining, household appliance manufacturing, and telephone communications, the overall rate declined.

production that
*produced, total value or
quantity of output*

Although the word **production** sometimes refers to the manufacturing process, concerns over productivity are not limited to manufacturing or heavy industrial organizations. In fact, it is not limited to the operative level either. There is as much need for concern about managerial and administrative productivity as about worker productivity. Productivity applies to whatever is produced—tangible product, service for sale, service for the benefit of society.

Some authorities believe that our decrease in productivity can be blamed on our shift from an emphasis on the production of tangible products to the production of services. We now employ more people in the "white collar" and service industries than in manufacturing processes. Because productivity is more difficult to pinpoint in the service areas, improvement is more difficult among these jobs. Nevertheless, any analysis of the productivity level must involve *all* productivity—not just industrial productivity.

Because productivity levels are closely tied to the economy as a whole, individuals also have reason to be concerned about productivity. Private ventures fail when their employees are not productive, because profits dwindle. Public organizations must provide their services with as few dollars (taxes) as possible. Recent cutbacks in government spending have eliminated many programs that were not "cost effective" (productive). Unfortunately, elim-

---

[3]"Productivity in Most Industries Fell in '80," *Washington Report* (January 1982) (Washington, D.C., Chamber of Commerce of the United States) , p. 5.

ination of some very productive programs also occurred. Governments, government procedures, and government employees are notorious for poor productivity. For many economically prosperous years, government budgets were routinely increased. This went on for so long that waste became rampant. Because each new fiscal budget was tied to the previous year's appropriation, government agency management was penalized for *not* spending instead of being rewarded for economy. Any budget item not fully spent in one period was reduced for the next period—even though the need might have been greater. Zero-based budgeting was an attempt to eliminate this situation by requiring that all dollars for each item in a budget be rejustified with each new budget period. The success of this practice at reducing government spending was minimal.

Whether an organization is private or public, better tools and better ways of doing things can enable one unit or the whole organization to produce more. Few people work themselves out of a job because they work too hard, unless the job was unnecessary in the first place.

Efficiency and economy aid everyone. Workers are more comfortable in an efficient operation, because they can see the results of their contributions to the success of the organization. In efficient organizations managers have fewer problems. Business ventures are profitable. Public ventures are successful. Successful organizations stay in business; successful workers keep their jobs—or get better ones; and efficient and economical units within organizations do not go unnoticed and unrewarded.

Supervisors may make their greatest contributions to productivity when they make concerted efforts to maintain realistic attitudes about the reality of organizational accomplishments. Organizations succeed when the people who make up those organizations recognize the value of their individual contributions. When individuals want the organization to succeed, they become concerned about waste and inefficiency. They don't view the organization as a "Big Daddy" who has unrestricted resources. Supervisors are not solely responsible for this attitude, but their close contact with workers suggests that workers' attitudes and perceptions will be influenced by supervisors. If the supervisor realizes that "there is no such thing as a free lunch," perhaps their subordinates will realize that too.

Consistent pro-productivity attitudes among supervisors appear to be contagious. If all supervisors believe that high-level, realistic standards can be met, then this attitude is passed to the worker. If part of the supervisory staff is negative or endorses lackadaisical attitudes, high standards are difficult for the remainder of the staff.

APPROACHES TO PRODUCTIVITY IMPROVEMENT

Throughout the history of the industrial movement various attempts have been made to increase productivity levels among workers. Many of these are discussed elsewhere in this book. They include employee incentives, "scientific" approaches to management, improved employee selection and training techniques, and external reward systems which were labeled "motivation" programs. These measures met varying degrees of success. While productivity levels climbed steadily, each technique experienced difficulty and workers seemed to eventually resent and oppose the techniques.

Later movements attempted to emphasize the supervisor as the key to productivity. The desire to maintain subordinates' approval, however, causes supervisors to overlook conditions which they know will enhance low productivity.

More recent efforts at improving productivity have emphasized worker participation in some way. The idea behind these efforts has been the belief that workers who are involved in decisions about how things should be done and about realistic expectations of worker groups would achieve higher productivity levels. Examples of these efforts include MBO (Management by Objectives), QWL (Quality of Work Life), job design, work measurement or time standard programs, and quality circle plans. MBO programs are discussed in Chapter Three of this book, and the following portions of this chapter contain discussions of quality circles, which are very similar to QWL, job design, and work measurement.

A current interpretation of the productivity problem suggests that the values of supervisors and workers and their resulting attitudes about work and productivity may carry the greatest potential for a turnaround of the productivity picture.

Quality Control Circles

quality control circle
small group of employees
who discuss problems,
pursue special projects,
and suggest changes

The **quality control circle** is a worker-participation activity that attempts to improve productivity. It is one of the techniques that has been used successfully in Japan. American chagrin at the

Whether or not you call it a quality circle or a production improvement team, regularly-scheduled, management-sanctioned problem solving meetings provide a system for enhancing productivity.

Photograph by Alan Baker, courtesy of FMC Corporation.

improved Japanese product quality and increased productivity levels during an era when productivity is falling here, has caused an emulation of their styles that might create similar results here. United States organizations in large numbers have endorsed the quality control circle approach in recent years. For the most part these have been industrial organizations, but a few attempts have been made to implement them in nonmanufacturing firms and government agencies.

A quality control circle (frequently shortened to "quality circle" in the United States) is a group of employees, usually ten or fewer, engaged in similar work. They hold regular meetings where they discuss problems and suggest solutions. The practice is based upon the idea that workers are closer to the real problem and are better able to suggest solutions.

In Japan, where quality control circles were developed, with the assistance of American statisticians, by the Union of Japanese Scientists and Engineers, the quality control circle is an institution which has been perfected over the past thirty-four years. More than one million circles were in existence by 1980. Employees are thoroughly trained in statistical techniques. Again, these are techniques that have been in use in the United States for a hundred years, but they are not understood by large numbers of workers here. Equal emphasis is given to quantity and quality levels, on the one hand, and worker pride in individual and group accomplishment on the other hand.

Each Japanese circle, headed by a foreman, meets weekly, sometimes on company time and sometimes on employee time, to identify problems and work on solutions. Some problems are complex and time-consuming. The circle may work on a solution for months. Their firms implement fifty–sixty suggestions per circle member annually. Problems which reach beyond the responsibility of a single circle may be tackled by representatives from several circles who form a new circle.

Success for quality circles in the United States will probably be long in coming or short-lived until employee and management attitudes and values are restructured. (This need is discussed in a later section of this chapter.) Several major differences between Japanese and American cultures will hamper the implementation of circles here. American circle members are frequently disgruntled and discouraged if their recommendations are not implemented. The Japanese accept the authority of the organization and probably would not question management's delay or refusal to implement a suggestion.

In Japan the circle is a small part of a larger productivity awareness plan. Careful planning, preparation, and nationwide recognition (including designating November as National QC Circle Month and a program of recognition for outstanding accomplishment by circles), and the sharing of benefits between worker and employer help to create a mood of acceptance and mutual trust. The ego-centered attitude of Americans and the adversary positions of management and employees would have to be altered before quality circles could succeed on a wide scale here. Too many of the existing circles have been created by management decree and have moved too rapidly to their tasks.

While we are generally skeptical about the prospects for quality circles in United States organizations, there is evidence that a philosophy of organizations which would be conducive to this approach is emerging. Labeled "Theory Z," this approach emphasizes worker involvement and harmony among workers and between workers and management.[4]

---

[4]See William G. Ouchi, *Theory Z: How American Business Can Meet the Japanese Challenge* (Reading, Mass.: Addison-Wesley Publishing Company, Inc., 1981, and New York: Avon Books, 1982), for a complete description of Theory Z and case studies of U.S. firms which have developed the approach.

IMPLICATIONS
AND
APPLICATIONS

INCREASING PRODUCTIVITY THROUGH JOB DESIGN

In some organizations the analysis of job content and the design of new jobs is associated with the personnel management function—more so than with supervision. However, the supervisor is the closest observer of operative jobs and the most likely person to accurately judge the desirability of job content. Because productive work is performed by people and will function well only when the right number of strategically-located people are cooperating, job design is closely related to attempts to improve productivity.

Job Content—Flexible or Fixed?

Some firms prefer to fit jobs to the worker—instead of seeking a worker to fill a described job. This practice may become more prevalent in the future as management styles become more people oriented and as organizations consider the long-range effects of their actions. Flexibility may better suit the worker, but it requires more participation by the supervisor.

Because of the rigidity of traditional job descriptions, firms which prefer greater job flexibility have been hesitant to prepare formal job descriptions. Organized labor and collective bargaining for job content usually force detailed descriptions. As mentioned earlier, EEOC regulations have also influenced this.

Even with the disadvantages of rigidity and the improvement to the working climate of flexible working arrangements, supervision is improved with written job descriptions. In situations where jobs are not clearly defined, especially where a supervisor is responsible for large numbers of employees, confusion and discord arise easily. Employee grievances frequently arise when workers are forced into work which they believe to be the responsibility of other workers. Such grievances also arise when workers must perform tasks which they don't find in their written job descriptions or perceive to be a part of their job content.

Harold McAlindon in a 1980 article pointed out that organizations which attempt to improve achievement should not stop with development of traditional organization charts, job descriptions, and rigid procedural descriptions.[5] He suggests a flexibility of organization that would also include key results documentation,

---

[5]Harold A. McAlindon, "Toward a More Creative You: Creating the Ideal Organization," *Supervisory Management* (January 1980), p. 30.

Job analysis may involve interviewing employees to determine actual job content.

standards of excellence for every position, maximum use of individual strengths (even for areas not covered by one's job description), and removal of obstacles to success as a part of the analysis procedure.

Job content should be identified. The language of the description should not be rigid or foreboding. It should allow for flexibility and application of individual talent. Employees and organizations can be most productive when workers and supervisors are equipped with a knowledge of job content, understanding of requirements and relationships which the job requires, and the realization that from time to time things which do not appear on anybody's job description must be done in order for an organization to function.

Tools for Defining and Clarifying Job Content

If workers are unsatisfied with their jobs or, at best, tolerant of the situation in which they spend one-third of their lives, the job

187

content may be the reason. Few supervisors have the freedom to affect their own jobs, and still fewer have the opportunity to determine their subordinates' jobs.

A few technical descriptions will enhance the supervisor's understanding of jobs. **Job analysis**, **job description**, **job evaluation**, and **job specifications** are terms that have distinct meanings but are sometimes confused. Job analysis and job evaluation are processes; job descriptions and job specifications are paper documents (perhaps electronic documents in the near future). The following discussion attempts to differentiate among these. Even though these terms are somewhat standard, written documents which outline job content are sometimes labeled "Job Analysis."

job analysis process of examining job content

job description document which describes job functions, responsibilities, duties, and relationships of a job

job evaluation process of assigning monetary value to specific jobs

job specification document which specifies education, experience, and physical requirements

Job analysis is the process of examining jobs to determine what is done in those jobs. As mentioned earlier, *analyze* means to take apart or to study the relationships among parts of something. Many people who hold jobs find it difficult to describe what they do. If the job is not analyzed and described, confusion and misunderstandings can result.

The process of job analysis has been around since the days of Frederick Taylor and his scientific management movement. As a part of the field of personnel management, it has enjoyed varying degrees of popularity since the 1920s. Recent years have brought renewed attention because of federal government regulatory policies and federal law. The Civil Rights Act of 1964, Title VII, the Equal Employment Opportunity Commission (created by the Civil Rights Act and strengthened by 1967 and 1978 amendments), and other laws and enactments have mandated attention to job content.

To some people job analysis is the process of describing what exists—the content of jobs at the time the analysis is being made. To others, the process should be broader in scope and should encompass information gathering about jobs and their relationship to the organization. This view sees jobs as vehicles to the functioning of systems within the organization. Because of the push by civil rights/EEOC laws and interpretations for employers to analyze jobs and better describe jobs, Ghorpade and Atchison attempted a *prescriptive* definition of job analysis (as opposed to *descriptive*). Their definition follows:

Job analysis should be a purposeful, ongoing organizational activity, performed by professionals in order to uncover, synthesize and disseminate information about jobs that can be used in deci-

188

sions relating to organizational planning and design, human resources management and other managerial functions.[6]

This approach to job analysis emphasizes the value of job analysis for understanding the total job. The authors of this definition would deemphasize time-and-motion-study approaches to analyzing jobs and would employ a variety of data gathering methods which produce valid and reliable results. They would emphasize research techniques that assure such validity and reliability. This approach suggests, however, that job analysis be performed by representatives of the personnel management department and not by first-line supervisors. Nevertheless, the more that supervisors understand about the process and the reasons for carrying out the process, the better able they are to cooperate in the analysis. This understanding will also enhance the supervisors' ability to communicate analysis details to employees.

Once a job has been analyzed, a job description is prepared. Job descriptions are documents which describe a job. As Exhibit 9.1 illustrates, descriptions frequently begin with a capsule statement that describes the overall job. Other sections of the document enumerate specific duties, tasks, and responsibilities. Job descriptions may specify the portion of time devoted to each duty or responsibility. Relationships with others in the organization may be spelled out. The immediate superior and subordinates, if involved, will be identified (by title or position—not by name) and contacts necessary between a person who holds the described job and others (inside and outside the organization) are listed.

Job analysis and *procedures analysis* are sometimes confused. While related, they are separate concepts. A procedure analysis examines how a major sequence of related tasks is performed. A job analysis examines all the functions, duties, tasks, responsibilities, and relationships of a particular job. It might even go into desirable additional responsibilities or promotional and developmental paths for employees holding that particular position. In an organization with standardized jobs, all employees with the same title would have identical or near-identical job descriptions.

written procedure
document which describes how to perform a specified set of routines

Likewise, *job description* and *written procedure* are sometimes confused. Job descriptions describe in writing *what* someone does because he or she holds a particular job. Written procedures de-

---

[6]Jao Ghorpade and Thomas J. Atchison, "The Concept of Job Analysis: A Review and Some Suggestions," *Public Personnel Management Journal* (August 1980), p. 136.

Job Description

Title	Word Processing Supervisor	Approvals:	Date
Unit	Word Processing/Admin. Secretarial Systems		
Location	Nashville		

Function

The Word Processing/Administrative Secretarial Systems Department provides complete word processing support for all departments designated to use the services. Supervisors provide work direction and training for one or more groups of from five to twenty correspondence secretaries who perform copy typing, transcribing, and composing activities. Other related employees may also be supervised.

Responsibilities

1. Methods Planning (5%)

   Establishes and revises internal work procedures and controls for electronic typing, editing, and composing equipment.

   Designs and revises subordinates' job descriptions.

2. Supervision (60%)

   Delegates work to and supervises the following personnel:

   (1) Senior Correspondence Secretaries
   (2) Associate Correspondence Secretaries
   (3) Correspondence Secretaries
   (4) One or more Word Processing Coordinators
   (5) One or more satellite Word Processing Center Supervisors

   Supervised employees provide complete typing support for a functional area or department, including correspondence, reports, memoranda, statistical documents, programming documentation, forms, invoices, manuscripts, and all other typing applications.
   Establishes and coordinates a system of work priorities among customer groups.
   Assures confidentiality of message content.

Exhibit 9.1
Job Description for a Word Processing Supervisor

190

3. Personnel Activities (5%)

Interviews and selects personnel for the unit.

Appraises unit employee performance.

Administers company merit pay program within the unit.

4. Other Responsibilities (30%)

Budget planning for the unit.

Staff planning—labor requirements, temporary help requirements, overtime requirements, special assignments, and coordination of interunit personnel sharing.

Determines standards of performance—quality and quantity—for unit.

Recommends, periodically, long-range program changes and physical space needs.

Provides orientation service for new users of the unit's services.

Resolves complaints from customer departments or functional areas.

With other supervisors and the manager of the department, selects, plans, installs, and coordinates word processing systems, including equipment and software selection.

Other necessary responsibilities deemed necessary to carry out the mission of the unit.

Relationships

1. Manager, Word Processing/Administrative Secretarial Systems
Reports directly to this person.

2. Customer management
Confers with managers of customer departments and functional areas served by the unit regarding WP services to that area.

3. Systems vendors
Maintains necessary contacts to keep abreast of technical, equipment, and software developments.

4. Other relationships
Maintains contact with supervisors and professionals in other organizations, makes presentations on WP to professional groups, and maintains membership and participates in applicable professional organizations

scribe *how* to perform specified procedures. A single employee might perform or assist in the performance of numerous procedures.

Job specifications are sometimes recorded on the job description, but they should be separate documents. They specify educational, physical, and experience requirements necessary for holding the described job. Job evaluation is a process which attempts to equate the monetary value of a job (a salary or wage range) to other jobs in the organization. Most job evaluation formulae rely heavily upon the specifications mentioned earlier and other factors, such as physical strength, required working conditions, exposure to hazard, and responsibility required. However, the supply/demand situation probably is still the greatest influence upon salaries and wages for operative level employees.

Practical Approaches to Improving Job Content

What can be done to make jobs more interesting? more challenging to the adult mentality? Chapter Four covered motivation and the supervisors' role in influencing workers' feelings and attitudes toward the organization and the work they do. From a practical standpoint, what can a supervisor do to understand the jobs of subordinates, to communicate job content to subordinates, and to redesign jobs believed to be ineffectively designed? The suggestions which follow summarize some of the things supervisors may be able to do to understand and influence job content in their departments.

First, one must understand existing jobs. Read job descriptions if they exist. Relate knowledge of what employees actually do with the described job. Interview employees if knowledge of what they really do is insufficient to judge the accuracy of the description. Pay particular attention to percentage of time devoted to major categories of responsibility. Serious deviations suggest that employees' work be redirected or that descriptions should be rewritten. Employees who do not know what is expected of them are frustrated unnecessarily.

Second, if any conditions suggest that employees are bored with their jobs or that job content is affecting employee morale, some consideration of redesigning jobs is desirable. Performance standards are helpful in determining how much a single employee can be expected to accomplish. Standard time data or work measurement results can also be helpful if the proper atmosphere and objectives for their use is maintained. The employee should not come out of such an experience believing that the effort was an attempt to learn how much additional blood the organization can subtly draw from his or her veins.

In response to increased volume, complaints, and concern over quality of the department, Monsanto Company initiated a job-restructuring plan in its St. Louis accounts payable department. In 1979 the company formed a task force to examine the department's mission and the contribution of jobs to that mission.

Using the Job Diagnostic Survey developed by Roy W. Walters and Associates, a management consulting firm, and interviews with employees by an in-house task force revealed employee concerns about growth needs, knowledge of overall work flow, and performance feedback. As a result, the department was restructured and jobs were redefined, using a "natural work unit approach" for processing invoices for payment. Employees were grouped by geographical area or specialty and one employee remained the contact for his or her group. A better rapport with clients developed.

Tangible results of the Monsanto plan included a productivity increase of 12.3 percent (measured in number of invoices produced) and a $15,200 annual saving in salaries and overtime wages. Less tangible results were employees' improved job satisfaction as jobs were expanded to take advantage of individual capabilities and definite efforts were made to communicate the department's mission.[7]

Third, with superiors' approval, experiment with some of the newer approaches to job design. Try a shared-job arrangement for jobs that are tedious or too detailed for eight-hour exposure. Flexible work hours for difficult-to-motivate groups may help. Use of temporary employees for seasonal fluctuations which are undesirable for regular employees might help.

The solution may be in the looking. If employees know that you are genuinely concerned about them and the content of their jobs, any attempt to improve the situation should be a real morale booster.

IMPROVING PRODUCTIVITY THROUGH WORK MEASUREMENT

If work is to be adequately supervised, the supervisor must have some concept of what to expect of workers and how much time

---

[7]"Job-Restructuring Plan Adds to Satisfaction of Monsanto Employees," *The Office* (March 1981), p. 63.

various quantities of work will consume. For most supervisors in settings other than industrial production, these expectations are based on estimates, whim, casual observation, knowledge of worker attitude and past performance, or periodic inspections to determine whether or not workers are on the job. In industrial environments, quality inspection of workers' efforts and production records are an indication of worker output—both quantity and quality.

work measurement
technique for quantifying employee production and establishing standards

Work measurement is a sorely abused and misused technique for determining productivity levels which may be expected. It was abused in the past when it was used as a device to get higher and higher levels of productivity from workers without adequately rewarding them for their efforts. Other applications have resulted in employee dismissals, incentive pay systems which increased standards after a majority of the workers were able to earn incentives, and abrupt changes in workers' jobs. Most of these efforts at work measurement dealt with quantity standards, highly routine jobs, and time and motion studies for the purpose of setting standards.

Work measurement involves quantifying work and establishing standards. In industrial environments, it has been called **time study** or **methods time measurement** (MTM). Many modern attempts at work measurement are carried out as much for planning, scheduling, and coordinating effort as for assessing worker performance.

time study *work measurement to set time standards*
methods time measurement (MTM) *process of measuring or quantifying work*
standard *quantity of specific work produced in a measurable time span*

The product of work measurement is a **standard**. A standard is some quantification of work—something that can be measured. It is based on the performance of a well-trained, average worker, working under usual working conditions. Knowledge of the expectations of such workers opens up all sorts of possibilities for planning and coordinating work.

Work volume in most environments can be related to other factors which are predictable. For example, if the marketing and economic forecasting departments of a firm can predict sales, many administrative departments can predict the volume of work which X dollars of sales will produce for them. The presence of standards will enable managers in each area to predict labor needs, schedule activities, increase or decrease staffs, or anticipate the adequacy of equipment capacities.

Where they are used, however, work measurement techniques often suggest ominous future events to employees—harder work for the same pay, loss of job, transfer to other departments. These fears can be overcome with careful planning, full disclosure, and employee participation in the process from the beginning.

The Supervisor and Work Measurement

Any supervisor can improve productivity through serious and patient efforts to examine what is done and to look for improvements. Real measurable results, however, need the impetus of a formalized effort of some type. That formal effort may come from an in-house group trained in systems and procedures analysis or work measurement techniques or from outside consultants.

An approach which has worked well for many organizations is an in-house group to handle the data gathering and analysis, guided by an outside consultant who can advise, offer suggestions, and provide instruments for gathering and analyzing information.

Many organizations have service groups which are available to either help departments study and improve various facets of work that they do or to actually handle certain kinds of work for them. These services are not fully used in some organizations. Examples are: methods analysts, forms design specialists, word processing centers, records managers, clerical assistance groups, and physical layout analysts. Some organizations require close association with these groups; others place them "on call" for those who request their services. They can usually help departments that have problems in the area for which they are specially trained.

Case Study *How Work-Measurement Can Control Costs* illustrates how a service group became so popular that departments requested its assistance. This reaction is the opposite of the typical reaction to a procedures analysis or work measurement group within organizations. They are typically viewed as "efficiency experts" or "trouble makers" who are sent in by top management to tell supervisors how to run their shows.

Although the approach used in the case is labeled a work measurement program, it is really a combination of the productivity improvement tools discussed in this chapter and Chapter Ten—procedures analysis, work measurement, staff redistribution, and the use of temporary employees. The most significant factor in the whole case is the management pledge that no employee would be terminated as a result of the study. Employees won't support a program and cooperate in assembling data if they think their jobs are threatened. Since attrition takes so many employees (without dismissals), there is really no need to dismiss employees whose jobs are eliminated by attempts to improve productivity.

IMPROVING PRODUCTIVITY THROUGH VALUE STRUCTURES

In the United States the Gross National Product declined again in the fourth quarter of 1981. The decline amounted to more than five percent. Experts suggest that the entire economic system may experience even greater difficulty than the 1981–1982 recession if there are not vast policy changes or orientations.[8] At the same time, the Consumer Price Index was still rising—113 percent between 1970 and 1980—from 116.3 to 247.[9]

During the last five years the basic response to the "red alert" created by declining productivity has been threefold. One approach has been a furious effort to produce greater numbers of items with too little attention to quality. The second approach has been to beef up marketing efforts to make people want to buy more. And the third approach has been to seek near-term gimmicks to bandage up the system. Those in Human Resources Development (HRD) areas have been guilty of the third.

Mini-approaches, which have been lauded as the answer to the problems, include such things as "back to MBO," "quality circles," "statistical quality control," "motivation seminars," and so on. For some organizations, this patchwork approach has been beneficial, depending upon the basic stability and the evolutionary stage of maturity of the organization. Production and marketing oriented approaches to improving productivity work less often than some of the HRD efforts. The mini-solution approach has limited value for solving long-term and basic problems that our industrial and organizational systems face.

To suggest that quality circles may be the answer to the production problems is naive and too simplistic an answer to a worldwide, complex problem that demands a total restructuring effort on the part of management at all levels. If, then, the picture is as bleak as it is perceived to be, what possible alternatives are available for a rational change orientation?

One suggestion that appears to be substantiated in the litera-

---

[8]"With Output Off Sharply, Experts Say Worse to Come," *Courier-Journal* (Louisville), January 21, 1982, p. A9.
[9]*Monthly Labor Review* (June 1981), p. 85.

ture is a wholistic approach based on systems that are currently working and that offer hope for continued success. Too much attention has been given to parts of organizations—at the expense of the whole. One obvious system that has been working in diverse areas of production is the Japanese model. While no evidence would suggest that this model is perfect, their approach appears to benefit all parties in the enterprise—the owner, the worker, and the consumer.

The West has long considered itself the leader in production and innovation, but adversary systems within organizations have slowed management's response time, reduced sales programs to short-term efforts and quality control to programs for which no person with real authority is willing to be responsible. Worker commitment is often non-existent.

Trying to identify one overall theme or summary statement that describes the difference between these two orientations (Japanese and Western) is dangerous, academically. However, based on combined experiences with private and public organizations, a judgment is represented by the following summary.

The Japanese model is based upon a long-term reinforcement system that is aimed at benefiting all participants of productive enterprises. The current Western model is based upon a short-term reinforcement system that is aimed at independent factions within the system. Technical differences between the two systems were discussed earlier; but because the discussion here is about productivity and values, two more fundamental issues need to be addresssed.

Until our value system changes to reflect major concerns for the welfare of owners, workers, and consumers, our industrial model will continue to flounder. Toffler's *Third Wave* has as a major theme the necessity for corporate entities to have multi-dimensional goals that far exceed the immediate goal of increased sales. There is little doubt that the managers of industry need to evaluate their organizational goals and to adjust those goals to a social world that is changing faster than it is doing anything else. Because this review and evolution must be wholistic, it will be complex; but a major value base must deal with all of the participants in the enterprise.

What, then, is the bottom line for change? There is no bottom line! There is a series of bottom lines that require a systematic evaluation of what any one organization can change to develop a commitment based on work that will, in Toffler's terms, both produce and consume for the welfare of the whole. The series of bottom lines is, the authors believe, identifiable and definable. The fundamental issues are Basic Value Dimensions (BVD's).[10] Two basic value dimensions which need some solutions to set the stage for increasing productivity are the immediacy orientation and the desire for short term individual gratification.

Immediacy Orientation Economic and business managers often complain that decisions are no longer made with the "bottom line" (profit) in mind. The reason generally given is that complex pressures from government and other external forces no longer allow the profit motive to come to the forefront. We agree that this is the case, but there is an additional ingredient which also affects productivity in the long run. That ingredient centers around professional managers (employees, too) who make the primary decisions for private organizations. These decisions, like the demands of unions, may be based on the potential for short-term personal benefit—or even short-term organization benefit—at the expense of other employees, stockholders, and customers. When decisions are based on short-term promotional opportunities for the managers involved, the competing values override even the basic profit motive. What should the bottom line be? The authors' response is that private organizations exist and prosper when owners, workers, and customers benefit and that there is probably no sequence to the importance of the three groups. They are equally important.

When decisions are made that compromise one of the three parties on a long-term basis, the decisions are bad. The bottom line is threefold: the worker's overall job satisfaction, the owner's profit combined with the organization's strength and stability, and the customer's product value.

Individual Gratification If there is anything to be learned from organized team sports, it is that unselfish teamwork is the only way to have a winning unit. In the United States, a myth has been perpetuated that everyone has the "right" to do his or her "own thing." The rights of the individual have been heralded. Special interest groups have been organized to carry the concerns of "individuals" to authorities—organized labor, consumer advocacy groups, faculty senates, legislative lobbies, associations for this

---

[10]A term coined by Dr. James Craig, Department of Psychology, Western Kentucky University (Bowling Green, Ky.), in 1981.

and that. The list is endless. Only in certain types of organizations has there been a truly functioning philosophy that the total is greater than the sum of the parts. Possible examples are Hewlett-Packard, Rockwell International, and Eli Lilly.[11] These organizations have attempted to work with all their staff members in developing a truly team-oriented approach.

The authors' basic suggestion is that *the team is more important than the individual*. Until all of the participants accept that attitude and until values which reflect this attitude guide their management, productivity as a bottom line on a long term basis will remain far removed from basic concern.

SUMMARY

People and the environments in which they work are the keys to productivity. Even though great strides in productivity levels have been accomplished in this century, rates of improvement have slowed or disappeared in the Western world in recent years. Supervisors greatly influence the attitude toward productivity among workers.

Many efforts have been made to maintain and improve productivity. The most recent productivity fad has been the quality circle, which has been a part of great productivity improvements in Japan.

Thorough worker knowledge of job content and performance expectations will probably enhance any effort to improve productivity. Job analysis and the use of job descriptions are one facet of this effort. Another program which can provide standards for performance and worker expectations is work measurement.

Job analysis is an attempt to define job content and, where necessary, to redesign jobs to fit the needs of the organization, its employees, and others served by the organization. While the standard has been rigidity in job content and the recruitment of workers who will fit into already defined jobs, the future is likely to bring greater flexibility as workers are assigned jobs that are, in some cases, tailormade for them. Even though flexibility of job content may be desirable for the worker, supervisors will continue to find job descriptions, job specifications, and the analysis process

---

[11]See William Ouchi, *Theory Z: How American Business Can Meet The Japanese Challenge* (New York: Avon, 1981) for a discussion of these and other organizations that endorse this philosophy.

199

to be helpful tools for planning and controlling work. Supervisors are likely to assist in the job analysis process—even if the major responsibility for this activity is carried out by professionals.

Work measurement, while frequently misunderstood and misused, is a valuable practice for establishing standards that are useful for planning, scheduling, and coordinating work and improving productivity.

While formal programs of job analysis, job redesign, and work measurement will be carried out by professionals, supervisors may be able to make contributions in these areas through informal efforts.

The most important need for improving productivity is a restructuring of the value system of managers and workers.

QUESTIONS FOR FURTHER THOUGHT

1. Since we are among the most progressive countries in the world, should we be concerned about increasing productivity? Is more necessarily better?

2. Do you believe that workers prefer to have their duties and responsibilities described in writing or to just do what they are told by superiors?

3. Assuming the use of written job descriptions, how does the supervisor handle the situation which requires that tasks not included in any worker's job description be performed? Create and discuss a hypothetical situation which might create this problem for a supervisor.

4. What are your opinions about the reason for declining productivity levels in the United States and Canada?

5. Explain the fact that office workers may be only fifty–sixty-five percent as productive as they could be, using the "average employee" standard as the measure of possible productivity.

6. What are possible reasons for low productivity among government workers?

7. Differentiate between job analysis and job description; between job evaluation and job specification.

8. Identify a job with which you are familiar and describe the possible effects of developing technologies and changing work habits on that job in the future.

10

SYSTEMS AND PROCEDURES ANALYSIS FOR SUPERVISORS

LEARNING OBJECTIVES

Upon completion of this chapter and related activities, you should be able to:

1. Explain the concept of systems as it applies to the performance of work.
2. Differentiate among the scope of the terms *system*, *procedure*, and *method* and give examples of each.
3. Interview people who perform standard procedures in organizations and write descriptions of those procedures.
4. Identify the basic tools of procedures analysis and their purposes.
5. Suggest simple approaches for simplifying the performance of routine work tasks.

CHAPTER OUTLINE

PROBLEM STATEMENT
PROCEDURES AS COMPONENTS OF SYSTEMS

BACKGROUND AND THEORY
AN INTRODUCTION TO THE SYSTEMS APPROACH
    Supverisor's Role in Improving Procedures
    Systems Analysis and Design
    Administrative Systems
    Professional Systems Analysts
    Systems, Procedures, and Methods
    Approach to Systems Improvement

IMPLICATIONS AND APPLICATIONS
INCREASING PRODUCTIVITY THROUGH BETTER SYSTEMS
    The Role of Information
    The Role of the Analyst
    The Role of the Supervisor
    Why Standardize Procedures
    Tools of Procedures Analysis
INFORMAL IMPROVEMENTS IN WORK
SUMMARY

QUESTIONS FOR FURTHER THOUGHT

PROBLEM
STATEMENT

PROCEDURES AS
COMPONENTS OF SYSTEMS

Supervisors can better control the productivity of people and the efficiency of processes if they view procedures as components of interlocking and interrelated systems. Combined with a concern for people and an environment conducive to harmony among management and worker, planned systems and standard operating procedures are integral parts of supervision and contribute to efficiency and economy. Procedures are seldom carried out independently. They affect other people and other procedures. Supervisors, assisted by specialists and workers as necessary, can analyze and improve existing procedures for performing the work assigned to their units.

BACKGROUND
AND
THEORY

AN INTRODUCTION
TO THE SYSTEMS APPROACH

Supervisors must understand the systems within which their subordinates function. In varying degrees they may have the freedom to examine systems and procedures and to develop new and improved ways of doing things. At least, they should refuse to accept the status quo until they have examined it for efficiency and harmony with the organization's overall objectives. Since employee productivity is a concern of every organization, efforts to enhance productivity are welcome in most organizations. Improving productivity is not a matter of cracking the whip or merely pushing employees. It is a matter of leading and providing mechanisms which make productive effort possible—working smarter, not harder.

Most of the suggestions made in this chapter deal with better ways of doing things—either because they can be done more efficiently or at lower cost. Lowering costs raises profits. Profitable organizations are better able to pay high wages or to keep paying wages at all. It's that simple.

In actual practice, many organizations make no formal attempts to analyze work procedures or job content or to establish formal standards. Formal standards of performance are limited to manufacturing concerns for the most part. Some organizations are making haphazard attempts at job analysis because of EEOC pressures. In these organizations where no formal attempts at improvement are made, supervisors and other managers—and occasionally the workers—informally examine these factors. Major problems and bottlenecks are dealt with as the problems surface. Subtle inefficiencies which lie dormant and quiet create no disturbances and continue to exist.

systems and procedures analysis *analysis of work routines to improve efficiency*

Systems and procedures analysis is an attempt to analyze what people do in a work environment. Their efforts to produce products and offer services are dissected and analyzed for possible improvement. This approach is a combination of the principles of scientific management, the systems approach to management, and computerized information handling technology.

In manufacturing organizations, the production processes are analyzed for possible improvement by industrial engineering specialists. In offices, information systems analysts, methods analysts, or work measurement specialists do the same things for information production processes.

Supervisor's Role in Improving Procedures

Supervisors are instrumental in the success of efforts to improve efficiency. They observe work from a vantage point which offers the best opportunity to evaluate systems and procedures and to improve production—whether that production involves producing tangible products, offering services, or processing information. Although their evaluations and suggestions are not always accepted by management, the supervisor should attempt to become as knowledgeable as possible about the reasons for established procedures and methods for improving them. Perhaps most important among supervisors' contributions is their effect upon employees' accepting or rejecting efforts to improve or change.

Changes in procedures are frequently necessary. New production techniques, mergers of organizations, governmental requirements, and different information processing routines are some of the things that require changes in procedure. Other changes are made to improve efficiency or reduce costs. Change for the sake of change is not adequate justification. Supervisors should wield whatever influence they can muster to assure that changes are carefully analyzed and systematically effected.

The natural reaction of employees and supervisors to analysis of the status quo is to resist such analysis. People get very comfortable with established procedures and easily convince themselves that there is no better way. If business and industry in this country had not looked for a better way, people would still be traveling in horse-drawn carriages and working in unairconditioned and poorly-heated buildings.

Even though change for the sake of change is not good, changes in work routines and working environments which represent improvements or necessities should be encouraged and given a chance to succeed.

Systems Analysis and Design

Systematic analysis represents an approach to change that yields positive results. The alternatives are the status quo or haphazard and unorganized change.

The availability of mechanized and automated devices for manufacturing and the use of computers for information processing have forced greater attention to systems and procedures analysis during the past two decades. Procedures must be visualized down to the most minute detail when computer programs are being designed to process the information created by the procedure. Otherwise the equipment will omit important information or will be unable to handle a given set of circumstances. The same detailed analysis is equally important for creating or improving any system—production or information, computerized or manual.

Systems analysts look with inquisitive eyes at whatever they see. They want to know who is involved, what they do, what documents are created, to whom they are distributed, what information they contain.

Because production systems improvement is largely the work of industrial engineers and requires extensive technical expertise, this chapter focuses on the systems and procedures that are likely to affect all supervisors—information handling systems.

Administrative Systems

Most supervisors are negative about what they call "paperwork," sometimes with good reason. Many supervisors, however, create and control miniature paperwork systems within their organizational units. Every supervisor will be exposed to information processing systems—receiving routine information, processing forms, providing information for distribution to others. Sales data, production data, financial information, inventory records, production scheduling information, claims data, order information, client records, progress reports, invoices, payroll data, quality inspection data, purchase requisitions, budget data, credit reports, preventative maintenance reports, safety inspections—all of these represent information systems with which organizations must deal.

The object of analysis is to create systems that will most efficiently and economically serve the objectives of the organization and to continually analyze existing systems so they remain efficient and economical. **Administrative information systems** are systems which provide information that enables the management of an organization to perform its functions. The systems may involve routine information procedures, such as sending a customer a bill at the end of the month. Other systems supply information for major decisions such as the need for opening a new branch or constructing a new office building. They affect planning and forecasting for the future and analysis of what the organization has done in the past.

Administrative costs have soared in recent years. Complicated by increased size and complexities of businesses, increased size and complexities of government bureaucracies, and governmental regulations which demand more and more information, organizations have sometimes found themselves expending more energy on administrative duties than on the basic purposes for which they exist.

A field of management variously called "administrative services," "administrative support systems," and "information systems" has evolved in an attempt to support and serve the administrative information needs of organizations. New technologies to support this movement are developing into major industries. Technologies which have emerged or greatly changed during this movement began with electronic computer data processing and have been followed by **micrographics** (microfilm and related document technologies), **word processing** (electronic processing of written communication), data communication systems, **telecommunications** improvements, and **reprographics** (document duplication and print technologies). Related administrative service groups have developed for such things as records management, forms design and control, communications management, secretarial and clerical services, physical layout and space planning, and office procedures analysis.

Some administrative support groups operate rather independently of each other within a single organization. Some of them serve only a portion of the organization. Multiple computers or word processing centers in one organization are not unusual. A more sensible approach is emerging as business firms, institutions, and governments combine these information and service groups administratively into a single unit headed by a high-level

administrative information systems *mechanisms for providing information needed by management, particularly those who manage organizationwide activities*

micrographics *records or documents on film, technology related to processing such records*

work processing *electronic processing of written communication*

telecommunications *voice, data, and image transmission by telephone lines*

reprographics *document reproduction: printing, duplicating, copying*

administrator. This person's title might be Director of Administrative Services or Manager of Information Systems or Vice-President—Administrative Services. This centralization of authority for all administrative information services does not suggest physical centralization for these activities. However, the cost of providing these services suggests that any method of coordinating their use and maximizing their effectiveness would probably keep the cost as low as possible.

Professional Systems Analysts

Systems and procedures analysts, both the analysts of computerized and manual information systems, are likely to appear in any large organization. If the firm employs its own systems and procedures analysts, they are likely to be a part of the administrative information systems group. Some organizations prefer to use outside analysts. Whether in-house employees or outsiders, their presence is the result of attempts to improve the speed and efficiency of information processing, to develop written procedures for job description manuals or training materials, or to develop standards which will enable management to predict personnel needs and schedule the work to be done.

Supervisors' natural reactions to the inquisitiveness of analysts is to regard them as intruders and potential troublemakers. The following discussion of systems, procedures, and methods identifies some of the basic theories and approaches to improving how we do things and attempts to prepare supervisors for analyzing their own procedures and methods. This knowledge should also be helpful for supervisors who work with analysts in examining the work of their departments.

Systems, Procedures, and Methods

As a basis for analyzing information, information systems, communication systems, records systems, or any established routine for doing something, definition of terms is necessary. To analyze work for possible improvement, the analyst must subdivide the work into distinct categories. A helpful set of categories for the sake of analysis is the division of work into systems, procedures, and methods. These categories identify the scope of the activities included in each.

As you read the following discussion of these categories, refer to the illustration in Exhibit 10.1, which depicts a set of specimen procedures and methods within a system.

The scope of activity covered by a system, a procedure, and a method, respectively, gets smaller. **System** is the broadest in scope and represents a family of related activities. **Procedures** are subdivisions of systems and, in turn, are dissected into **methods**, or subdivision of procedures, for the purpose of analysis.

system family of related work procedures

procedure subdivisions of a system

method subdivision of a procedure

As was discussed in Chapter Three, a popular way to view organizations is to consider them as one huge system of interrelated subsystems. Organizations have been equated to the human body with its nervous system, digestive system, circulatory system, and so on. Even though one system experiences difficulty, the body can survive. A healthy fully-functioning body, however, is one in which all systems are in harmony with each other. The same is true of business firms and other organizations. Information systems analysts prefer to identify major functioning systems within organizations for the purpose of analysis—rather than viewing the whole organization as one system. Thus, the typical organization might have a personnel management system, a production system, a financial system, a marketing system, various patient and/or client service systems, an accounting system, and others. Because collective and simultaneous examination of all these systems is impossible, they are subdivided into smaller components for analysis. The word *analysis* itself means breaking apart for study or identifying subportions of a whole.

Approach to Systems Improvement

For the purpose of improving communication and the flow of information, major systems are identified and targeted for analysis. In a bank these systems might be customer services, checking accounts, savings, consumer loans, commercial loans, trust and estate management, personnel, and so on. In a hospital, the systems might be patient care, surgery, medical records, administrative services, pharmaceutical services, and emergency medicine. In a city government such systems as financial and budgetary planning, parks and recreations, utilities, street department, sanitation, fire protection, and police would be functioning as individual components of the larger organization.

All systems in an organization need information from others in order to operate. All of them provide information to and interact with others. It is obvious that this approach applies the word

	This System	Involves These Procedures.	The Methods of One Procedure
Exhibit 10.1 **Specimen System with** **Related Procedures** **and Methods**	Receiving System	1. Receiving raw materials 2. Receiving packaging components and product containers 3. Receiving merchandise 4. Receiving equipment and components 5. Receiving miscellaneous shipments	1.1 Receive phone call from security guard that shipment has arrived 1.2 Meet driver at dock 1.3 Secure shipment documentation from driver 1.4 Return to receiving office 1.5 Retrieve purchase order copy 1.6 Verify quantities 1.7 Write receiving report 1.8 Write short or over report (if necessary) 1.9 Initial and distribute documents 1.10 Log shipment on daily receipts log

For the purpose of this illustration, only one of the five procedures is broken into methods. These methods might differ from one organization to another. Similarly-detailed procedures would exist for each of the other four procedures.

system to identifiable parts of the whole, which must work together in order for the objective of the whole to be reached. The "whole" can be an entire organization; it can be a department, branch, or other unit within the organization; or it may be a unit of work within one of these. Whatever the scope of a particular system, it should embrace all the people, equipment, facilities, and processes associated with the identified whole.

When a system has been targeted for analysis, the next step is to identify each procedure or subdivision of that system. To illustrate these concepts, we will apply them to a specimen system that follows. Assume that the system targeted for analysis is the receiving department of a small manufacturing concern. (Refer again to Exhibit 10.1.) This department's work could be subdivided into five categories: receiving raw materials, receiving packaging components, receiving merchandise orders, receiving equipment, and receiving miscellaneous other shipments. Conceivably, the same procedure might be followed for all of these activities. However, different requirements may necessitate different approaches. Raw materials may require special inspection and laboratory or quality control tests. Merchandise and equipment shipments require notification to the department which ordered them. So the question "What do you do when something arrives?" may be answered with "That depends upon what is arriving."

The number of procedures into which a system is divided usually increases as organizations grow in activity and number of employees. A single, simple procedure for doing something (in our specimen system, the documentation and processing of goods that arrive) may cause difficulties and create the need for two or three separate procedures which are dictated by circumstances. For example, the procedure might require that all goods received be held for inspection by the quality control department. An engineer who needs a replacement part for a piece of equipment may complain that his shipment is held unnecessarily until a quality control employee initials a piece of paper. Soon, his complaint is heard, and a new procedure is born. Now we have one procedure for receiving raw materials, which need inspection, and another for receiving equipment parts, which do not need inspection.

If left uncontrolled and unchallenged, individual whims and uncoordinated development can result in too many procedures which unnecessarily complicate the system. Illustrations of this type of complication are the firm that used twelve different forms and methods for logging long distance telephone calls and the supervisor who created six copies of a form—three of which were filed in his office. When we asked the supervisor why the three forms were all being filed within ten feet of each other, he said that this was done so that any of his three assistants could retrieve them without moving from their chairs.

Procedures-conscious people recognize that separate procedures for different situations may improve employee productivity and the system's efficiency. They must also recognize that too much subdivision may have the opposite effect. To improve systems, identify and examine the procedures which make up the system. Then, systematically examine each procedure.

Procedures are examined by dividing them into *methods* or individual components of each procedure. In our specimen system, receiving raw materials is one procedure. All the methods of this procedure might be performed by one person in the receiving department, or they may be shared. Various other methods could involve additional departments before the procedure is complete— accounting, inventory control, quality control, and production scheduling are possibilities. Those who pay for the goods must know that they have arrived, and those who inspect the goods for quality must approve them before they are used. Even though the list of methods is incomplete, it illustrates the multiple methods that might be involved in a single procedure. Procedures for processing an insurance claim, a deposit to a checking account, or the payment of a property tax bill might be similarly subdivided for analysis.

IMPLICATIONS AND APPLICATIONS

INCREASING PRODUCTIVITY THROUGH BETTER SYSTEMS

The Role of Information

Information management is sometimes considered a function of "the office" or the computer department; however, any productive system involves information handling and processing. Even the smallest business or the smallest department of any organization creates, records, transmits, and receives information. Sometimes this is done for the benefit of the processor; sometimes it is a requirement of the job; sometimes it is done to satisfy an outside agency, such as documenting deductible expenses for the Internal Revenue Service. Whatever the reason for its existence, supervisors who recognize the value of information and are able to see its role in a total system are able to analyze the procedures with which they deal and to appreciate the need for accurate and complete information. Those who do not see the value of the information with which they deal should seek interpretations and

Supervisors sometimes resent the procedures analyst who asks probing questions, but their interviews are necessary to determine what people do and to mesh procedures into smoothly functioning systems.

justifications and perhaps uncover new approaches to handling information in the process of probing.

Computers and other technological developments speed the processing of information; but, unfortunately, they may create so many data in the process that systems are actually weakened by the abundance of data. Supervisors who request information from these sources must work closely with the technicians and explain the nature of the information need and how it will be used.

The Role of the Analyst

Those who analyze systems, procedures, and methods ask questions about every step. Who, what, when, where, and how questions are usually appropriate. An alert analyst would question the reason for each method and the technique for carrying out each method. Why are discrepancies reported on a separate form? Why not provide that information on the receiving report? Could some of these data be keyed into a computer terminal to eliminate some of the forms? Who gets the four copies? Why?

Without planning or analysis, procedures grow and sometimes become very complicted. The reason for doing something in a particular way is frequently "That's what the guy who had this job before me told me to do." Some organizations have professional procedures analysts on their staffs. Others employ outside specialists to do this. The supervisor can be the analyst for his or her own area. Those who have examined what is done, how it is done, and have questioned the reasons can improve productivity and efficiency and can work easily with staff analysts or outsiders who may come in to do this work. The tools and practices which are identified and discussed in a later part of this chapter are intended to sharpen supervisors' ability to work in either of these capacities.

The Role of the Supervisor

Part of the supervisor's role is to examine the procedures that function within his or her jurisdiction—whether or not any formal attempt is in progress. Worker frustration can be minimized by smooth operating procedures and jobs that contain a variety of activity. Alert supervisors will tackle observed procedural difficulties. If correcting the difficulty is too great for the supervisor and subordinates who work with the procedure, the help of internal systems specialists or outsiders should be sought. Management is usually receptive to a supervisor who recognizes a problem and seeks a solution.

Today's supervisors are on the threshold of many new and exciting developments and different approaches to work. Some of the things likely to develop in the next two decades may alleviate some of the disadvantages of present systems. Shared jobs, home work stations, flexible work hours (sometimes called **flextime**) and electronically joined facilities are some of the things now in practice which may become more widespread as technologies improve. Supervisors may work from their homes in the very near future. Picture phones, data transmission, cable TV systems, and all sorts of microprocessor-assisted devices may make physical proximity of supervisor and subordinate unnecessary in the future. Even if the supervisor does go to the office or plant, the subordinate may stay at home or may work in a neighborhood center or in a different city. Technologies which will change our entire approach to living and working are already developed. Successful supervisors will be ready to retool and adapt to the changes which these technologies will bring.

Anticipated changes will probably bring certain frustrations and problems, but they may also bring the need for increased standardization of procedure. "The computer won't accept that

flextime *flexible work hours*

214

information" is a standard phrase today. That's because the computer operates on a planned procedure, but procedures can be changed.

Why Standardize Procedures

Standard practices manuals, office procedures manuals, sales manuals, and other written descriptions of procedure reflect attempts to standardize ways of accomplishing tasks. The assembly line is the ultimate standardization. Why standardize? Is it still a practical approach to work?

Throughout this century managers of all enterprises have increasingly believed that standardization of products and procedures enhances economical production. And there is little doubt that it has. It was also thought to enhance quality, and for many years it may have done so. This factor is sometimes questioned because of lax quality control and lack of employee attention to assembly line detail.

In addition to making possible the mass production of goods and services that make our standard of living possible, standardization offers many other benefits. Workers can be trained easily, labor needs can be predicted accurately, employees can change jobs readily, and scheduling can be more accurate when standard procedures for performing tasks are followed. Extremely routine jobs do create boredom and other problems for some workers. Although procedures can be easily analyzed, measured, and improved when something is done the same way every time, the employee who follows a repetitive routine may feel unchallenged and question the worth of his or her contribution.

From the management standpoint, standardization is valuable. From the worker's viewpoint, it may be questioned. Careful planning of job content and employee responsibility and the matching of employee personality and preference to job assignments can overcome some of the difficulties created by standardization.

With organizations operating on the scale at which today's work is accomplished, the absence of standardization would bring chaos. The challenge, then, is to bring quality to the process of standardization and to use the technologies we already have to improve productivity and eliminate the disadvantages of standardization. Productivity and worker satisfaction can both be improved without causing either to suffer. Many workers reject the idea of "robot welders" and other technological improvements,

Flowcharts make it possible for the supervisor and the analyst to depict the details of an entire procedure. Identifying potential areas for improvement is then easier than with oral or written descriptions of procedures.

Photograph by Alan Baker, courtesy of Lord Corporation.

because they see them as replacements for human employees; but these advances can result in more challenging jobs for people.

Tools of Procedures Analysis

While space does not permit an extensive treatment of procedures analysis here, identification of some tools which are used in such analysis follows. Even if the supervisor does not use these instru-

216

ments and processes, in-house specialists and outside consultants are likely to use them when analyzing supervisors' departments. A basic knowledge of what they are and how they are used will enable the supervisor to better understand the process.

The most effective approach to systems and procedures analysis begins with personal interviews or observations to document existing procedures and methods. They answer the question "What do you do to carry out this procedure?" Interviewing is necessary even when written procedure descriptions exist, because actual practice may vary from prescribed practice.

Numerous flowcharting techniques may be used to depict a procedure once data regarding the procedure have been gathered. The **flowchart**, a symbolic description of a procedure, is better than a textual (sentences and narrative) description, because the analyst can visualize an entire procedure or major portion with the aid of a flowchart. Exhibit 10.2 illustrates American Standards Association symbols which are drawn with the aid of a plastic template and are valuable in charting procedures. Exhibit 10.3 illustrates a simple flowchart using these symbols to represent the methods of a procedure. The symbols save time and improve understanding of the procedure because they represent verbal descriptions of methods. Two symbols, a double circle and a document symbol, replace the sentences "The first thing done is to type a Credit Memorandum. This is typed on Form No. 6032 in this firm. The form is a two-part forms set."

flowchart paper drawing, using symbols and words to depict methods in a procedure

Specialized applications may combine these symbols and add others in the flowcharting technique. Just as the procedures being charted are standardized, the procedure for charting itself is somewhat standardized so that analysts can "read" charts prepared by others. Flowcharts have become such a part of our communication today that most textbooks—at least, business texts—contain numerous flowcharts describing theories, practices, and procedures.

Exhibit 10.4 illustrates a simpler method of flowcharting called the **block diagram flowchart**. Each block represents a method and contains a sentence or sentence fragment describing the method. The objective of any chart is to depict the entire procedure in as little space as possible so that it can be visualized as a whole and improved upon.

block diagram flowchart paper drawing using sentences and phrases to depict methods in a procedure

Whatever the technique used to chart a procedure, there is value in constructing a chart, because in the process of charting, one frequently discovers unanswered questions or the lack of uniformity in handling procedures. Attention to these observations is helpful in creating revised or proposed procedures. Charts may

217

Exhibit 10.2
**Flowchart Symbols
used in Charting
Procedures**

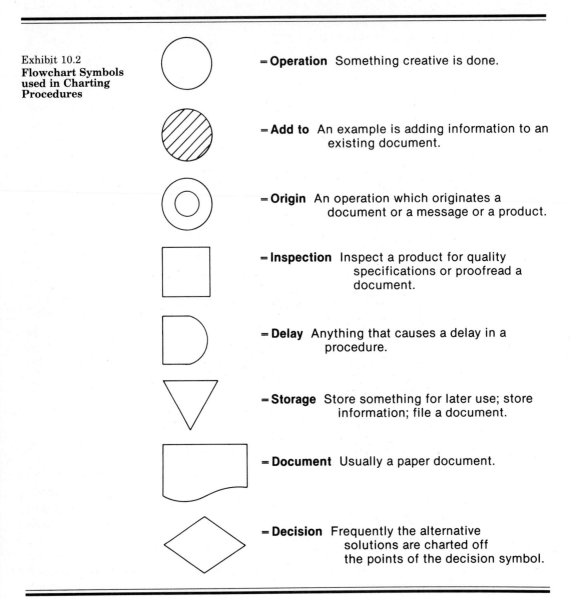

= **Operation** Something creative is done.

= **Add to** An example is adding information to an
existing document.

= **Origin** An operation which originates a
document or a message or a product.

= **Inspection** Inspect a product for quality
specifications or proofread a
document.

= **Delay** Anything that causes a delay in a
procedure.

= **Storage** Store something for later use; store
information; file a document.

= **Document** Usually a paper document.

= **Decision** Frequently the alternative
solutions are charted off
the points of the decision symbol.

also be used as training devices which enable new employees to
visualize a routine procedure. Even during chart construction, the
analyst is continually probing, questioning—Why? How? Who?
Why does Accounting get four copies of this form? Why does Data
Processing produce a 160-page printout *and* a microfiche of this
information? Where does Department A get the information on

Exhibit 10.3
**Flowchart of
Procedure for
Processing a Credit
Memorandum**

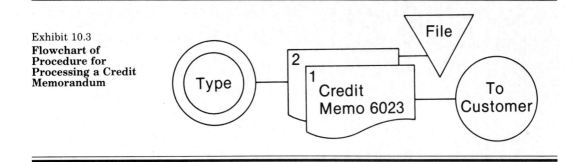

this document? Do all twenty-three of these executives really need a copy of this report?

Once data regarding current procedures are gathered, analysis and examination of answers to the above questions aid the preparation of revised procedures. Analysts of manual procedures are especially concerned about procedures which involve a large number of documents, large numbers of document copies, people who travel great distances to complete a procedure or gather information, documents which travel to a single work station several times, and justification for the distribution of document copies.

INFORMAL IMPROVEMENTS IN WORK

Somewhere between the formal procedures analysis, at one extreme, and no attempt to improve productivity, at the other extreme, is the application of common sense in an attempt to improve productivity of supervised workers and processes. Relatively basic work simplification techniques and application of logic to working situations can result in efficient and productive environments. Some ideas which grew out of early attempts at efficiency improvement in the early days of the industrial revolution remain appropriate today. Depending upon the nature of the job, some of the following suggestions may simplify work.

1. Examine the workstation. Is it comfortable and conveniently arranged? Does it meet the special needs of the worker who occupies it?

2. Is the employee required to waste time and effort traveling to materials which could be brought to the employee? Human or

219

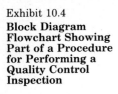

Exhibit 10.4
**Block Diagram
Flowchart Showing
Part of a Procedure
for Performing a
Quality Control
Inspection**

**Quality Control
Inspector**

Draw four samples of product from one production line. Label samples. Send to lab.

**Laboratory
Technician**

Perform Test A, Test C, and Test E

Record results in permanent lab book. Complete six-part lab report (4682-C)

Distribute 4682-C copies

mechanical messengers or conveyor systems might expedite such transportation.

3. Do the tangible objects with which employees work (products, documents, raw materials) return to workers for additional work? Could all the work be done with a single exposure?

4. Do products or documents travel the most direct route throughout their routine paths?

5. Examine delays. What are the reasons?

6. Document errors, difficulties, or confusion for a period of time. Look for patterns, associations with particular employees, outside influences.

7. Is the productivity of some workers reduced because they spend long periods of time waiting for something? Could they work on another task in the meantime?

8. Is equipment among the most efficient available? How would a new piece of equipment affect productivity? Compute the payback period (time needed to pay for the piece of equipment through increased productivity).

9. Examine the physical layout of the plant, shop, or office. Is it physically attractive? Is it comfortable? Are environmental characteristics (air quality, temperature, sound control, color selection, cleanliness, and so on) conducive to productive work? Are workstations and general layout conducive to high productivity and a satisfied staff? Was the workstation designed for the *particular* type of work being performed at the workstation? Or was the employee merely placed in some standard workstation? (For example, many people view office workers in standard traditional desks—all in a symmetrical row like tin soldiers.) In most cases a different workstation for each separate job description is desirable.

10. Examine the flow of information into and out of the organizational unit and physical layout for which you are responsible. For major information flows, chart the paths of information or products or documents on a drawing of the physical layout of the department. Does the path cross itself anywhere? Does it return to the same work station repeatedly? Is it a straight line?

These questions represent the type of inquisitiveness with which any department may be examined. The nature of the work in some organizations may suggest completely new questions, but these give some idea of the nature of attempts to simplify work.

Organizations are people; people are efficient when they are rewarded for their contributions, when they are well trained and fairly treated, when they are provided with adequate equipment and physical environments, and when there are good systems for carrying out their duties. In the final analysis, all of these factors determine the success or failure of systems; but if every factor except the system is present, the venture will struggle.

SUMMARY

The systems approach to viewing organizations sees the whole organization as a combination of major systems which may be subdivided into procedures whose components are labeled methods. Attempts to improve productivity must consider the total system, and changes must be associated with effects on other facets of the system. At the procedures and methods level, improvements are made by questioning the reason for performing each current method. Specific tools and approaches to systems analysis exist, and knowledge of these should benefit the supervisor even if formal analyses are made by other staff members or outsiders.

Data for analyzing procedures are gathered by interviewing and observing workers. The flowchart is a tool for depicting the steps followed in performing a procedure. It may be used as a preliminary step to writing standard operating procedures.

Many organizational procedures involve the processing of information in some manner, and this information can usually be processed more effectively if it is carried out in a standardized fashion.

Supervisors may be able to improve the standard procedures in their work areas by following informal approaches to identifying inefficiency, waste, and time-consuming activity.

QUESTIONS FOR FURTHER THOUGHT

1. Compare the basic meaning of *analysis* and the meaning of systems and procedures analysis.

2. Identify systems in a business or other organization with which you are familiar. Select one or more systems and divide into procedures and methods. Chart a specimen system in pyramid fashion—system on top, procedures on the next level, methods on the bottom level.

3. Compile generalizations about the nature of procedures analysts and their approach to improving work.

4. What is an administrative information system? Is there any involvement in such systems for those who are not part of the organization's "administration"?

5. To what extent are supervisors also procedures analysts?

6. Do the workers you know prefer to make their own decisions about how to do the things their job involves, or would they prefer being told how to do things?

PART FOUR

PERSONNEL MANAGEMENT FUNCTIONS FOR SUPERVISORS

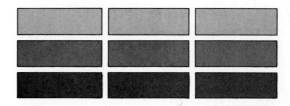

11

EMPLOYEE SELECTION

VOCABULARY TO MASTER

Turnover rate
Valid
Reliable
Predictors
EEOC
Discrimination
Quota systems
Norms
Affirmative action
Sexual harassment
Cognitive differences
Criterion
Placement
Orientation

LEARNING OBJECTIVES

Upon completion of this chapter and related materials, you should be able to:

1. Define the supervisor's role as a liaison between personnel staff and the operative.
2. Describe the personnel functions—selection, placement, orientation, and services.
3. Develop a philosophical orientation that will reflect the value of personnel actions as a maintenance function of the organization.
4. Describe the value of selection systems for the benefit of employee and employer.

CHAPTER OUTLINE

PROBLEM STATEMENT
SELECTING THE RIGHT PEOPLE

BACKGROUND AND THEORY
MAINTENANCE FUNCTIONS
    Goal: Low Employee Turnover
    The Ideal Selection Model
EXTERNAL INFLUENCES
    Equal Employment Opportunity
    Testing and EEOC
    Interviewing and EEOC
    Dismissals and EEOC
    Affirmative Action
    Women's Roles Have Changed

RESEARCH AND PRACTICE
CURRENT SELECTION AND PLACEMENT PRACTICES
    Recruiting
    The Employment Process
        Application
        Interview
        Testing
        Placement
EMPLOYEE ORIENTATION
PERSONNEL MAINTENANCE SYSTEMS
    General Climate
    Employee Benefits

IMPLICATIONS AND APPLICATIONS
NEW DIRECTIONS FOR PERSONNEL
SUMMARY

QUESTIONS FOR FURTHER THOUGHT

SELECTING THE RIGHT PEOPLE

Personnel management is a broad area of functions that must endeavor to select and place appropriate individuals to carry out major efforts of the formal organization. In addition, it is a function that must have adequate resources to provide fringe benefits and internal reward systems for the total organization. How this system provides for both the explicit and implicit maintenance activities (or behavioral regularities) is also of prime importance.

MAINTENANCE FUNCTIONS

Personnel management is a field of professional management which deals with the function of staffing and caring for the needs of people who work for an organization. In large organizations a personnel manager or a director or perhaps someone with the title *Vice-President—Personnel* directs a complex system of personnel management activities and numerous personnel staff assistants. The range of activities administered by this group includes all of the procedures necessary to select, hire, and train new employees. Training functions will be considered separately in Chapter Twelve. In addition, the personnel group is usually responsible for administering programs which benefit employees. Insurance, compensation plans, employee safety programs, and affirmative action programs are some of the benefit programs that frequently fall under the realm of personnel management.

In small organizations, some of these activities are shifted to other supervisory managers. Human relations programs, collective bargaining, and contract administration may also fit into these responsibilities.

In any organization supervisors will be involved to some extent with this effort to hire and serve employees. Regardless of the degree of involvement, supervisors should be knowledgeable about personnel management principles and practices. Supervisors are employees, too. They are served by the personnel management effort. The chances are considerable that they will actually perform many personnel management activities.

Among the activities most likely to be carried out jointly between supervisors and personnel management are 1) selection and placement of employees, 2) employee orientation, 3) training programs, and 4) administration of employee benefit programs. With the exception of training programs, these activities are dis-

226

cussed in this chapter. Even though not all of these functions are performed by *every* supervisor, information about them and knowledge of the principles upon which they are based are essential if supervisors are to accomplish the fullest benefit for employees and the employer. A positive, free, and open relationship with personnel managers can result in a pleasant atmosphere for the supervisor and employees directed by that supervisor. The climate that surrounds the personnel activities has a considerable impact upon the workers' perceptions of management. Personnel is one area in which management can demonstrate in a tangible manner that it cares for the employee. The supervisor in turn can convey this climate to the operative. If workers observe management's concern through a positive personnel services program, the workers' perception of management will be positive.

Goal: Low Employee Turnover

Although the *selection* and *placement* of employees is handled formally by personnel departments in many organizations, supervisors are frequently involved at some state of the process. The supervisor's participation may range from merely advising the personnel manager to assuming major responsibilities for finding, interviewing, and hiring employees. Whatever the level of involvement of the supervisor in this aspect of management, the overall goal is minimum employee turnover. **Turnover rate**, expressed quantitatively, is the percentage of the work force which must be replaced annually. If a department with 20 operative positions must replace three of them during a one-year span, the turnover rate in that department is 15 or 15 percent ($3 \div 20$). Turnover rates vary among types of workers, but sound management practice suggests that every effort should be made to keep this rate as low as possible. Whatever the reason for employee separations and dismissals, the firm or organization would be better off if they could eliminate most separations.

turnover rate percent of work force replaced in a year

Low turnover results from a combination of good employee selection procedures, fair and equitable compensation of workers, and a working climate that staff and managers find pleasant and productive.

The employer's choice of employees to hire and the hiring practices used may be affected by legislation requiring equality in employment opportunity. The recommended practices discussed in this chapter must be applied within limitations imposed by such legislation. A later section of this chapter presents an analysis of the impact of equal employment legislation on personnel decisions and other areas of supervisory management.

The cost of replacing an employee is significant. Contributing to this cost are the expenditures necessary to find, hire, and train a replacement. Additional cost is due to lost productivity between the day a new employee is hired and the time when that new employee is fully trained and productive—at least at the level of the previous employee in that position. Firms that attempt to measure the cost of turnover believe that the cost of one turnover may range from $500 in small organizations to several thousand dollars, depending upon the training needed and the effort required to find the right employee.

Finding employees may be a simple task. But finding employees who are qualified and who will remain with the organization is sometimes quite complicated. The supervisor is probably in the best position to advise those who perform initial screening of applicants and those who make the final decision to hire. They are better acquainted with the job and its requirements than anyone in the organization. Although supervisors may have had little professional training in creating formal job specifications, they can provide valuable advice to those who do produce these documents. (See Chapter Ten for a discussion of job analysis, job descriptions, job evaluation, and job specifications.) Formalized education and experience specifications, recommendations from references, and test results may be woefully inadequate in selecting one candidate from five or six whose "paper" qualifications are similar. High turnover rates and poor employee performance may not be the result of poor training or poor management but may be the result of inadequate selection procedures and failure to involve the people who will work most closely with the new employee.

The Ideal Selection Model

Anyone who has been involved in the business of selecting people for jobs or placing individuals within the organization has wished dearly for a method that worked reliably. What is needed is the identification of specific job behaviors that are most important and the formulation of questions for predicting which applicants will behave in those ways. Another way to say this is that if one knew exactly what needs to be predicted, related to job performance, or if one could devise a test or method that would identify the best applicants, personnel selection would be easy.

valid a test that measures skills required in a job

reliable a test that measures required job skills consistently

predictors indexes of future job success

The ideal selection system would be one that is easy to administer, **valid** (tests the skills required), and **reliable** (consistent from one time to another). A hypothetical outcome from such an ideal system is reflected in Exhibit 11.1.

Exhibit 11.1 indicates an ideal situation, where people who score high on the **predictors** (tests or interviews or application analysis) would also do well on job performance. In addition, it shows that the hypothetical female high school graduates as a group would score best on both the test (predictor) and in job performance (job skill). As the figure also indicates, however, this ideal outcome seldom occurs. Because this is the case, hiring judgments must still be made by management—often by the supervisor. Even in the example, if the test scores were considered by themselves, a personal judgment would have to be made among X_1, X_2, and X_3. As supervisory judgment will be called upon, it becomes necessary to have an understanding of what job skills must be considered and what kind of person will most likely have and/or develop these skills. Therefore, the selection process is one of predicting job performance based on a limited amount of information. The more sophisticated the organization's personnel system, the more information there will be available to aid in the decision. The hiring decision, however, will be made by people and the supervisor often participates.

EXTERNAL INFLUENCES

Equal Employment Opportunity

EEOC Equal Employment Opportunity Commission, oversees plans to prevent discrimination in employment

Supervisors are directly involved in many activities which are subject to and affected by legislation. The impact of law upon employment practices varies with the inclinations of the administration in control in Washington at a particular time. Federal and state laws prohibit discrimination in a broad range of employment practices, including hiring, firing, paying, training, classifying, and promoting employees. The most powerful federal legislation dealing with employment originated when the Civil Rights Act of 1964 created the Equal Employment Opportunity Commission (**EEOC**). The Commission's powers were increased by the Equal Employment Opportunity Act of 1972. Court rulings and administrative actions have interpreted and changed the effects of the laws, and the Age Discrimination in Employment Act of 1967 added age as a forbidden discriminatory practice. Other legislation added the handicapped to the list.

Exhibit 11.1
**Hypothetical Outcome
of an Ideal Selection
System**

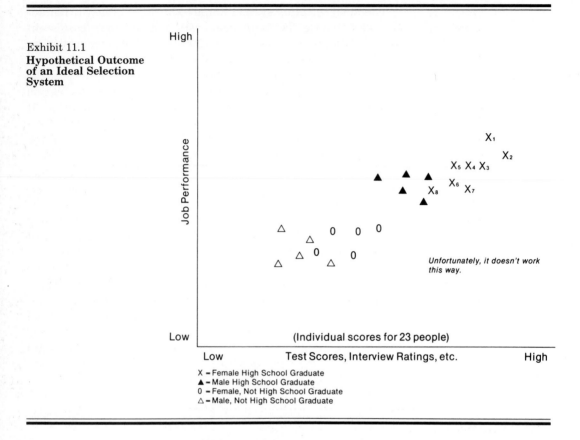

X – Female High School Graduate
▲ – Male High School Graduate
0 – Female, Not High School Graduate
△ – Male, Not High School Graduate

discrimination an illeg-
*al act when race, color,
religion, sex, national origin, age, or handicap are
used in employment*

Any good system for staffing is a discriminatory process—an attempt to select the best qualified people to fill positions. The laws which affect this process, however, identify illegal discriminatory practices. Illegal **discrimination**, as defined by legislation, involves singling out applicants for employment or employees for special (different) treatment because of their race, color, religion, sex, national origin, age or handicap. Only when these factors are bona fide occupational qualifications (necessary for the performance of a job), can they be used. They seldom are necessary. A sometimes forgotten portion of legislation dealing with these factors also prohibits retaliation against employees who have opposed illegal employment practices or who have testified or participated in legal action that attempts to eliminate such practices.

By necessity, any discussion of legislation and employment practices sounds very legalistic. To help unravel the legal entanglements which may result, three factors should be considered. First, laws sometimes state prohibitions in rather vague and general terms. Only through court cases and the resulting strings of appeals and decisions do the specific meanings of the law become clarified. Second, *prohibit* does not necessarily mean eliminate. Illegal discrimination has been identified and prohibited, but it has not ceased to exist. Third, the laws and, to a great extent, the court interpretations of those laws have dealt with the result of employment practice—not the intent of that practice. Therefore, many employers who consider themselves fair and open in their employment practices may actually be discriminating without knowing it.

quota systems *hiring a specific number of people from minority groups*

To illustrate one of the many complexities of dealing with EEO matters, the Civil Rights Act specifically forbids required **quota systems** (hiring a percentage of minorities equal to the percentage of the population represented by that minority). Yet the courts have encouraged "voluntary" affirmative action plans which do just that. Quota systems have become commonplace. Counter charges of reverse discrimination have been lodged.

Another complexity evolved from the fact that employee appraisal systems are now generally interpreted to be selective devices and subject to the *Uniform Guidelines in Employee Selection Procedures*, the federal government's guide to employment practices. In this text, we have used the term "employee selection" to refer mostly to initial selection of employees. Legally, however, selection may involve any vacancy that is to be filled. Because vacancies may be filled by current employees and because employee appraisal may affect whether those employees are selected for promotion to new openings, the appraisal system is considered a selection device. Nevertheless, we treat appraisal systems as a separate topic in Chapter Thirteen.

Although illegal discrimination may exist in a system for selecting workers, it may also exist in the manner in which a system is applied. Supervisors are very much involved in applying the system. Managers at any level who wish to avoid discrimination and who wish to prevent legal actions should be knowledgeable about illegal discrimination as it relates to the staffing function.

Testing and EEOC

Tests can be used effectively in the employment process to diagnose an applicant's knowledge and abilities, but they can be

norms *average test re-sults from large numbers of people*

discriminatory unless they are valid (measure job-related skills). *Validity* must be established, and **norms** (test results from large numbers of similar people) must be established. The wording and the vocabulary used in test questions can discriminate in circumstances where they cause an applicant to score low. The solution is to use a professionally validated test.

Interviewing and EEOC

Interviewers of job applicants may hold prejudices against minority groups—consciously or subconsciously. Others may imply prejudices by the questions they ask and the statements they make, even if no such implication is intended. Avoiding statements and questions which involve race, sex, handicap, or age is recommended. Even casual references to the problems of a working mother, for example, may suggest that you would prefer a male who would not be expected to have these problems. There is no assurance that this will be the case, though.

Interviews should be planned. They need not be stiff and formal, but the interviewer who has carefully considered the questions to be asked is less likely to violate regulations.

Dismissals and EEOC

Every organization must occasionally terminate the employment of some workers, even though replacing them may be expensive. Here too, the criterion for the decision to fire an employee cannot and should not be discriminatory. Many organizations have established procedures for terminations. The procedures, especially in government organizations, may be very time-consuming. Some consider it impossible to dismiss a civil service employee, for example.

Even if the procedure permits it, haste in terminating employees should be avoided. Supervisors who have the authority to fire or recommend firing employees must make special efforts to handle these situations fairly. At best, they represent difficult emotional conditions for everyone involved. If there are difficulties with employee performance, the existence of documentation which substantiates such difficulty is necessary. Putting together these materials at the time of the dismissal is insufficient. A formal procedure, consistent treatment of all employees, and objective explanations of the reasons for dismissal are recommended. Third-party (supervisor's superior, for example) observation of discussions relating to the employee's termination will discourage legal action.

Affirmative Action

*affirmative action em-
ployer action to provide
jobs for identified minority groups*

Through Executive orders, various U.S. presidents have used powers granted by the Civil Rights Act to require government agencies and private employers with government contracts to not only refrain from illegal discrimination, but to take positive steps or **affirmative action** to provide jobs for identified minority groups. Any employer may voluntarily engage in affirmative action plans, of course. These plans spell out details of hiring, training, and promotion which will include minority groups. Various regulations define minority groups.

While affirmative action plans are not supposed to be quota plans, they do "measure progress" by examining the numbers of minorities employed, the distribution of minorities among the various job types and levels, and the uniformity of these numbers throughout the organization (including number of applicants). Here too, a formal plan can be designed so that discrimination is diminished. Also, a formal written plan is easier to defend. Plans are less likely to discriminate if they provide public announcement of job vacancies, written descriptions of the forms and procedures used in the application process. Detailed written job descriptions and specifications, and details of questions which are asked and those which are not asked of applicants could also be included.

Women's Roles Have Changed

*sexual harassment
annoying the opposite sex
in working environment*

Within the past twenty years there has been a drastic change in the way the Western world views the importance of women in the work force. The push for equality between the sexes has to some extent been achieved in a few settings. Newspapers and magazines frequently print data on salary comparisons, percentage of women in jobs by type of job, and status associated with women being afforded specific positions. **Sexual harassment** and the development of programs to curb this type of discrimination became a major topic of interest during the 1970s and it continues to gain the attention of more and more employers.[1] Attitude changes are dif-

---

[1]See *Sexuality in Organizations: Romantic and Coercive Behaviors at Work*, Dail Ann Newgarten and Jam M. Shafritz, eds. (Oak Park, Ill.: Moore Publishing Co., 1980), for additional material relating to this topic.

Women are now full members of management teams in many organizations.

Photograph courtesy of Citizens National Bank.

ficult to bring about, but change has come and is continuing to come. Besides the social expectation that women should stay at home there has been a prevailing attitude that women don't have the ability to compete with men in areas that require considerable intellectual skills. The obvious question is what does the research indicate?

cognitive differences
recognizable differences between groups

Janet Hyde (1981) has done a superb job of reviewing the literature about differences between men and women (**cognitive differences**) on such areas as comprehension of written and verbal material, ability to use numbers and geometric forms, understanding object relationships in space, and ability to disregard misleading visual information.[2] In general terms, the findings are that the differences are virtually meaningless, are mostly due to learning experiences, and are of questionable value for selection purposes.

---

[2]Janet Shibley Hyde, "How Large Are Cognitive Gender Differences? A Meta-Analysis Using W^2 and d," *American Psychologist* (August 1981), pp. 892–901.

234

All of this should not be taken to imply that sex discrimination no longer exists in many of our cultures. For example, the lifelong employment system in Japan is practiced predominately for the male worker. The supervisor should be aware that sex discrimination, as a matter of policy, has become unacceptable in the United States, not only in the selection and placement areas but also in all areas of personnel management.

RESEARCH AND PRACTICE

CURRENT SELECTION AND PLACEMENT PRACTICES

Large organizations maintain contacts with potential employee sources which have proven to be effective in finding good employees in the past. Some jobs may be filled by promoting or transferring someone already employed by the organization. Some organizations seek recommendations from current employees. However, two problems may result from heavy dependence upon such recommendations. Employees may be unable to evaluate their friends and relatives objectively, and the use of this method may violate equal employment opportunity regulations.

Other sources of employees include public and private employment agencies, colleges, universities, high schools, and vocational-technical schools offering educational opportunities for the types of employees needed. Contacts with educational institutions are likely to produce inexperienced applicants. However, experience may be less important than education and general ability in many positions. Advertising in newspapers, trade publications, and professional publications is more likely to attract appropriate applicants when work experience is a desirable qualification. Public and private employment agencies may be able to refer qualified applicants.

Recruiting may merely involve attempts to inform potential applicants about vacancies. If this produces quality applicants and the number of applicants needed, employees can be selected from those who respond and those who make unsolicited applications. A more aggressive approach is to send recruiters to the potential employee, particularly in educational institutions. Supervisors may not engage in such recruiting practices, but they should closely advise recruiters who go out looking for employees.

Two employer practices indicate the importance which some organizations place on finding the right employee. For positions that are particularly difficult to fill with qualified employees, the employer may be willing to pay employment agency fees. This may

be worth the cost if a particular agency has a positive past record of providing quality applicants for the firm. Another practice is payment of travel expenses for qualified out-of-town applicants. Both of these practices are expensive for the employer, but the expense may be less than the cost of frequent turnover. They are more likely to be used by employers seeking supervisory and managerial job applicants than those who seek operative-level employees.

The Employment Process

The typical employment process will involve several steps: completion of a formal application form, initial screening, preliminary interviews, testing, contacting references, additional interviews, and final selections. Prior to the supervisor's participation in the employment process, a personnel department may have carried out several steps. Included in these preliminary steps are accepting and processing routine application forms, screening applications against technical, educational, and skill requirements for the job, and perhaps preliminary interviewing and testing programs.

In a large organization promising applicants may be employed before they are placed in a specific job. A training program is usually involved. During the training period, decisions will be made regarding specific placement as supervisors in departments having vacancies get an opportunity to meet, work with, and evaluate trainees. The objective of the initial employment process for these organizations may be simply to find qualified and promising office employees, production employees, or staff—particularly if a large number of vacancies exists in each category. In a small organization, applicants for specific job vacancies would be sought.

Another approach is to offer promotions and/or transfers to capable current employees in cases where a move to a vacant position would be desirable for the employee. Then the firm would concentrate on hiring a new person for the job vacated by the promotion or transfer. This practice has many advantages for the supervisor who must work with the promoted or transferred employee. The supervisor may be well informed about the person's abilities. The need for orientation to the firm is unnecessary. Instead, supervisory efforts are directed toward training the new employee for the specific job. This practice has the drawback of a high turnover among low-level jobs. Supervisors of transferred employees must spend more time training and orientating replacements. Sometimes employee piracy is charged against de-

partments that lure the more capable employees away from other departments within the organization.

Whatever the method of filling vacancies, the supervisor should play some role in the process. Although supervisory participation may begin as early as initial screening of applicants, it is essential that supervisors enter the process at the final interview stage. Few supervisors would push for the right to make the final decision, but their evaluations of candidates certainly should be considered. As long as they realize that professional personnel managers and, in some cases, supervisors' superiors have had greater experience in employee selection and a broader understanding of job specifications, their participation will be valuable. Certainly their suggestions should be sought and considered.

Application The formal application for employment is the first official communication with employees. The major objective of this document should be to identify people who are available for employment and to gather major categories of data that would permit initial screening. This screening should involve only bona fide job specifications. Consequently, initial applications for employment are frequently rather brief. The gathered data are limited to basic personal information, education and experience, and, perhaps, career plans.

Interview Your first interview of a job applicant may be as disconcerting for you as for the applicant. What do I ask? How do I select one or two from among several interviewees who appear to be equally qualified? If applicants have been screened for "paper" qualifications (education, experience, and so on), you may face several technically qualified persons. Yet differences may be revealed through interviews. Employee potential rather than accumulated training and experience may be the distinguishing factor.

A major concern for supervisors interviewing applicants is to make the applicant feel comfortable and at ease. You will learn more about the applicant and he or she will learn more about the job if the interview takes place in a relaxed atmosphere.

The second objective of the interviewer should be to ensure that something is learned about the applicant. Small talk may be acceptable during the first few minutes, but the interviewer must pose stimulating questions that will help to differentiate among applicants. Experienced interviewers do not agree on the nature of the questions that should be asked. Some of them believe that the interview should be direct and that questions should be pointed to show the applicant's ability to think and to handle questions. Others think they learn more about the applicant when more general questions are asked. For filling most operative-level positions, the latter approach is more productive. If the position being filled requires professional training or a person who must perform under pressure, there may be some merit in seeking answers to difficult, job-related questions. Even under these circumstances, there is little to be gained in trying to put the applicant on the defensive.

The interviewer should prepare a checklist of questions to be covered during the interview. The applicant's answers to one question usually will trigger additional questions. The interviewer should record reactions to the applicant immediately following the interview. Valuable information will be lost if this chore is postponed.

Testing The supervisor probably will not administer tests or interpret results. This should be done by professionals. However, in organizations where testing is used in the employment process, supervisors should understand the nature of the tests that are given and how they are used. Tests are a *supplement* to the selection process. They are at best only an estimate of an individual's future performance. They should be treated as an aid and never as the sole **criterion** or basis for making the selection decision.

criterion basis against which an employee accomplishment can be measured

Testing in the employment process became an issue following the enactment of equal employment legislation in 1964. Many tests were discovered to be culturally biased. They eliminated persons on bases other than factors which would determine probable job performance. However, most commercially marketed employment tests have been reconstructed to eliminate these biases.

Placement In some cases, where employees are not placed in specific jobs until after orientation and training, the supervisor may participate in the **placement** process. At this point, the most important consideration should be related to placing the employee in a position where he or she will be productive and satisfied with the job. This means that the employee possesses at least the minimum qualifications for the position and feels comfortable about the position. Some placement processes should take into consideration the personalities of people with whom the new employee

placement situating people in specific jobs

238

must work in a particular job and the probability that the new employee can be trained adequately for the position. For operative-level jobs, the job content usually is not altered to fit a particular applicant. Instead, applicants who fit the job are sought. In small organizations or in positions where a wide range of responsibilities, duties, and tasks are required, however, it may be foolish to insist that one employee perform all tasks identified in a job description if others are more capable of performing some of those tasks.

EMPLOYEE ORIENTATION

orientation introducing a new employee to the work environment

Orientation includes those things that are done to introduce a new employee to the work environment, to fellow employees, to the work station, and to general policies and procedures that a new environment creates. Orientation does not include training in the performance of job tasks and responsibilities. That comes in the training program. A surprising number of organizations pass up the opportunity to get employees comfortably settled in new jobs. They are allowed to stumble around and fend for themselves without adequate guidance.

The employee's immediate supervisor is the person most likely to conduct orientation. Sometimes fellow workers are also involved. There should be a planned sequence of activities for every new employee. Otherwise, supervisors and others who share in the orientation process will forget many important details. Even people who have suffered through embarrassing and frustrating experiences as novices in new positions forget that agony and, when promoted to supervisory positions, inflict the same misery on new employees for whom they become responsible.

Even though it may last only a few hours, a thorough orientation acquaints new employees with their work environment and other employees with whom they will work. If the place of employment involves a large facility (such as a plant or office building) a general tour of the facility should be included. Other orientation activities would include identification of facilities and services at the disposal of the employee, introduction to fellow workers, and explanation of routine requirements and practices.

An account of a predicament faced by one new employee illustrates the danger of putting a new employee to work without orientation. An employee in a financial institution wondered why she was not given a mid-morning break as other employees in her section were. She was a new employee, however, and thought she

Employee orientation acquaints new employees with their work environment and other employees with whom they will work.

Photograph by Alan Baker, courtesy of FMC Corporation.

shouldn't complain. In the meantime, fellow employees labeled her a "do-gooder" because she worked all morning without a break. After several weeks of increasing discomfort and obviously poor personal relations with fellow workers, she managed the courage to ask the supervisor if there was something wrong. By questioning other workers, the supervisor discovered the real reason for the bad start. An effective orientation to policies and practices would have prevented this uncomfortable situation. Of course, an alert supervisor would have observed the difficulty long before this.

Some orientation programs deal with factors involving employee safety, use of recreational and health care facilities, payroll and financial arrangements, a historical summary of the organization, and explanation of the employer's general philosophies. A discussion of the organizational structure and introduction to key supervisory and managerial personnel are desirable components. The better the new employee understands the employer's objectives, purposes, products or services, and philosophies, the more

240

likely he or she will feel a part of that organization. Thorough orientation, combined with adequate training for the job, will help the employee to begin to visualize promotion possibilities and a potential career path within the organization. The thoroughly oriented employee feels welcome and comfortable, a member of the team.

PERSONNEL MAINTENANCE SYSTEMS

General Climate

One of the most neglected areas of personnel management is the overall climate or philosophy regarding the personnel function. Personnel functions should be a service arm of management provided for the benefit of the entire staff. Recall the discussion about job dissatisfiers. Those organizational procedures which provide staff benefits, for example pay, fringes, overtime, and training, are areas that can lead to considerable discomfort for the employee if care is not taken to provide those benefits in a sincere, positive and service atmosphere. All of the maintenance functions are for the benefit of the employees or staff and do not exist for the benefit of the personnel clerks or managers.

Employee Benefits

Provision of specific employee benefits which, in effect, supplement the wages and salaries of employees is a high-level personnel management activity. In many cases the decision to provide a benefit involves organization policy and decisions at the highest levels. Although most supervisors do not participate in such decisions, they are in close contact with the recipient of such benefits. The supervisor should assume the role of liaison between the employee and those who do provide benefits. If a choice of one benefit or another is being considered, the supervisor is the one most likely to be able to represent the employees' interests, desires, and needs. On the other hand the supervisor is in the best position to explain benefits to employees. Some employees may have difficulty understanding that an employer-purchased insurance policy, for example, may have greater value to the employee than what the employer paid for it, because the employer buys a large quantity of insurance at lower premiums. If employees bought insurance as individuals they would probably pay more for the policy than the employer is paying.

While benefits are meticulously negotiated one by one in a union contract situation, in the nonunionized working environment management offers whatever benefits it deems necessary in order to remain competitive with other employers and in order to maintain low employee turnover ratios.

Among the financial benefits which may be provided are health and life insurance, medical and dental care facilities, vacations and off days with pay, provision of uniforms, profit sharing plans, stock purchase plans, pension plans, and educational tuition for employees. Many benefits are required by law, including unemployment tax payments, workmen's compensation insurance, and social security contributions.

Many benefits are not financially measurable to the employee, but they are expensive for the employer. They include employee development programs, seminars and institutes on special aspects of the job, safety programs, recreational programs, sponsorship of athletic competition for employee teams, and memberships in professional organizations for employees. While these benefits are labeled *employee* benefits, they are mutually beneficial for employee and employer. They produce more capable employees and give employees a sense of identification with the organization. If they contribute to the loyalty of employees and help to retain employees who might otherwise have left the organization, they are as valuable to the organization as to the employee.

The supervisor's role in a benefit program involves awareness of the various benefits and how they are administered, an awareness of employee needs and evaluation of benefits being provided, and assistance with the administration of benefit programs whenever that becomes necessary.

The supervisor should consider that one of his/her tasks is to assist personnel in providing these services. Not only does this orientation provide a climate of "we-ness" (we are all in this together), but each employee is treated with a certain degree of dignity. This last item is not an unimportant factor. Researchers and industrial administrators who have traveled to Japan to review their systems often ask who are the most respected members of the management team. The answer is generally the same. The personnel manager is the most respected (maybe most important). The entire climate that reflects a concern for the individual worker may have its origin in the personnel services function of the organization and the supervisor plays a part in building that climate.

IMPLICATIONS
AND
APPLICATIONS

NEW DIRECTIONS FOR PERSONNEL

One of the most interesting things about the societies we live in is that we go through one cycle after another, but some general trend is in the making. It is almost as if we are copying the spiral of the expanding universe—always in a cycle but always expanding or evolving. Personnel systems during the 1970s were greatly influenced by government regulations dealing with appropriate methods for selection, affirmative action, hiring quotas by race, discrimination policies, hiring of handicapped, hiring of veterans, sexual harassment, wage determination levels and on and on. The 1970s also was a period when the government made available considerable sums of money for the enforcement of these regulations. It has been our observation that personnel managers went into a state of withdrawal and became quite bureaucratic. The emphasis became one of "Is it legal?" and not one of "Is it best for the participants of the system?" Service could no longer be the primary interest; rather fear of the enforcer was the major influence.

The early 1980s will bring a change to this emphasis because of reductions in federal funds for enforcing regulations. Certainly a future change in administration policy could return us to a major emphasis on minority rights oversight by the government, but in all likelihood enforcement actions will be limited until the late 1980s. The point is that at some point in time government influence on personnel systems will stabilize and personnel managers can go about their business of developing more effective and sophisticated selection, orientation, training, evaluation, and maintenance programs.

Some organizations have quite sophisticated personnel systems, where the staff is up to date on new selection techniques, new training programs, and other personnel functions. Supervisors are mostly at the mercy of the system; however, they should stay abreast of approaches being taken and contribute their part as the occasion arises.

It is personnel's job to keep employees informed as to what jobs are open, what training or on-the-job training programs are available and in general what services are provided by their function. Personnel activities are easy to forget about until their services are not provided. Because the supervisor is one major link between the worker and the personnel system, it is incumbent upon him or her to keep track of what activities are provided.

SUMMARY

This chapter dealt with three primary functions of the personnel management staff. These three functions are the personnel selection and placement system, the orientation programs, and the employee services programs. All of these functions can be categorized as maintenance functions (in the open systems model) and are activities that all management staff should consider important for the general good of the organization.

Often the supervisor takes part in the selection of employees and he/she should have a general understanding of management expectations of new operatives. In addition, the supervisor may be the most knowledgeable about job requirements and therefore has important input in the selection process.

Often, to a greater degree, the supervisor will have a major role in orienting the new employee. This includes not only the formal procedures and work-a-day regularities, but the more hidden informal lines of communication that expedite the processing of information and services. Many of the do's and don'ts of everyday work are informal and can be passed along to the new employee.

Finally the supervisor can be an important liaison between the personnel services activities and the worker. They can act as a conveyor of information as to what services are available. In addition, the supervisor can provide an atmosphere of interest in the welfare of the operative. Without a doubt, the principle of reciprocity fits this topic quite well. If the organization is concerned about the staff and shows it with positive and beneficial personnel services, the employee is more likely to provide a service for the system when the occasion arises.

Because personnel systems will continue to be in a state of change, probably for some time to come, the supervisor needs to be attuned to these changes and be a source of assistance to their workers.

QUESTIONS FOR FURTHER THOUGHT

1. Describe the concept of personnel services as a maintenance function.

2. What are the consequences of large turnover rates within companies or other organizations?

3. *Cognitive differences* is used to describe "differences" between male and female intellectual abilities. What are the findings by Hyde relating to this topic?

4. Of what value can a supervisor be in employee orientation programs?

5. Of what assistance can the supervisor be in personnel selection programs?

6. What does organization climate have to do with personnel services?

7. What has been the overall effect of antidiscrimination legislation by the federal government?

8. Identify employment practices which can be discriminatory under existing laws and interpretation.

12

EMPLOYEE TRAINING

VOCABULARY TO MASTER

OJT (on-the-job training)
Apprenticeships
Vestibule training
Job rotation (JR)
Programmed learning
Reaction surveys
Comparative performance measures
Long-term appraisal
Interference
Learning curve
Concrete reasoning
Formal reasoning
Operant conditioning
Insightful learning
Cognitive participation
Spaced learning
Transfer
Feedback

LEARNING OBJECTIVES

Upon completion of this chapter and related assignments, you should be able to:

1. Describe several training program options available to organizations to train and upgrade employees.
2. Identify five guidelines for developing and sequencing effective training.
3. Describe and discuss three principles of learning that apply to training programs.
4. Explain the concept of learning curves and relate this to employee training.
5. Describe the influence of feedback and motivation on learning tasks for the trainee.
6. Describe several limitations that the trainee has in terms of learning, retention and recall.

CHAPTER OUTLINE

PROBLEM STATEMENT
WHAT IS THE SUPERVISOR'S ROLE IN TRAINING PROGRAMS?

BACKGROUND AND THEORY
EMPLOYEE TRAINING
    An Overview of Training Programs
    Approaches to Training
    Training Methods and Materials
    Guidelines for Effective Training
    Evaluation of Training

RESEARCH AND PRACTICE
THE NATURE OF LEARNING
    Levels of Learning
    Principles of Learning
    Motivational Operations

IMPLICATIONS AND APPLICATIONS
WHAT DOES THIS MEAN FOR THE SUPERVISOR?
SUMMARY
QUESTIONS FOR FURTHER THOUGHT

WHAT IS THE SUPERVISOR'S ROLE IN TRAINING PROGRAMS?

Supervisors will as a matter of routine find themselves in situations that call for training employees. Whether the training is for a transferred employee or a worker who is new to the organization, effective training techniques and a general understanding of how people learn will be of considerable assistance to the supervisor. In today's organizations there is no question that there will be training programs; supervisors and other managers must work together to provide the most functional training process possible. Supervisors not only need an understanding of the specific learning-training interaction skills required, but they also need a perspective of the overall training effort of the organization.

EMPLOYEE TRAINING

Just as new employees must be thoroughly oriented to the organization, they must be trained to perform in the particular jobs to which they are assigned. Some jobs require long, complicated training processes, handled by professional employee training staffs; others require less complicated training which may be provided by the new employee's supervisor. Training may involve on-the-job approaches, special in-house formal training, or outside formal training sessions. Off-site programs may be operated by the employer or contracted out to private groups or institutions.

An Overview of Training Programs

Today's firms and organizations are expanding into the realm of in-house training. The main reason is that most jobs are seen as being so task specific that vocational schools, colleges, and other generalized instructional systems do not provide appropriate specific training needed by today's organizations. The high school or college graduate cannot enter a job at XYZ Company and start producing at the level required, so the company sets up some form of task-specific training. Employees who complete these programs not only are well informed on the company's task-specific needs, but they are indebted to the company for additional education and may feel a loyalty to that organization. Many moderate-sized organizations have their own training staffs and fairly well-established programs. The main concern for small to moderate-

When you become a supervisor, you may become involved in a variety of formal instruction, including in-house training programs in a classroom setting.

Photograph by Alan Baker, courtesy of Bowling Green Board of REALTORS.®

sized organizations is that training programs often are needed to meet the needs of personnel on the job. There are several approaches to meeting those needs; and a systematic approach to developing, implementing, and evaluating programs is needed.

Whether the supervisor is actively participating in the training process or supervising the "finished product" of that process, a knowledge of alternative approaches to training and guidelines for effective training will make supervision of the newly-trained employee easier. An understanding of how people learn, at what pace they learn, and how well they retain what they have learned will make a more effective supervisor.

Approaches to Training

OJT (on-the-job-training) *training while on the job*

apprenticeships *training alongside an experienced worker*

vestibule training *training prior to being placed*

On-the-job training, apprenticeships, and *vestibule training* programs are three labels that have been used to identify three popular approaches to employee training which are likely to involve the supervisor directly.

On-the-job training is self-explanatory. OJT has its origin in the apprentice and guild systems where individuals learned a trade as they worked alongside a craftsman. Military organizations in many countries have well-defined task specific OJT pro-

249

grams for their enlisted personnel. Each job is divided into skill levels that are progressive in nature, tied to promotion possibilities, and required levels of study and task completion. Supervisors are assigned trainees and are supposed to guide their trainees through the job skill requirements. Small business firms often use this approach because it is inexpensive. The idea is that the employee is providing some service to the organization while he/she is learning the job.

After initial orientation, the trainee goes to work. The supervisor assumes major responsibility for training. The employee actually produces while learning, beginning with simple job tasks and progressing to more complicated ones. Apprentices learn by assisting experienced employees (in some cases, one who holds some license, certificate, or union status) and learning from those employees. Even though major training tasks fall on experienced employees in these cases, the supervisor is still responsible for the success of the effort.

Some short training programs, which must be completed before job entry, have been labeled vestibule training programs. Just as one enters a building via the vestibule, one enters the job via the training program. It differs from on-the-job and apprenticeship programs because it is completed before the employee begins to work on the job. It may then be supplemented by some on-the-job approach.

In-house, formal training facilities, complete with classrooms, multi-media instructional aids, and teachers (training directors) are common today. Participation in training programs that use these facilities and a formal approach to learning the job may be combined with part-time performance on the job. The employee may attend formal classes for part of the day and perform some phase of the job for the remainder of the day. The length of such classes and training may vary from a few days to many months of instruction, depending upon the technical nature of the job for which the employee is being trained. The supervisor should be fully aware of the nature of the instruction being offered to employees and should supplement it with on-the-job instruction.

JR (job rotation) rotation form one job to another during training

Another approach to on-the-job training is **job rotation** (JR). In this approach the concern is the development of a diversified employee who can perform more than one set of tasks and who has a greater commitment to the organization than just one job. In this situation the trainee rotates from one job assignment to another and masters portions of each job. JR should be tailored to the individual. However, in recent years assembly line workers have been exposed to this training program to improve their job satisfaction.

Training may be provided through an off-site program of full- or part-time instruction. Very intensive full-time instruction is common for employees who will work with specialized equipment or use technological processes on the job. These programs are almost always financed by the employer, but they may be contracted out to private training groups. In some cases, manufacturers of equipment provide such programs for the employees of organizations who use their equipment.

Training Methods and Materials

Training methods may include "buddy" systems (new employee assigned to experienced employee), individual instruction (self-guided instruction), demonstration, or group instruction. Group training may involve lectures on the basics of particular jobs, followed by demonstrations and trainee applications of what has been learned. Any of these methods may be supplemented and greatly enhanced by individualized training methods and materials.

The old and standard approach to training is the lecture. Instruction by a specialist, telling something to a group, is often in a one-way communication process. If the trainee is required to do outside reading and individual study, and if the lecturer provides an opportunity for interaction with the trainee, the training process is enhanced. Simply providing for a transfer of information in a lecture setting does not ensure that learning takes place; and unless the trainer can take the information and apply it within a short period of time, little gain is likely to occur. For certain types of jobs, about the only way the operative can stay abreast of the changing technology is through lecture, individual study, or programmed special media instruction.

programmed learning
self-directed instructional
materials with self-
analysis

Programmed learning devices are self-directed programs which the learner may follow. They involve study, self-testing and feedback throughout a prescribed learning sequence. They may involve printed instructions supplemented by questions which must be successfully answered before the next step. The learner is provided necessary materials for this step. More complicated programmed training devices may involve computers to accomplish the same task. With this futuristic approach to training, the learner receives instruction and reacts to that instruction via some

251

Many supervisors participate in formal training programs as instructors. Simply providing for a transfer of information in a lecture setting does not insure that learning takes place. Practice and opportunity to apply learning are necessities for the learner.

computer terminal (usually a combination of a typewriter keyboard and a cathode ray tube display screen). Computerized standard reactions to learner responses tell the learner whether or not a particular phase of the training has been mastered. Several companies sell or rent systems that can be used to tie into broadcast centers whereby instruction in specific areas can be selected. This, however, is still expensive or out of the question for many organizations and has some of the weaknesses of the lecture option. Of greater interest are the minisystems that can interact with the trainer and are available twenty-four hours per day with programmed instruction for specific task development skills. The expansion in this area will be interesting to observe; and the more sophisticated the personnel training function is, the greater will be the emphasis toward utilizing computerized learning systems. Programmed approaches to training require very little supervision while the employee is learning, but the initial production of the material is very time consuming and expensive.

Films and video taped programs have been produced for specific topics of instruction. Not only can the product be professional

Training should involve an identification-demonstration-application-evaluation sequence. The trainer identifies the job segment to be learned, demonstrates its performance, allows the learner to perform, and follows up with evaluation.

in nature but the materials can be highly organized, thus reducing the time required to present a considerable amount of content.

Training materials for many types of jobs are available from commercial firms that specialize in their production. Those who produce such material should be thoroughly familiar with the job and with learning theory. Otherwise the materials will be ineffective. Supervisors should be familiar with the content of such material and should be available to help trainees interpret and apply what has been learned.

Guidelines for Effective Training

Although the need for training, the type of training provided, and the materials and methods used for training change from time to time, several appropriate guidelines have been developed throughout the past forty years. Whatever the program, these guidelines should help to produce effective programs.

1. Early portions of the training should preview the entire job for

the employee and help the employee to visualize the general nature and scope of the job and how it fits in among the total organization's efforts.

2. Training should be subdivided into manageable segments—small enough in scope and detail to be easily grasped by the trainee. The sequence should allow learning at one phase to enhance learning in future phases.

3. Training should involve an identification-demonstration-application-evaluation sequence. The trainer identifies the job segment to be learned, demonstrates the performance of that segment, allows the learner to perform the segment, and follows up with evaluation and constructive criticism.

4. Responsibility for training for every job in the organization should be specifically assigned.

5. The nature, duration, and expected outcome of training experiences should be identified in writing.

Evaluation of Training

The main questions to be answered in a training evaluation plan are quite simple. Those questions are: 1) Does the training lead to the desired change in behavior? and 2) Is the training reasonably efficient?

The most obvious response to both of these questions is "Compared to what?" Is the desired *change in behavior* and increase in employee production compared to the employee's beginning level or compared to personnel already "on the line"? The answer to that is, perhaps, both! Does *reasonably efficient* suggest a comparison to no training, to OJT, or to other training programs? The answer, again, may be all three.

One possible way to view the issues that revolve around these two major questions can be described as follows:

		Compared with
	Is behavior changed?	1. beginning level 2. "on-line" personnel 3. those not trained 4. those otherwise trained
Training Program		
	Is training efficient?	1. cost vs. production increases 2. OJT program 3. no training 4. other training programs

Certainly there are other possibilities that might need to be considered. However, if the focus is on those two main questions and one wishes to evaluate them within the organizational setting, there are three basic approaches that can be used. No one evaluation procedure will get at all the questions, so the task is to use as many as are allowable, given the organizational constraints.

reaction survey evaluation of training programs

1. **Reaction Surveys**. Simply use a pencil and paper survey to get the views of participants, supervisors, and others regarding the outcomes of various approaches to training.

comparative performance measure evaluation of trainees vs. nontrainees

2. **Comparative Performance Measures**. Various tools and instruments are available or can be created to evaluate performance. The main thrust is to determine whether performance is adequately affected by the training program. If possible, performance of employees who have not had the training should be compared with those who have.

long-term appraisal evaluation beyond time of training program

3. **Long-term Appraisal of Training Impact**. This evaluation deals with the concept of the effect of training over time. Do employees who receive a particular training exhibit behaviors that significantly influence production, improved procedures, promotion, organizational climate, and satisfaction on the job? Again, this might be approached with survey instruments, interviews, or operational audits.

RESEARCH AND PRACTICE

THE NATURE OF LEARNING

Man is basically a creature of learning. The learning process varies with the individual's approach, but in general it involves the establishment of responses to stimuli. Or you may prefer to call learning any change in behavior due to some experience.

In the context of an organizational setting, training programs are geared toward one of several outcomes. One is changing or adding behaviors that will permit learners to perform tasks. Another is describing organizational systems so that employees can function within the units of the system. And another would be the persuasion of employees that the organization within which they work is meaningful. These three outcomes might be abbreviated into task-skills, system-procedures, and motivation-persuasions. The techniques for increasing the learning process may vary (see training methods). With few exceptions, however, most of us have similar limits as to how rapidly we can master and learn a new set of responses to a new set of stimuli.

Any general psychology textbook will provide more information on learning theories and ways to look at the learning process. In addition, numerous studies in learning, models to explain the learning process, and to explain the physiology of the brain have been written. However, on a day-to-day basis most of that information is of little interest to supervisors. The supervisor, though, should be aware that very few people are able to learn rapidly without several conditions being met: the element of interest or motivation, some ability to acquire new information, an opportunity to learn, and practice.

What does that mean for the trainer? First of all, the training package or approach must allow ample time to assimilate and practice the item(s) to be learned. This, obviously, takes time. In addition, repetition of short-duration tasks is often the best approach. Second, the learner has to be interested in the tasks to be achieved. Some form of reward system will be needed to motivate the desired behavior. Third, certain physical tasks are simply beyond the capability of some people. Likewise, many mental tasks are beyond the capability of some people. To go one step further, some people deal best with "concrete" relationships, while others think in "formal" terms and, thereby, test hypothetical relationships.[1] Often what touches one mind does not have any influence on another.

One of the interesting things about the learning process is that people are not very efficient at obtaining, storing, recalling and implementing the new "stuff" they have learned. Recall learning how to ride a bicycle. For some of us it came within three or four hours; for others it may have taken weeks. For all of us, there were some falls along the way. Or how about the time you had to learn a part for a school play? It probably took hours of trial and error and trial and success before the total piece was learned. The next day you probably made some mistakes when you tried to recite the whole piece. Most learning, manual or verbal, takes place in the same fashion. You learn a little; you forget a little; and each time you work on the same task you get better; but the whole process takes time and practice.

When people try to learn job tasks, those tasks must have meaning both from a motivational and an intellectual standpoint. In addition, new information that is "entered" into the brain creates an electrochemical process that takes not moments but hours.

---

[1]Hans G. Furth, *Piaget and Knowledge: Theoretical Foundations*, (Englewood Cliffs, N.J.: Prentice-Hall, Inc., 1969).

interference factors which complicate learning

learning curve graphic representation of achievement

Information already in the system (brain and/or total nervous system) and later experiences will often act as **interference** in the total recall process. The older people get, the more confusing the interference can become. Not only can it be difficult to get information into the system, it can also be difficult to get it back out in a useable form. On the input side, learning curves might give us some insight into the process of obtaining information. **Learning curves** generally take on the shape of a ski slope. With repeated attempts, there is a reduction in errors (see Exhibit 12.1).

After initial training on day one, the learner is eventually able to perform the task without error. On day two, when he or she resumes task performance, errors will crop up during first attempts because of forgetting. An initial period of relearning is required to perform the task error free.

Another way to look at the learning process is in terms of number of correct responses over time or by number of trials. If a trainee is given a task to perform that is repetitive, the number of correct responses may be counted over a day's time or some other time period. Exhibit 12.2 is a representation of that learning process. Notice that there is a period of time when a plateau or a leveling off is apparent. This often happens in assembly line work, sales, and many short-duration jobs. What is happening is that there is a period of time when the learner is consolidating past experiences and possibly seeking new or advantageous ways to complete the task. In any event, the supervisor should expect some leveling off of performance with trainees, but that does not mean that improvements are not forthcoming.

Levels of Learning

concrete reasoning thinking in terms of tangible phenomena

formal reasoning problem solving using abstractions and indirect relationships

One of the more interesting areas of learning theory has been the spin-off from Jean Piaget's developmental theories of learning. The development of reasoning in science teaching expresses an approach to learning that has considerable value and usefulness in the world of work. Most people operate on a **concrete reasoning** pattern; that is, they relate to observable conditions or tangible things, simple relationships, one-to-one relationships, and object grouping. Others operate on this concrete level but also use **formal reasoning** to learn and to solve problems. They test hypotheses, consider numerous combinations of abstract ideas, control variables, and attempt to consider indirect relationships.

In reality on the job, most of a supervisor's tasks will be to deal with information transfer on a concrete basis. If that is the case,

257

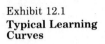

Exhibit 12.1
Typical Learning Curves

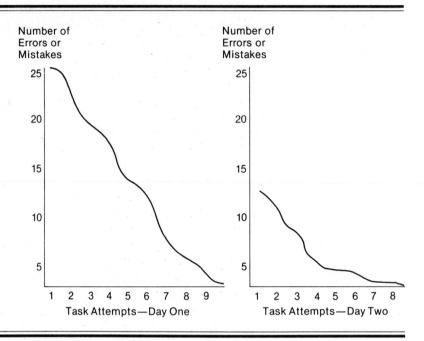

the learning system needs to be object-oriented, descriptive, simple, and repetitive.

Please note, however, that "boring" is not included in the list. And that is where motivation or interest comes in! One of the big problems with training and learning is that human behavior is dependent upon a number of interrelationships. For example, a person learns at different rates depending on the interest or internal motivation which is a function of external rewards—past, present, and future. And much of that interest can be affected by the organizational climate. Any organizational climate is affected by both the real and the perceived reward systems which influence workers to achieve some degree of excellence. In addition, that climate is a function of the leadership styles within the organization. What, then, are the combined factors that lead to behavior change? The question is not an easy one to dissect. Because of the interplay of a number of variables, a picture of those interrelationships might be helpful. In an attempt to build that picture, an approach to each of the major components must first be considered.

Learning can be discussed in terms of three levels: classical, operant, and insight. These three basic levels of learning may be considered distinct entities, but they are really units of awareness

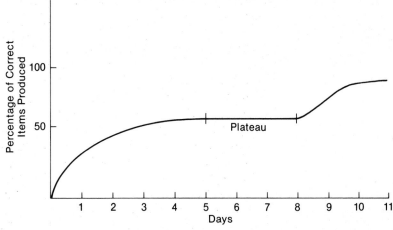

Exhibit 12.2
Representative Learning Curve with a Plateau

that fall on a continuum of the process of learning. The last two levels are important for trainers.

operant conditioning stimulus influenced responding to our world

Operant conditioning, or operant behavior involves responses for the receipt of a reinforcement or reward. This kind of learning can be described as trial and success behavior—whatever worked in the past is likely to be repeated. The learner isn't aware of the reason for reacting this way. Habit or repetition are important factors in performance at this level. This type of learned behavior is a simple "getting along in the environment" kind of responses and habitual in nature once established.

Most of the wakeful day is controlled by past learnings due to operant learning and habitual responses. The work setting is a series of rewards and punishments that are inherently operant in nature. The person on the assembly line makes moves because of a specified reward system. So many units produced during a period of work yield a paycheck which provides food and shelter and other things for the worker. If some other value is added to the unit produced, the reward system is even greater; but whatever the incentive, the worker is performing for a reward or gratification or satisfaction of an actual or perceived need. In other words, people do things to get something in return.

insightful learning personalized responding to our world; beyond situlus-response behavior

Insightful learning or higher order learning is a style of behavior change that requires putting together various stimuli (information, conditions) and perceiving (seeing) possible outcomes (results). Insightful learning may be broken down into

259

seven separate levels in terms of individual participation. This "Evaluation Model of **Cognitive Participation**" is suggested by Crumb and is as follows:[2]

cognitive participation degree of involvement from awareness to changed behavior

Level	Descriptor	Action
1	Awareness	Attends to and tolerates information
2	Interest	Seeks more information to find meaning and function
3	Evaluation	Mentally questions information and relates it to own concepts
4	Trial	Tries out information on actual problem—sees if tool works
5	Adoption (Rejection)	Accepts information as useful tool and considers self for using the information
6	Promotion	Becomes a verbal proponent of information; seeks to lead others in use of information
7	Changed Behavior	Endorses information and actively elicits refinements and development of new behaviors

Again, these seven levels are on a continuum from awareness to changed behavior and may be difficult to separate into finite categories when evaluating any one set of individual behaviors. The more complex tasks within organizations will fall under insightful responding/learning; and within an increasingly sophisticated society of workers and managers, any appeal for change in behavior should take an insight approach into consideration.

Principles of Learning

There are at least three basic concepts that the trainer needs to keep in mind when teaching a worker a new set of tasks.

spaced learning learning interspaced with rest periods

Spaced learning schedule. Under most conditions for most types of training situations, there is ample research documentation that short training and practice sessions with short rest periods are far superior to continuous and massed training periods. This has to do not only with the short attention and interest spans that most of us have, but also with the memory consolidation process. That is, time is required for it all to sink in and become a part of our response system. The rest periods also allow us to "think" about what is being learned and associate those

---

[2]Glenn H. Crumb, "Evaluation Model of Cognitive Participation." (Paper presented at the Regional Meeting of the Association of Educators of Teachers of Science, Emporia, Ks., November 1972).

items with past experiences. In a sense it allows us to do what may be called "messing around" (experimenting) with the information and "testing" its usefulness.

transfer ability to apply that material learned in one situation to another

Transfer of training. Any trainer must realize that telling a person how to do something is vastly different from having the person actually perform the task. If training takes place in one setting (not the workplace), and the trainee must take what has been learned back to the job site, the transfer process is not always easy. Something is lost in the process, because the actual job task cannot be exactly duplicated. Transfer of skills is always best when the stimulus and response conditions for training and work task are most nearly alike. That is why on-the-job training programs work well.

feedback reaction by receiver in a communication cycle

Feedback. Knowledge of the results of a trainee's efforts is necessary for learning to take place. The sooner the feedback is forthcoming, the more rapidly the learning will be verified. The process of knowing that a correct response has been made is reinforcing and valuable to the learner. Not only is there a motivational component to immediate feedback, but response corrections can be made quickly. Practice or hands-on activity is, therefore, an important part of any training program. Only by "trying out" what has been learned, can we get feedback so as to make subsequent corrections or adjustments. The learning package is one of:

Training ⟷ Practice ⟷ Feedback ⟷ Adjustment

Motivational Operations

Another dimension that needs to be considered is the nature of reinforcements that have an impact upon any changed behavior or new set of responses. Reinforcements are individual, unique and, therefore, can only be considered in terms of the individual needs or goals system. A reasonable approach is one that describes a hierarchy of needs with primary needs having the greatest impact, followed by secondary or social needs. Again, rather than elaborating on a more complicated descriptive approach, the Maslow model (see Chapter Four) will suffice. His model, starting with the most potent needs and following in a prescribed sequence, is:

1. Physiological needs
2. Safety needs
3. Belongingness and love needs

4. Esteem needs

5. Self-actualization

This approach suggests that we attempt to satisfy each need before we become interested in taking care of the following need. For example, if our need for safety is not met, we are not very concerned with being loved or striving for fulfilling our potential as a human being. A look at the activity of labor unions in the United States and Canada shows that this model is right on target. Safety and job security are of primary interest; and only after those conditions are worked out, do worker concerns center around pay or expected productivity. Motivational operations, then, are one aspect for consideration when dealing with learning and training issues; because if the employee concerns are not with task functions, the training activities will be handicapped.

IMPLICATIONS
AND
APPLICATIONS

WHAT DOES THIS MEAN FOR THE SUPERVISOR?

There are several basic factors to consider or try to focus upon when supervisors participate in training programs.

1. There are learner limitations that require well planned, task specific training with considerable practice opportunity. Practice and hands-on applications allow for immediate feedback which allows for adjustment.

2. Most training provided by first-line supervisors requires concrete, direct results, and a simple approach. Much of what the supervisor knows will appear second nature and very simple. However, the new trainee may be working from ground zero. The task is often to *assess* the capability of the trainees and then to select either concrete training or formal training.

3. Trainee motivation is a factor that must be considered. If trainees are not interested and have limited external reinforcements which encourage their staying on task and learning, the trainer's job is almost impossible. Outside of using additional hands-on activities, the only solution may be to advise management and start back at ground zero.

4. Any training activity that is not just a stimulus-response action, such as putting one nut on one bolt and passing that item on down the line, may require a sequence of events for the training to be complete. Time for presentation of information

needs to be devoted to this process. That process has been described in seven steps by Crumb and any training program can be developed around those seven ideas. This step by step process for building a training package is:

a. Awareness—Explain background, history, and reasons why the task is done this way. Allow trainee to "mess around" with information.

b. Interest—Show how task activity will provide solutions to problem. Fully instruct trainee on task activity.

c. Evaluation—Get trainee involved with task intellectually and force him or her to relate to personal experiences.

d. Trial—Have trainee try out process. Require practice. Ensure some failure and some success.

e. Adoption—Require the trainee to use task activity as a way to provide outcomes.

f. Promotion—Have the trainee verbalize task processes and explain the reasons why the activity is to be done this way. Have the trainee assist others in doing the task.

g. Changed Behavior—Elicit refinements to the activity. Have the trainee try to improve on the system. Compare starting point of the trainee and the outcome after training.

Obviously not all training tasks need to be this elaborate; but as the task or job requirements become more complex, this full-blown approach will take care of most of the problems encountered with training employees.

SUMMARY

Employee training programs are essential for most organizations. Whether the training system used is one of on-the-job experience, formalized instruction, or off-site professional instruction, there are some principles of learning that need to be considered.

The supervisor needs to realize that the learning process entails a trainer-trainee relationship that facilitates training—practice—feedback—adjustment. Both success and failure are part of the process, and there are different learning rates and styles for individuals. As complexity of learning tasks increases, so can the method of presentation. No matter what the training system is (OJT, TV, lecture, programmed instruction, microcomputer, or others) consideration should be given to the various levels of cognitive participation on the part of the trainee. Not only must the trainer remember that learning comes in bits and pieces, but that the arrangement of the bits is a function of the individual's motivation. Meaningful information is arranged in a meaningful fashion with many associations. In addition, the more one values certain information, the more he/she will use that information.

What are the keys to learning? There are many, but three are as follows: *content* that has applicability or functional worth; *presentation* that includes the whys, the hows, and feedback; and *motivational involvement* of the trainee.

These factors cannot be accomplished if the approach is haphazard. They can be learned and developed by the supervisor.

The supervisor is an important link in the training situation and can, through effort, master an understanding of the learning-training process.

QUESTIONS FOR FURTHER THOUGHT

1. Define the terms operant learning, insightful learning, concrete operations, and formal operations.

2. Job rotation is a type of on-the-job training but it has been used for other purposes. What are those other purposes?

3. What are three basic principles of learning that the trainer needs to consider when working with trainees?

4. One model that has been proposed for developing a training package describes seven levels of cognitive participation. List and define those levels.

5. Explain the concept of a plateau in learning curves and why they appear.

6. What is a programmed instruction approach to training?

13

APPRAISING EMPLOYEE PERFORMANCE

VOCABULARY TO MASTER

Performance appraisal
Performance review
Performance planning
Ranking
Checklist
Rating scale
Performance management
Narrative evaluation
Goal setting

LEARNING OBJECTIVES

Upon completion of this chapter and related assignments, you should be able to:

1. Define performance appraisal and contrast this process with related employee evaluation processes.
2. Cite legislative requirements and legal implications which have created recent interest in performance appraisal.
3. Review the general history of performance appraisal techniques.
4. Contrast traditional methods of performance appraisal with contemporary approaches to appraisal.
5. Identify essential ingredients of an effective appraisal system.
6. Develop a foundation for the formation of a philosophy of performance appraisal.

CHAPTER OUTLINE

PROBLEM STATEMENT
WHAT IS THE PURPOSE OF PERFORMANCE APPRAISAL?

BACKGROUND AND THEORY
AN INTRODUCTION TO PERFORMANCE APPRAISAL
　　Renewed Interest in Appraisal
　　Employee Attitudes about Appraisal
TRADITIONAL VERSUS CONTEMPORARY APPRAISAL SYSTEMS
　　Traditional Systems
　　Contemporary Systems

RESEARCH AND PRACTICE
HISTORY AND CURRENT STATUS OF APPRAISAL
APPRAISAL TECHNIQUES
　　Ranking
　　Checklist
　　Rating Scales
　　Narrative
　　Goal Setting
　　Interviews

IMPLICATIONS AND APPLICATIONS
INGREDIENTS OF AN EFFECTIVE APPRAISAL SYSTEM
　　Supervisor-Influenced Ingredients
　　Organization-Influenced Ingredients
SUMMARY

QUESTIONS FOR FURTHER THOUGHT

<table>
<tr><td>

PROBLEM
STATEMENT

</td><td>

WHAT IS THE PURPOSE OF PERFORMANCE APPRAISAL?

All supervisors will be required to evaluate subordinates, either formally or informally; and they should understand some of the issues and problems associated with various methods and techniques of appraisal. *Performance appraisal* should be a part of the plan for employee development. Appraisal is an ongoing process which creates benefits for the organization as it facilitates employee growth.

</td></tr>
</table>

BACKGROUND
AND
THEORY

AN INTRODUCTION TO PERFORMANCE APPRAISAL

Supervisors evaluate subordinates. Sometimes they use a formal system and special instruments, but always they use subtle, informal techniques to evaluate subordinates' abilities and overall worth to the organization.

This chapter's presentation on appraisal is intended to introduce supervisors and potential supervisors to some of the issues, problems, and background of this complicated process. Perhaps this presentation will spark an interest in evaluation systems and techniques and an interest in securing professional training in the appraisal of employee performance. The treatment of the subject here does not constitute such training. Important additional appraisal skills are needed in order to develop proficiency in this activity. Depending upon the organization and the nature of responsibilities, specific training in interviewing techniques, job analysis, management by objectives, development of performance standards, and employee counseling may be desirable. Extended (40 hours or more) workshops or in-house training programs in these areas are often required by employers.

performance appraisal
employee evaluation system

Many definitions of employee **performance appraisal** exist. They vary from specific, discriminating definitions to broad, all-encompassing approaches to the process. Some focus on the past; some, on the employee's future. Performance appraisal can be thought of as any exchange between supervisor and subordinate which provides feedback about current and recent performance and provides a basis for future development of the employee.

performance review
formal review of employees by superiors

Some consultants and writers such as Yager prefer to differentiate among the processes of performance appraisal (informal day-to-day feedback), **performance review** (periodic formal reviews

268

In some organizations, performance appraisal stresses the day-to-day, informal feedback from subordinate to supervisor.

Photograph by Alan Baker, courtesy of Speakman Electric.

performance planning
defining future expectations of employees

of performance), and **performance planning** (outlining the employee's future and the consequences of alternative directions).[1] A more common practice is to lump together the three under the umbrella of "performance appraisal." In most cases, this broader meaning is employed in this chapter. Almost every "expert" agrees that using performance appraisal for salary and wage increment decisions destroys the value of the appraisal. However, business firms, institutions, and governments continue to do just that on a very large scale.

Many organizations which evaluate employees do not subscribe to these objectives. It should be assumed that the goal is employee development and that employees prefer feedback regarding their performance if it is provided in the proper perspective. Other factors, such as government requirements which have caused organizations to improve or begin evaluation programs,

---

[1]Ed Yager, "A Critique of Performance Appraisal Systems," *Personnel Journal* (February 1981), p. 129.

have overshadowed this basic objective. For some reason, many organizations still do not evaluate their employees and most of those who do evaluate do not train the evaluators (supervisors). The report card of employee appraisal systems has not been good.

Renewed Interest in Appraisal

Businesses and government agencies appraise the performance of between 30 and 40 million employees annually, and this number will grow substantially in the near future. Two factors have created greater interest in employee appraisal systems in recent years: 1) a federal government mandate for evaluating certain employees and 2) court decisions which have criticized appraisal systems involved in EEOC cases. The Civil Service Reform Act (CSRA) required that all federal employees be under performance appraisal systems by October 1, 1981. Performance standards and evaluation of employees' accomplishment of these standards will be used to determine promotions and merit pay increments for federal employees.

Although legislation has not outlawed poor appraisal systems, court cases have blamed them for discrimination because of race, sex, and age. Examples are *Mistretta v. Sandia Corporation* (1977) (layoffs of older employees) and *Brito et al. v. Zia Company* (1973) (layoffs of Spanish-surnamed employees). The faults found by the courts were in the nature of the systems and the factors evaluated—not in the existence of a system.

In addition to firms that are encouraged to establish or revamp appraisal systems for fear of legal action, many organizations voluntarily evaluate their own appraisal systems. People-oriented management techniques and less paternalistic management styles have led some organizations to re-evaluate their appraisal of employees and to change from a criticism of past performance to an employee-development approach. Emphasis is on helping employees to evaluate their work, to establish personal goals, and to chart future progress and growth within the organization.

Employers can actually prepare to defend themselves against suits which claim bias and discrimination if a system which is straightforward and job-oriented is in place. If an objective appraisal system exists, documentation to justify personnel decisions will be abundant. Some employers have been able to successfully argue in court cases that EEOC guidelines and those imposed by other government agencies may contribute to illegal and unfair labor practices. A fair and equitable appraisal can support such arguments; but one that bases judgments on subjective data and vague characteristics, such as attitude and personality, defeat these arguments.

Employee Attitudes About Appraisal

One researcher, Henderson, believes that employees are very knowledgeable about the fairness of systems, about the real uses of appraisal data, and about the differences among different raters' evaluations.[2] That is to say, employees know whether or not a system is fair. Even though workers are generally negative about performance appraisal systems, they know that they are going to be evaluated under any circumstances. If there is no formal system, employees know that informal evaluations may be less accurate than a good formal system.

Employees fight appraisal systems, Henderson believes, because they think the systems don't use objective criteria or equitably distribute whatever rewards the systems provide. They believe that supervisors can "rig" the system in favor of their favorites and that factors other than real performance dominate the evaluation. Whether or not these beliefs are justified, any evaluation system is going to cause employee concern.

The task of evaluators, then, is to develop a system that eliminates these faults and to convince employees of the merits of the system. In the discussion that follows, both "traditional" and "contemporary" approaches to appraisal are discussed. The system which includes the characteristics and techniques that have been labeled "contemporary" would eliminate most employee fears. The system needs to exist in a favorable communication climate and under open-systems conditions of mutual trust and understanding. For some supervisors, however, implementation of such a system may present a dilemma. Supervisors may not be in positions to influence the system used. They may be handed a system and told to work with it. What then?

The remainder of this chapter presents what are believed to be accurate descriptions of various systems and techniques and the implications of their use. Other chapters have presented ideas about the necessity of free and open communication and the need for developing an environment of trust among management and

---

[2]Richard Henderson, *Performance Appraisal: Theory to Practice* (Reston, Va.: Reston Pub. Co., 1980), pp. 9–10.

271

employees. These additional ideas should assist supervisors in developing their own philosophy of employee appraisal. Those who are given the opportunity to influence the systems used in organizations must weigh the alternatives carefully. The sources cited in the appendix provide excellent food for additional thought. If employers provide or permit training in employee appraisal, take advantage of such an opportunity.

TRADITIONAL VERSUS CONTEMPORARY APPRAISAL SYSTEMS

Even though a particular appraisal system may not fall neatly into either of these categories, they tend to emphasize characteristics from one of these two. They are either highly subjective in their evaluation of general factors or they lean toward objective and goal-oriented evaluations.

Exhibit 13.1 identifies some of the differences between appraisal approaches. Appraisal systems and techniques seem to generate more employee resistance and more difficulty with government regulations and the courts if the system carries elements listed here under the traditional category.

Traditional Systems

Traditional appraisal systems force supervisors to rate subordinates periodically (annually, or semiannually), usually with little or no specific training for the supervisor. A three-step system is likely to be employed: 1) supervisor rating of employee; it may be quantitative, narrative, or a combination of evaluations, 2) the employee reacts in writing to the evaluation, and 3) supervisor's supervisor reviews both (the secondary review). Both the supervisor's rating and the employee's reaction are likely to be written for the benefit of the supervisor's supervisor. The whole process often becomes a complex game in which everyone is trying to impress the "boss" who makes the ultimate decision.

The traditional systems (regardless of instrument or technique) emphasize the supervisor's overall impression as influenced by past events. Some traditional systems are labeled merit systems and are directly associated with pay raises. They give the impression that performance is the only official criterion for pay raises. Because employees realize that many other factors influence pay (such as economy, nature of job market, cost of

272

	Traditional Systems	Contemporary Systems
Exhibit 13.1 **Characteristics of Traditional and Contemporary Employee Appraisal Systems**	Past performance emphasized	Goals oriented
	Combined with wage/salary reviews	Future emphasized
	Includes secondary review	Behavioral criteria, evaluation
	Not related to job description	Narrative evaluation about job-related material
	Little or no training for rater	Time consuming for rater
	Quantitative results based on general criteria	Rater training included
	Little employee participation	Ongoing process
	Periodic with little intervening activity	Includes coaching as well as evaluating
	Consumes little rater or employee time	Separate from salary review
	May involve combination of all ratings into one overall rating	

ranking grouping employees in a sequence, best to worst

checklist evaluating employee on a list of traits

rating scale a scaled instrument which measures multiple characteristics

living) they may be discouraged by the pretention that the evaluation is for the purpose of determining pay increments.

Even though a **ranking**, **checklist**, or **rating scale** (techniques which tend to quantify the evaluation) may be employed, the outcome of traditional systems is likely to be highly subjective. Subjectivity itself is not a fault, but no one should pretend that subjectivity does not exist when a quantitative system is used. Subjectivity is an element of any person's evaluation of another person. But if the rater is forced into a scale or a ranking on a vague criterion (industriousness) or a nonjob-related approach (initiative), the result may not evaluate how well the employee has performed what he or she was supposed to perform. If no job description or performance standards exist, neither the rater nor the rated may know whether or not performance has been acceptable.

Another problem which frequently arises is that raters are required, as a final step in the process, to assign a single overall rating for each employee. This practice is more likely to be associated with the systems that we have called traditional. Raters are likely to average the employee's evaluations for individual factors to get this overall rating. If the factors were not equally important, this results in an inaccurate rating.

Contemporary Systems

Contemporary systems attempt to evaluate employees at all levels in combination with overall organization management. The spirit and mood of systems that are placed in this category emphasize **performance management** instead of strict appraisal. They incorporate mutual (supervisor/employee) identification of expectations for the future (relatively short term) and the means of accomplishing these expectations. Continual appraisal and periodic formal reviews assess progress toward achieving expectations. Employees know what the reviews are going to produce. There are no surprises. Expectations are based on written job descriptions and specific performance standards. They attempt to mold overall organization objectives and individual employees' objectives when identifying expectations.

Perhaps the biggest advantage of contemporary appraisal systems is their expression of expectations in terms of observable and identifiable behavior. Behavioral statements describe specific behavior (performance) rather than making personality-related general statements. Exhibit 13.2 provides a contrast between *behavioral* and *nonbehavioral* statements from a performance documentation.

Because application of these systems requires specific training for raters' descriptions for jobs, and standards of performance, they are more expensive to initiate and manage than traditional systems. The counseling, interviewing, and documentation required to make these systems work will consume supervisors' time.

performance management mutual identification of expectations of employee by supervisor and employee

RESEARCH AND PRACTICE

HISTORY AND CURRENT STATUS OF APPRAISAL

Although workers have always been evaluated, more formal appraisal systems have been employed in the past fifty years; and those are the ones reviewed here. Early systems concentrated on desirable characteristics in good performers. Because good performers were stable, mature, committed, and loyal, these were assumed to be measures of performance. Evaluation systems ranked and rated employees on the extent to which they possessed these characteristics. Techniques employed were similar to those labeled traditional in the previous section of this chapter.

By the 1950s many firms were using narrative evaluations instead of or in combination with quantitative evaluations. The 1960s brought management by objectives (MBO) techniques. Management by objectives is more than an appraisal system; it is a

<table>
<tr>
<td>

Exhibit 13.2
Comparison of
Behavioral and
Nonbehavioral
Appraisal
Documentation

</td>
<td>

Behavioral:

Technician developed and prepared two technical reports during this period. She prepared these reports on time, in a concise and clear fashion. She developed and used charts that highlighted the changes experienced by her group during the period.

Nonbehavioral:

Technician's "pushy" attitude interferes with her work.

or

Technician accomplished tasks in an exemplary fashion during the period.

</td>
</tr>
</table>

whole approach to management planning. The term is applied to many variations of the technique, but it involves organizational, departmental, and individual goals which are in harmony and periodic reviews of progress toward accomplishment of those goals.

Using specific expected behaviors for goal setting and review has been more popular since the 1970s. This practice has been encouraged by regulation, by court decisions, by changing employee life styles, and by progressive management techniques. It is an approach that is people oriented.[3]

Research such as that reviewed by Rendero which has attempted to reveal the nature of current appraisal systems shows that most systems are young (in effect for less than ten years) and that many firms (twenty percent in this study) have no systems at all.[4]

Although it is more than an appraisal system, management by objectives remains popular and is frequently identified as the method or technique of appraisal. "Almost 50 percent of new performance appraisal systems are objective-setting in nature."[5] For almost thirty years, firms have used MBO as a means of establishing goals and evaluating accomplishment. Because the term is associated with so many different approaches and because it is limited to management-level appraisal in some firms, it is safe to assume that many firms which identify their system as an MBO system are not actually using a goals-oriented approach to appraising operative employee performance.

---

[3]This history adapted from a review of performance appraisal by I. Lazer, "Performance Appraisal: What Does the Future Hold?" *Personnel Administration* (July 1980), pp. 69–73.
[4]T. Rendero, "Performance Appraisal Practices," *Personnel* (November-December 1980), pp. 4–12.
[5]Rendero, "Performance Appraisal Practices," p. 6.

APPRAISAL TECHNIQUES

Other sections of this chapter refer to and evaluate the use of these techniques, but the following brief descriptions are offered for the purpose of clarification. Techniques should not be confused with systems; techniques involve the nitty gritty documentation of the appraisal process. A variety of techniques may be employed in a single system. The list is not complete, but it contains most of the popular techniques employed in current and recent-past systems.

There are almost as many different evaluation instruments as evaluators, but most of them fall into one of two categories— objective and subjective. Some instruments require objective data, based upon direct productivity such as number of items produced, volume of sales, or performance of specified number of tasks. Objective data usually say nothing about the quality of the performance, but they give a quantitative base for comparison. Subjective instruments, such as the rating scales discussed below, allow the evaluator to consider quality factors of performance.

Ranking

Employees in a particular group, usually those reporting to one supervisor, are ranked from best to worst. The ranking may be a pure sequence or the system may force the rater to put a certain percentage of the subordinates into varied categories. There are many faults with this system. It assumes that some employees are "worst"—a negative assumption. It allows for petty feelings to enter easily. And it may assume that no two employees deserve equal treatment.

Checklist

Checklists involve series of employee traits. The rater checks the items which are closest to his or her evaluation of the employee based on that set of traits. Exhibit 13.3 contains sample items from such a checklist. Exhibit 13.4 represents a forced-choice checklist.

Rating Scales

The rater is given a numerical scale, ranging from high to low performance. The employee is rated by selecting the point on the scale which represents the rater's evaluation of the trait being scaled. Sometimes guideline statements are given at various

Exhibit 13.3
**A Portion of an
Employee Traits
Checklist**

Check the box which represents your opinion of this employee:

10. Is courteous to customers:

Strongly agree	Agree	Undecided	Disagree	Strongly disagree

11. Keeps poor sales records:

Strongly agree	Agree	Undecided	Disagree	Strongly disagree

12. Completes customer transactions adequately and quickly:

Strongly agree	Agree	Undecided	Disagree	Strongly disagree

Exhibit 13.4
**A Forced-Choice
Checklist**

Place a check in front of the statement that best characterizes this employee:
(Check only one item)

6.____is patient with customers.
____reaches conclusions logically.

7.____accepts responsibility for own action.
____is fair with subordinates.

8.____sets an outstanding example.
____meets job tasks with care.

points on the scale to guide the rater's evaluation. Exhibit 13.5 is a portion of such an employee rating scale.

Narrative

*narrative evaluation
written description of
employee performance*

The **narrative evaluation** requires a textual (sentence) evaluation of the employee on each factor or criterion. It is sometimes referred to as a prose evaluation. This method requires written evaluation, using a set of specific criteria. The process is very time consuming for the rater.

Goal Setting

*goal setting employee
appraisal and perform-
ance planning involving
end objectives*

In addition to MBO, several other variations of the **goal-setting** technique are used. SDR (staff development review), PM (performance management), BARS (behaviorally anchored rating scales)

277

Exhibit 13.5
A Portion of a Rating Scale Used for Employee Appraisal.

Codes: 1—Superior; 2—Above Average; 3—Average; 4—Below Average; 5—Unsatisfactory; NA—Not Applicable

	1	2	3	4	5	NA
Job Knowledge (Extent of theoretical knowledge and practical know-how)	✓					
Judgment (Obtains, analyzes and uses appropriate information)	✓					
Attitude	✓					
Dependability	✓					
Creativity		✓				
Relationships with Others	✓					

	1	2	3	4	5	NA
Professional Development		✓				
Initiative	✓					
Effective Leadership		✓				
Planning and Organizing Effectiveness		✓				
Delegation (Appropriate delegation of authority and responsibility)		✓				
Insert any other factors unique to this position and evaluate. If additional space is needed, use reverse side of form.	1	2	3	4	5	NA
	1	2	3	4	5	NA

and other systems emphasize the goal-setting technique. They deal with plans for the future and concentrate on the present to some extent. They deal minimally with the past. Self-appraisal, as well as supervisor appraisal, is included in this technique.

Interviews

Most appraisal techniques incorporate some type of interview session between the rater and the employee. These may range from brief communication of the results of checklists or rating scales to extensive discussion sessions. The goal setting techniques are more likely to include extensive interviews.

IMPLICATIONS
AND
APPLICATIONS

INGREDIENTS OF AN EFFECTIVE APPRAISAL SYSTEM

As mentioned earlier, the supervisor may not have the authority or the freedom to develop a plan for evaluating employees in his or her part of the organization. To the extent that one is able to influence whatever plan is used or to develop a system for evaluating subordinates, the following suggestions should be helpful. They are intended to help in understanding appraisal systems and to make supervisors more comfortable in evaluating those systems. This discussion is not unbiased, as it emphasizes elements that could be associated with the previous discussion of contemporary approaches. Labeling the preference "contemporary" does not mean that these philosophies and practices dominate current systems. There are still many elements of traditional practice being used in today's appraisal systems. Every management must develop its own philosophy, and this will greatly influence the system chosen.

This summary of ingredients is divided into those which are more likely to be influenced by the supervisor and those which must depend upon the organization as a whole for direction.

Supervisor-Influenced Ingredients

A performance planning approach and climate should prevail. Performance planning systems involve goal setting for organizations, for units within organizations, and for individual employees. The supervisor can determine his or her own goals and assist subordinates in developing their goals. Formal, written

In an effective appraisal system, the performance review is a conversation which stresses the future, with the employee providing as much input as the supervisor.

Photograph by Alan Baker, courtesy of Lord Corporation.

goals may be parts of some systems; but this activity may be a subtle, everyday process of helping subordinates to think through what they have to offer and to make plans accordingly.

Employees know what is expected of them in a performance planning atmosphere. Daily "coaching" provides continual feedback. Periodically formal performance reviews are held between subordinate and supervisor. They cover the period of time since the last review, but the formal review receives secondary emphasis—secondary to the future oriented (such as goals, plans) portion of the system. The performance review takes on the mood of a session to identify and deal with objectives which have not been met if such conditions exist. Preferably the employee will identify problems and suggest solutions. Sometimes this involves mutual agreement about dealing with an undesirable situation or condition. The supervisor avoids direct criticism, fault finding, or placing blame for failure to meet objectives.

Problem solving of a disciplinary nature and wage-salary reviews should not be combined with goal-setting and performance reviews. These are topics for separate sessions. When disciplinary evaluation is necessary, be specific and direct; avoid vague suggestions and sarcasm. Evaluate behavior (performance)—not the employee, per se. Evaluation involves what the employee has done or

281

failed to do—not the kind of person he or she is. Discipline which concentrates on finding a way to change future performance is better than belittling the employee because of past performance.

These are ingredients which would be difficult for supervisors to inject into highly structured and traditional appraisal systems; but, even in those systems, these suggestions can influence individual supervisors' approaches to dealing with their subordinates. They are much easier if the organization (employer) provides the following ingredients. Many who work in highly-structured organizations may question the possibility of using this approach and label it idealistic. Some environments make this approach impossible, but that's one of the challenges of managerial positions— how does one make the workplace a more rewarding environment?

Organization-Influenced Ingredients

Successful appraisal systems depend upon administrative support from high-level management. The climate for evaluation is affected by the same factors that affect the communication climate—trust, respect, and concern for employees; honesty and integrity in dealing with all groups; and a belief that supervisors who develop their subordinates will be rewarded—not punished.

Organizational philosophy affects the climate also. Even though a system of appraisal is initiated to comply with some federal guideline, the underlying objective can be staff development and it can focus on meeting employee needs for nurture, growth, and belonging. Perhaps it is idealistic to assume that all employees want this type of treatment, but it appears that to use any other approach assumes employee laziness and a Theory X attitude, and the authors do not believe this represents today's employee.

Beyond the philosophical climate provided by the organization are some tangible ingredients which must be provided. Supervisors can't provide their own training and the instruments and procedures for implementing systems, because these should be consistent throughout the organization. All supervisors should have a thorough training in following specified appraisal procedures and administering appraisal instruments. They should be trained in interviewing and counseling techniques. They should be taught to "coach" employees—how to act and react to anticipated situations. Organization should provide for written job descriptions and employee expectations in behavioral terms. The organization should also provide the mechanics of the system, so that it will consume as little of the supervisor's time as possible. Some documentation of employee appraisal is desirable. The organization provides the system of record keeping and helps supervisors learn to use the system effectively. They should help the supervisor to work with individual subordinates in applying job descriptions and requirements to the development of mutually agreed upon goals for that individual.

Evaluation instruments, like employment tests, should be job related, reliable (consistent), valid (evaluate what they are supposed to evaluate), and standardized (applied in the same manner wherever they are used throughout the organization). The organization's overall management must provide these assurances. Individual supervisors can recommend attention to such detail, but they probably won't be in a position to control them.

Lazer's "ideal system," which is outlined in Exhibit 13.6, and Henderson's "major components", which are presented in Exhibit 13.7, summarize the ingredients of successful systems. Lazer's recommendations emphasize his "no surprise" theory and incorporate many of the ingredients recommended in this chapter. He believes that with an effective system employees expect the appraisals they get and that supervisors at all levels can, with the

---

The Ideal Appraisal System Includes:

Exhibit 13.6
Ingredients of an Ideal Performance Appraisal System

There will be an agreement between the manager and employee on the employee's job responsibilities and how the boss and employee want to work together. This understanding is the cornerstone of the whole system.

Based on the function's and department's objectives, which flow from corporate objectives, there is agreement on the employee's expected results and performance, including what is to be done, how it is to be done and an understanding of the manager's performance standards and reward criteria. It is here that dynamic top-down and bottom-up interaction occurs.

There should be an ongoing review of work progress and of the agreed-to working relationship. This is nothing more than day-to-day communication and updating of goals, objectives and priorities. Some companies formalize this into a quarterly review that becomes a performance posting or a problem-solving discussion around each objective.

The next step is the actual performance appraisal for purposes of compensation. If the first three steps have taken place, there should not be any surprises for the employee. The appraisal discussion should be objective, that is, based on the individual's results against objectives. This session should be a small piece in the total performance appraisal system; it is the day-to-day contact which is the real substance of a working relationship.

Source: I. Lazer, "Performance Appraisal: What Does the Future Hold?," *Personnel Administrator* (July 1980), p. 72. Reprinted by permission.

Exhibit 13.7
Components of a Performance Appraisal System

Major Components of a Performance Appraisal System:

1. Identifying job responsibilities and duties and performance dimensions, standards, and goals.

2. Prioritizing and weighting performance dimensions and performance goals.

3. Determining appropriate methods for appraising performance.

4. Developing suitable appraisal instruments and scoring devices.

5. Establishing procedures that enhance fair and just appraisals of all employees.

6. Providing performance feedback to all employees.

7. Relating observed and identified performance to the rewards provided by the organization.

8. Designing monitoring and auditing processes to ensure proper operation of the system and to identify areas of weakness.

9. Granting employees opportunities for appeal whenever and wherever such action is appropriate.

10. Training involved employees in all phases of the appraisal system.

Source: Richard Henderson, *Performance Appraisal: Theory to Practice* (Reston, Va.: Reston Pub. Co., 1980), pp. 8–9. Reprinted with permission, Reston Publishing Company, a Prentice-Hall Company, 11480 Sunset Hills Road, Reston, VA 22090.

aid of past performance appraisal, aid subordinates in planning their own development, career paths, and future goals.

Many business firms and other employers are beginning to build into their systems some mechanism for employee appeal. Arbiters, ombudsmen, and appeals committees offer employees third-party devices for instances where the supervisor and the subordinate disagree on evaluation or any aspect of the appraisal system. Collective bargaining arrangements have traditionally provided such mechanisms, but voluntary installation of such a procedure is less likely to kindle an adversary position between supervisors and subordinates. It is one more positive element for the climate that is so critical for organizational survival and growth.

SUMMARY

Supervisors are a vital ingredient in any appraisal system. All supervisors appraise their subordinates—informally, if not with a formal appraisal system. They are not likely to be responsible for developing systems, but they must work within such systems. A basic understanding of appraisal system history, legal implications, and issues regarding their use should make supervisors more comfortable in administering their organization's appraisal plan.

Legislation, court decisions, and development of behavior-oriented management systems have encouraged renewed interest in appraisal systems.

Early and traditional systems of employee evaluation were characterized by criteria which evaluated the nature of the individual, rather than the performance of the individual. When they did evaluate performance, they concentrated on the past and gave little opportunity for employee input. Contemporary systems emphasize forward-looking approaches, setting of goals, and plans for accomplishing expectations. They are more likely to be continuing processes than periodic exercises. Elements of both categories of systems are present in plans that are in operation today.

Appraisal techniques involve a variety of instruments and approaches, including informal interviews, checklists, rating sheets, rankings, and goal-setting techniques. Supervisors may not participate directly in the selection of appraisal systems, but they are involved in implementation of systems and should know as much as possible about issues, trends, and ingredients of systems.

QUESTIONS FOR FURTHER THOUGHT

1. Review reasons, other than the desire to provide feedback to employees, for recent interest in employee appraisal.

2. Differentiate among performance appraisal, performance review, salary review, and performance planning.

3. What is a behaviorally-oriented goal or evaluation statement? Give examples.

4. Why do employees, as a rule, oppose the use of evaluation systems?

5. As a supervisor, would you object to your superior's rating you and discussing the rating with you? Elaborate.

6. What are the three steps in a traditional, secondary review appraisal? What faults might be associated with this system?

7. Why do many authorities recommend that wage and salary review processes be separated from performance appraisal systems? Is this separation possible? Elaborate.

PART FIVE

THE SUPERVISOR'S CAREER

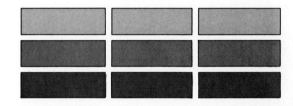

14

CAREER PATHS
FOR SUPERVISORS

**VOCABULARY
TO MASTER**

Career development
Growth mapping
Vertical promotion
Diagonal promotion
Lateral transfer
Career transition
Interrole transition
Intrarole transition
Career path
Linear
Steady-state
Spiral
Transitory
Resume
Targets
Activity evaluation quadrant

**LEARNING
OBJECTIVES**

Upon completion of this chapter and related assignments, you will be able to:

1. Outline a personal philosophy of employment success.
2. Identify the values of planning career moves.
3. Anticipate the possible impact of career transitions and identify possible adjustments that transitions require.
4. Differentiate between self-directed career development and employer-assisted career development.
5. Develop your own three- and five-year career plans.
6. Identify the possible elements of a formal career development program.

CHAPTER OUTLINE

PROBLEM STATEMENT

BACKGROUND AND THEORY

GROWTH MAPPING

    A Philosophy of Career Planning

    Value of Planning

    Career Options

RESEARCH AND PRACTICE

IMPACT OF CAREER TRANSITIONS

    Preparations for Transition

    Changes in Role

    Adjustments to Functional Changes

IMPLICATIONS AND APPLICATIONS

ALTERNATIVE PLANS TO CAREER DEVELOPMENT

    Self-Directed Plans

        Self-Appraisal

        Opportunity Appraisal

        Coordinate Self-Appraisal

        and Opportunity Appraisal

    Formal Plans

        Formal Program Elements

        Employee Self-Appraisal

        Targets and Paths

        Preparation

        Orchestration

SUMMARY

QUESTIONS FOR FURTHER THOUGHT

PROBLEM STATEMENT

career development
planning one's employ-
ment future

growth mapping iden-
tification of possible
career changes; planning
experiences to achieve
goals

Career development is planning for the future. This primarily rests upon the shoulders of the individual who must define the directions, jobs, paths, and learning experiences that will complement desired employment changes. Supervisory management is a position from which individuals often expect to move into middle management positions. The organization can facilitate career development by outlining the potential moves; however, the individual frequently must take the initiative in selecting alternatives and seeking paths to these alternatives. This **growth mapping** process entails a view of the future in terms of one's own skills and interests and the jobs likely to complement and challenge the individual.

BACKGROUND AND THEORY

GROWTH MAPPING

The process that we call growth mapping (career planning) can be discussed from several perspectives. Of course, every worker is interested in his or her own career. Some people plan careers methodically; others just let them happen. Regardless, one approach to career planning can direct attention to individuals as they plan their own careers. A second approach can examine career planning as a personnel service within organizations.

In increasing numbers organizations are offering formal *career development* programs for employees. Career development is different from training programs, which attempt to better prepare workers for the jobs they are in or, in the case of initial training, to find a niche for new employees. Career development as a formal employee service includes long-range plans and may involve planned or potential job changes.

A discussion of career development could involve a description of desirable elements of formal programs, suggestions for the administration of such programs, or issues surrounding programs and trends. Our approach concentrates on the first two items. Because students of supervisory management are not likely to be in positions that would require or permit them to create career development programs for others or to significantly alter existing programs, this approach emphasizes the supervisor's own career planning. This chapter contains material that should help you to analyze your own desires about the future and to begin serious planning for that future. It also discusses formal career development programs.

Your approach to career planning will be greatly affected by your current status. If you are a practicing supervisor or an employee who hopes to land a supervisory position, your current employer may have a formal plan or at least some informal assistance for helping you to chart a future with the organization. If you are a full-time student and are not currently employed, you have greater choices; but the variety of directions available and the scarcity of jobs that fit your "mold" may be frustrating. Don't assume that lifetime career plans are absolutely essential or that they are fixed in early jobs. However, serious thinking about general directions and the nature of the work you want to do should make for smoother sailing in the future.

Popular motivational programs and one-shot speakers who use hype to get people aroused to their own potentials (and leave town) create the impression that anybody can do anything. Further, they leave the impression that one who does not have grandiose plans for personal "accomplishment" is lacking in personal initiative. While anything that improves our self-esteem may give us courage to do the things we have wanted to do, excessive determination to "succeed" may drive us into endeavors which do not fit reasonable criteria for success.

A Philosophy of Career Planning

The best career is the one that will match your skills, interests, and expectations. The answer to successful early career planning is the foresight to know what will bring job satisfaction in the future. How will you measure success for yourself? For too many college students the answer to this question tends toward one of two extremes. At one extreme such motivators as money, prestige, and status (whether or not these are conscious motivators) dominate the thinking of students. At the other extreme is the group that refuses to make any plans for the future. This group concentrates on what they *don't* want to do—not on planning for the future. They don't want to be like some segment of society which has turned them off or rejected them.

If you can escape the notion that your future must fit a mold that has been sculptured by others (parents, friends, teachers, spouses, children, or mentors), you are more likely to plan a successful (satisfying) career. Define success for yourself, then seek it. Although we believe it extremely naive to suggest that you can be *anything* that you wish to be or do anything that you wish to do, there is very little chance that you will achieve something that you don't attempt. Serendipity is a scarce commodity.

On the assumption that you will not sit around waiting for success to fall into your lap, career planning will be discussed from the following perspective. We are assuming the supervisory level; you are now a supervisor—what next? We will present career planning under two sets of assumed circumstances: 1) you are charting your own course for the future, taking advantage of any employer assistance which may come your way, or 2) you are participating in some employer-sponsored career development program.

The American economic system was founded upon the basis of individuals supporting themselves to the best of their abilities. If you can accept the responsibility for your own destiny, you can define success for yourself and plan a career that will achieve it.

Although you must provide your own philosophy, you might find aid in a professional career development specialist's ideas about success. John Leach, a career consultant and director of career studies at the University of Chicago's Human Resources Center, identifies four elements of a work experience that he believes generate the feeling and perception of success: belonging, growth, self-esteem, and personal significance.[1] Leach offers these observations after a four-year career studies project. "Employees need to be able to identify with the groups in which they work and to feel a part of the organization. The career plan should enable the employee to grow and to contribute. We feel better about our working lives if we perceive jobs as useful." Collectively, Leach believes, these elements of career success bring about the fourth element—personal significance. "Everyone is looking for that piece of turf that is theirs and no one else's. Everybody wants to be a 'somebody.' Fortunately, because people are different, everyone's definition of 'somebody' is relatively different. Herein lies the key to career planning. What kind of career will make you feel that you are the 'somebody' that you want to be?"

Keep in mind that mobility and ladder climbing need not, necessarily, be a part of career planning. There isn't enough room at the top for everyone. Level of management isn't necessarily the measure of success either. Many people would not enjoy the challenges and the pressures that high-level positions bring; others thrive on such pressures. Likewise, do not assume that financial success is dependent upon "getting ahead" or prestigious jobs. Personal financial success can be managed apart from or in addition to the income generated by salaried employment. (Assuming

---

[1]John Leach, "The Career Planning Process," *Personnel Journal* (April 1981), p. 283.

"reasonable" definitions of success, of course). For some people, success and personal growth may come from development of a current position, through assuming additional duties or responsibilities, or by pursuing an avocation.

Value of Planning

Because many supervisors observe colleagues' and friends' careers developing "by accident," they may lack an appreciation for the value of career planning. Why not just do your best in your current job and wait for opportunities to present themselves? Career advancements that appear to have come about by chance may have been more carefully planned than the casual observer can detect. The supervisor who took advantage of a training program, a college course, or a seminar series—even though there was no apparent need for such training, may have been the "natural" choice for a promotion, while those who were waiting for opportunity to assert itself were left waiting still longer. Whether you are a practicing supervisor, a supervisor trainee, or a student, some serious thought about your future and, at least, the general directions it might take will enable you to chart the course for that future. When opportunities appear, you will have a set of criteria against which to measure them. Even if you decide to reject an option you will feel better if you did so with full information about whether or not it would have offered you what you wanted at a particular time.

There is probably no need for students and young employees to map an entire career, but they should begin identifying strengths and interests and cataloging these for future application. Because firms are beginning to recognize that career development activities are desirable and profitable, employees who have made preliminary career plans are in a better position to participate in formal programs that might be offered. Career planning without the aid of the employer is possible, but it is more meaningful when there is a cooperative and supportive employer and preferably some formal program.

Career Options

As a basis for developing a career plan, a supervisor should consider the several options available. These are summarized below and discussed in the paragraphs that follow.

vertical promotion *movement to a higher level position within current unit*

diagonal promotion *movement to a higher level position in another unit*

lateral transfer *job change to another unit but at same level*

vertical promotion by current employer

diagonal promotion by current employer

lateral transfer with current employer

transfer to a similar position with another employer

transfer to a position with another employer that represents a promotion to a higher-level position

transfer to a position with another employer that represents a diagonal change in level and job nature

other changes (such as moves to lower positions)

Vertical promotions are considered to be within the same discipline, technical area, or type of work. The supervisor who experiences such a promotion usually moves from first-line supervision to a middle management position in the same area of specialization. *Lateral changes* (sometimes called horizontal) may involve changing one's area of specialization to a related or different area. Individuals may purposefully seek such changes because they open up new career possibilities which might not have been available if they had waited for vertical moves to become available. *Diagonal moves* represent a higher level and a different specialty. Of course, many people change employers frequently. Such moves may involve similar work with a different employer, a higher position in the same specialty or a change in both the level and the specialization. Moves which involve both a new employer and a new specialization may offer difficult and frustrating adjustments.

Career changes and career plans may not involve any of the above changes. Those currently working as supervisors may seek employment in jobs which do not involve direct supervision of other employees. Some may even elect demotion because they do not enjoy supervision or the options available from the current position. Many staff jobs which do not require supervision of large numbers of people may be preferable. All of these are options and should not be ignored. Another option for career planning is no move at all. Twentieth century values have so ingrained "getting ahead" into society's thinking that it has made that term synonymous with success. Success may be staying where a person is and making the job the most effective position that it can be. As stated earlier in this chapter, every person must define success and seek it. If that definition includes changes which create different and challenging situations, many options for finding such challenges are available.

RESEARCH
AND
PRACTICE

career transition *a
significant change in em-
ployment status or
condition*

IMPACT OF CAREER TRANSITIONS

Career planning can prepare an individual for the impact of the transitions that will almost surely occur in any field of employment—particularly if the person is already in a supervisory position. **Career transition** means some important change in one's career; this does not necessarily mean a new or different job. Research reveals that job changing is becoming more prevalent, more accepted, and more expected than in the past. People are no longer considered restless and unstable just because they want to change jobs. Nevertheless, changes produce stress for individuals and their families.

Preparation for Transition

The rate at which life-style change is taking place today and the indication that future changes will come even more rapidly creates a need for workers at all levels to consider the impact of such changes on their working and personal lives. Whether or not job changes are anticipated, other changes are sure to occur in most working environments as a result of changing technologies and changing life styles.

There is every indication that technologies already developed and nearing widespread application (particularly computer, communication, and information handling technologies) may drastically alter our working environments, the nature of our responsibilities, and our life style. Instant communication, information handling networks, and satellite transmission of information may make it possible for organizations to function from dispersed physical locations without the barriers that are currently encountered by multilocation facilities. At-home jobs, neighborhood "departments," and supervisors who never see their subordinates "live" are just a few of the changes that may come about. Add to these the responsibilities of a new job, and you have a frustrating situation. Frustrating, but certainly not unsurmountable. And the rewards of increased productivity and effectiveness may be far greater than the cost in frustration. The implication is that everyone must prepare for change—whether or not change is built into one's career plans.

Changes in Role

Some transitions involve changes within existing roles. Examples are the assumption of an additional responsibility, an adjustment

295

outside the working environment (family, or spouse employment), and passage through various career and life stages. Changes in the degree of importance placed upon individual careers by employers may occur without the individual knowing it. Changes within existing roles can be anticipated, but they are not specifically planned.

interrole transition
employment changes
involving major role
changes

intrarole transition
changes which affect
one's employment without
role change

Planned changes may be viewed within the context of the role change involved. Louis discusses several **interrole transitions** and compares them with the above **intrarole transitions**.[2] Louis' research revealed five such interrole changes which may be anticipated and planned:

entering or re-entering the labor pool

assuming a different role within one organization

moving from one organization to another

changing from one profession (discipline or specialization) to another

leaving the labor pool

Every role change brings adjustments, some of which are expected. To the extent possible, supervisors who anticipate role changes should expect and prepare for confusing and frustrating situations. If these are anticipated, they are easier to handle. Without the comfort that comes from complete knowledge of people, their predicaments, and the procedures they follow, we sometimes misinterpret actions and intentions. People in new environments and new roles should refrain from snap judgments of people and their motives. Actions and reactions which seem unacceptable to newcomers may appear perfectly logical once full information is available. Expect a change to create the need for special adjustments, watch for the needed adjustments, and the transition will be smoother. Likewise, when you work with others who have experienced transition, remember their plight and help them to adjust.

Adjustments to Functional Changes

"Costs" of promotion from supervisor to middle management may take the form of sacrifices. Even though monetary reward should

---

[2]Meryl Reis Louis, "Toward an Understanding of Career Transitions," *Work, Family, and the Career: New Frontiers in Theory and Research* (New York: Praegar Publishers, 1980), pp. 200–218.

improve, promoted individuals should expect to spend more time on the job, to experience less routine and more uncertainty, and to have less time available for away-from-the-job activities. Careful time management may be necessary to cope with the demands of a more responsible job. Just as the change from worker to supervisor involves adjustments, promotion to other positions may require greater delegation and more dependence upon others. The "do it yourself if you want it done right" adage becomes less and less possible as more responsible jobs are assumed.

Middle managers perform the same functions as other managers, including supervisors. However, the proportion of time devoted to each function will likely change. Exhibit 14.1 compares the proportion of time spent in various managerial functions at supervisory and middle management levels. Middle managers spend considerably less time in the function of directing because they have lost the direct contact with operatives. Instead of directing the work of others, they are likely to spend greater amounts of time planning, organizing, and leading, and about the same proportion controlling. Duties and specific responsibilities will change accordingly. "Paperwork" and reporting activities are likely to increase.

Involvement with other employees' career plans also represents a change, even though supervisors are somewhat involved in the careers of subordinates. Employee appraisal and counseling sessions offer opportunities for supervisors to identify promotable subordinates. This opportunity for assisting others in career development will increase in middle management positions, because middle managers' subordinates are supervisors; and many of them will have definite ambitions for the future.

IMPLICATIONS AND APPLICATIONS

ALTERNATIVE PLANS TO CAREER DEVELOPMENT

Tradition has set the responsibility for career planning and development squarely on the shoulders of the individual. Career planning and "getting ahead" have been synonymous. "Career" was the working part of one's life and was separate and distinct from other parts of life. For some, there were few other facets to their lives.

Current definitions of *career* adapt a broader view that includes, in addition to the working life, relevant life aspects not directly associated with the job; for example, family, private life activities, multicareer households, and general life style. With this new definition of career has come organizational involvement

Exhibit 14.1
**Proportion of Time
Devoted to Basic
Management Functions
by Supervisors
and Middle Managers**

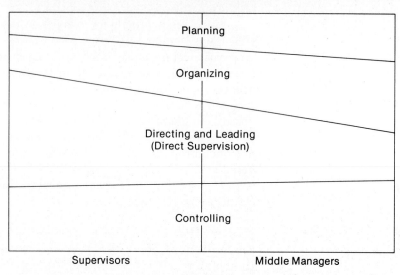

in career planning and development. Organizations now operate career development programs which are formal portions of the personnel management function in the organization. The leaders of such organizations recognize the value of retaining valuable employees and the effect of assistance in career charting to accomplishing retention. Programs exist in a variety of stages, ranging from "paper" programs which offer very little real assistance to complex systems of counseling, self-analysis, target setting, and selection processes.

Whether you plan your own career independently of your employer or take advantage of career planning services available to you, many of the steps involved will be similar. Because of the probability that many individuals will not have the benefit of employer-assisted planning, the following materials suggest a framework for individual career planning.

Both approaches to career development (self-directed and employer-directed) involve three basic steps:

1. Appraise yourself.
   Interests
   Skills

2. Appraise career opportunities.
   Present organization
   Outside organizations

3. Coordinate self-appraisal, career opportunities, and career plans.
   Personal program
   Organization program

Self-Directed Plans

Self-Appraisal As discussed in another chapter, th Window represents the "arenas" of your existence—those characteristics which are known to others and to you, th are known to others but not to you, those which are kno but not to others, and those which are unknown to y others. Self-appraisal in preparation for career plannir take a serious look at all of these arenas—particularly th ities which you know that you have but are unknown Likewise, don't ignore the possibility of unknown quali may have skills and talents that you don't realize.

Local colleges or universities usually have testing that may be an aid in this area. Of specific help might be inventories and achievement test batteries. Interest attempt to compare your likes and dislikes with those viduals who are successful in specific fields of work. Achi tests may identify skills which you possess for specific tions—skills that were previously not considered.

With the precaution that you be honest with yourself you think positively about your own capabilities, self-app the following areas should provide a realistic backdrop fc plans. Written statements about these factors are pre What are your preferences with regard to a job? What a interests, your values, your skills? List your strengths as and as an employee. List the weaknesses which need at Don't dwell on your weaknesses (some would say that you not even bother to identify them), but a realistic view c things that can be improved—particularly as you plan fc demanding jobs, is healthy.

State three- and five-year career goals as specifically a ble. List your past experiences (job duties, responsibilities required) which qualify you for that first goal. Groupir experiences according to the nature of the activity may be h If available, past performance appraisals by superiors ma you to evaluate yourself realistically.

If you are a student, do not assume that you have had n valuable experience. In what student organizations have yo a member? If you held offices or important committee a

ments, what were the responsibilities? What part-time or volunteer work experiences have you completed? List past work experiences (full-time, part-time, volunteer) by employer, job title, responsibilities, and skills required.

Michael Driver's research at the University of California at Los Angeles has utilized four distinct **career paths** that might help to categorize your own style.[3] They are linear, steady-state, spiral, and transitory. Based on research in 1,000 firms, Driver's four personality profiles with regard to career paths are described as follows. The **linear** path represents climbers—people who are aggressive, energetic, confident, highly competitive, and desire achievement, power, and wealth. **Steady-states** are interested in a single discipline or employment area; they want clearly-defined jobs. Steady-states are more concerned with security in the job than upward mobility; they strive to perfect their performance in a job. **Spirals** are capable of turning their energies and talents to several disciplines at once, but "they don't tend to mesh well in organizations that have elaborate rules." **Transitory** types are divided into two categories: one subgroup within this category is motivated essentially by challenge. They will become bored if the challenges don't persist. Once things are running smoothly, they move on to a new job. The second subgroup changes jobs frequently, but for a different reason. They have low self-esteem, little energy, and lack self-direction. They job hop in search of the right niche.

Opportunity Appraisal Begin appraising the opportunities available by considering your current employer or prospective employers. If the employer is a private business, investigate the industry in which it operates. What are the employer's stated objectives? Examine trends in their volume of business, size of operating budget, revenues, profits, turnover of employees, turnover of management-level personnel. Are changes expected (mergers, product introductions, new facilities, expanded operations)? How does the employer's status compare to the industry as a whole?

A little library research may give some clues about the future of the industry and the firm for which you work if it is a large or

----

reer path the stages
one's employment life
route to ultimate goal

near career path of one
ho seeks advancement,
aggressive, confident
eady-state a career
th of one interested in
single discipline con-
rned about job security

piral career path of one
pable of attending to
veral disciplines at one
me
ansitory career path
sociated with one who
anges jobs and/or em-
oyers frequently

----

[3]Michael Driver, quoted from *American Way* (September 1980), in "Research Spotlight," *Management Review* (January 1981), p. 57.

national organization.[4] Firms and industries that are in their early lives are more likely to offer advancement opportunities than those which have progressed to declining status or old age.

If your current or prospective employer is a government agency, what is the track record for that agency? What determines their funding levels? What is their reputation for efficiency? How vulnerable are they to budget reductions or changes in national politics?

Sources of information about current employers and the opportunities that exist within those organizations are: the organization chart, job descriptions, job specifications, and manuals of policy and procedure. How many jobs exist for which you can qualify? What do the jobs involve? What skills do you already have which qualify you for those jobs? What training and additional skills must you acquire? Who currently occupies each of those positions? What are their ages and ambitions? The chances for promotion within a single organization may be a simple problem of arithmetic. Each higher rung on the chart involves fewer spaces.

Discuss career planning with the personnel department and, with caution, with your supervisor. Be aware that personnel departments, in many cases, may themselves discuss some of your plans with your supervisor. Also, some supervisors feel threatened by subordinates who talk of career plans, because the supervisors assume that the subordinates have an eye on the supervisor's job. If they are good supervisors, however, they too will have plans and they will expect others to have plans. If their plans do not involve a move from their current positions, they should be actively involved in helping capable subordinates to prepare for moves to other areas. Seeking a superior's assistance in career planning, however, must depend upon your interpretation of that person's ability to deal with the fact that you want to plan your future. In all cases, use tact, judgment and discretion in these discussions.

Future plans may include the possibility of a change to another employer or you may be a student seeking your first permanent employment. If so, consider some additional factors. Assuming that you seek employment in the specialty in which you are now employed or in which you are studying, identify any geographical restrictions which would affect your accepting a job. Then identify firms within the desired geographical designation

---

[4]See *Standard and Poor's Industry Surveys* for industry data and *Moody's Manuals* or other corporate information services for data about individual corporate firms.

that employ persons with your qualifications. Again, the local library can help. Are there other restrictions which you would apply to any opportunity? Salary? Job pressures? Travel?

resume description of personal qualifications for prospective employers

Job seeking strategies involve the preparation of personal data sheets (**resumes**) which outline educational experiences, work experience, and other growth activities and, sometimes, names of people who can evaluate your qualifications. Such a document may be requested in addition to the completion of a formal application for employment. The appendix contains two sample data sheets to guide your preparation. Even if a prospective employer does not request a data sheet, providing a quality document which outlines your qualifications will be helpful for those who consider your application. It might be the factor which separates you from other similarly-qualified applicants. The quality must be impeccable, however.

During the interview with prospective employers, check on such things as career development plans, opportunities through job posting and training programs, transfer and promotion policies, and education assistance programs. Not only are these equally important to salary and fringe benefit packages, but they also signal prospective employers that you are thinking beyond the immediate future. Written descriptions of such programs are preferable to oral discussions.

Coordinate Self-Appraisal and Opportunity Appraisal Once you have completed your self-appraisal and opportunity appraisal, you can identify *targets*—positions for which you may wish to prepare. You should probably identify several targets at various levels. Identify typical paths to the target positions. How long should you expect to stay at each level, each position?

targets employment positions to which one aspires

What are the needed skills in the target positions? Which of these skills do you already have? Which will require additional training? Is there related general knowledge that would aid your movement into these positions? Knowledge of computer technology, studies that will aid understanding of people and their behaviors, and training that improves oral and written communication skills are sure to be valuable in most middle management positions.

activity evaluation quadrant matrix of past experiences

Preparation of an **activity evaluation quadrant** may assist in matching your self-appraisal with job opportunities.[5] A sample

---

[5]Based on a matrix presented by G. Rowland Phare in "Career Planning: A Do-It-Yourself Approach," *Managerial Planning* (July-August 1980), p. 39.

Exhibit 14.2
**Activity Evaluation
Quadrant**

	Activities Liked	**Activities Not Liked**
Activities Which I Consider To Be Personal Achievements	A	B
Activities Which I Consider To Be Nonachievements	C	D

is given in Exhibit 14.2. Begin by making a list of the things that you have done that you would consider memorable activities. Where you have been, what you have done, activities which have interested you most, accomplishments, travels, sports, jobs. As you list them, categorize them into achievements and nonachievements. List each achievement that you liked in the "A" quad, the achievements that you did not like in the "B" quad, the nonachievements that you liked in the "C" quad, and so on. Investigate job opportunities related to the things which you have recorded in the "A" quadrant.

Coordination plans should include such activities as membership in professional associations, participation in available seminars and workshops, and completion of additional college work that would fill gaps in your preparation. A steady program of professional reading and specific plans for correcting any recognized weaknesses or deficiencies will further prepare you.

Answers to these questions should enable you to prepare those three- and five-year plans mentioned earlier. The number of changes anticipated for the next five years may be less important than the nature of your growth and development during those years. One, two, or no changes may be involved. If your plan will bring growth, and feelings of belonging, self-esteem, and personal significance, your chances for success, as you define it, are great.

Formal Plans

Programs that are labeled "career development" can involve elaborate and complex systems and represent a genuine concern for serving the growth and future needs of employees. On the other hand, informal, haphazard and unplanned attempts to find a niche for more aggressive employees, while ignoring others, may also be labeled "career development" or "employee development." Employees in organizations which fit the latter descriptions would do better to follow the suggestions in the earlier portions of this chapter and make their own plans.

The following description of a formal program represents the authors' interpretation of a desirable program. Factors which affect the success of any employee service would also affect this one: climate, top-level support, carefully-considered objectives, adequate planning, and specific responsibility for the program. Beverly L. Kaye presents a convincing argument for considering career development efforts as the integrating force that can weld together other employee services.[6] Without integration, such services as training, promotional planning, personnel audits and forecasts, job posting, performance appraisal, and the preparation of job descriptions, job specifications, and organization charts are carried out independently.

Viewed as an integrating force, career development can become a part of the total management picture, rather than still another independently-operating program. It is meshed with overall organizational objectives and visible enough that every employee knows of its existence and availability.

Obviously, larger organizations offer more opportunity for growth and development through job changes than do small organizations. If growth is to come from upward movement, simple arithmetic may point out the futility of planning such moves in some organizations. Formal programs can exist in small organizations, but growth in such firms is likely to come in the breadth of responsibility rather than through job changes.

Formal Program Elements Some elements of a formal program are similar to the previously-described elements of a self-directed plan. Those will be treated briefly here. Other elements, which can exist only in formal programs, are discussed more thoroughly.

---

[6]Beverly L. Kaye. "Career Development: The Integrating Force," *Training and Development Journal* (May 1981), p. 37.

Career development programs offer employees the opportunity to complete in-house training programs, courses, and institutes. Completion of such formal studies contributes to the supervisor's promotability.

Photograph by Alan Baker, courtesy of Lord Corporation.

Career development is a service and as such is usually offered to those who volunteer to participate. Careful planning goes into the establishment of such a program. Its availability and nature may be explained in meetings for employees who meet basic requirements for participation.

Employee Self-Appraisal Employees who participate are assisted in a self-appraisal of interests, talents, experiences, values, and ambitions. Materials are developed or purchased for assisting employees in this activity. Rather elaborate sets of programmed self-evaluation materials or notebooks may be completed by employees and/or supervisors. The results are used to form an employee profile. Meetings, workshops, or in-house career planning seminars may be parts of this process.

Targets and Paths Employees, with the help of program directors or professional counselors, select targets—positions for which they are prepared or for which they wish to become prepared.

Because of the uncertainty of future vacancies and timing, several alternatives may be selected. They may involve vertical, horizontal, and diagonal moves within an organizational unit. Lateral moves may be encouraged in order to provide a breadth of understanding for future assignments. Rough time tables for such potential moves may be worked out.

Some bold plans may include moves to other divisions of an organization or to a different employer. Many organization executives are not comfortable with the knowledge that an employee includes as a part of his or her formal plan a move to another employer. Admission that such moves are possible and probable, particularly when inside paths don't open up, is merely a recognition of reality. Although there is no need for employees to pretend that they are permanently attached to an organization, they should avoid antagonizing management by threatening to seek employment elsewhere. Naturally, organization managers hope to attract and keep promising employees, and career development is one factor that might keep employees from "jumping" to other organizations. It should be noted that the tendency to change employers frequently is greater in the Western culture than in other parts of the world.

Preparation Employees must prepare themselves for their potential changes. The authors continue to stress that word *potential*. Formal programs do not promise participants that they can take other people's jobs. Rather, they develop potential candidates for positions which might become available. While some vacancies can be anticipated through retirement, recent changes in mandatory retirement laws make predictions more difficult.

Preparation may be totally provided by the organization or financed by the organization through some outside agency. The range of developmental activities includes in-house seminars, classes, work experience, and outside activities such as college courses, institutes, and workshops. Training is expensive; therefore, employees are selected carefully.

Orchestration Coordinating a group of employees, all with plans for job changes, is no small feat. Elaborate mechanisms may be developed to inform employees about available jobs and their requirements. Job posting, not only immediately-available jobs, but also future vacancies, is a communication task of the program. Identification and publication of job requirements, "ladders" to

The supervisor's professional development will cut across many topic areas, such as ethics, finance and budgeting, psychology, and communication.

Photograph by Alan Baker.

certain jobs, and experience/preparation requirements make employees aware of opportunities.

What happens when an employee selects a target, prepares for a job change, and then is not selected for the position? Without counseling for such employees, the program could actually be counter-productive.

Coordination of formal programs must assure that all managers, including supervisors, are fully aware of program elements and procedures. They must understand the philosophy and objectives of the programs, the mechanics of the system, the role of departmental and unit managers, and the services which the program provides.

SUMMARY

Career development is a growth mapping, planning activity for one's future employment. The process may involve a self-directed program or one provided as a service by your employer.

Individual interests and preferences in work and careers vary greatly and significantly influence career plans. Every supervisor should think through his or her own career planning philosophy. This philosophy will form the basis for either a personal career planning process or participation in an employer-sponsored activity.

Multiple options for career moves are possible for supervisors. They involve vertical, lateral, and horizontal moves with the current employer or similar moves with a different employer. Career progress may depend upon specific preparation such as training programs, special education, and identified work experience.

Career changes involve transitions in the nature of work performed and should be anticipated in the planning process. While some of the changes experienced may be temporarily stressful, careful planning will lessen the impact of such experiences.

Self-directed and employer-sponsored career planning usually involve three facets: self-appraisal, opportunity assessment, and coordination of individual talents and expectations with available positions. Counseling centers and interest-appraisal instruments may be helpful in the self-appraisal phase.

Many employer-sponsored programs of career development are inadequate and poorly managed, but supervisors should accept opportunities to participate in such programs. There will always be some uncertainty involved in the long-range formal plan, and such plans may cover several years and extensive training and other learning experiences. Good formal programs make all employees aware of the existence and nature of program elements.

QUESTIONS FOR FURTHER THOUGHT

1. What is career planning and how important is it for supervisors?

2. What are Leach's four elements of a work experience that affect the "success" of the individual who encounters that experience? Name and briefly discuss what you think each element means.

3. Is there a difference between the feeling and the perception of success? Is it possible that identical experiences for two supervisors can be successful for one and unsuccessful for the other?

4. To what extent should career planning involve changes from one job to another and from one employer to another?

5. Identify and discuss at least six options available for career paths.

6. In what ways is the working environment changing? How will these changes affect your future? What environmental changes will be involved in job changes?

7. Contrast the role of a supervisor with the role of a middle manager; describe the probable differences in the quantity of time devoted to various managerial functions in the two roles. What other differences might be expected by one who moves from supervisor to middle manager?

8. What is the difference between *interrole* and *intrarole* transitions? Are both involved in career planning?

9. Is *career* limited to your working life? Discuss.

10. What are the three basic steps to a self-directed career development plan?

11. Differentiate among linear, steady-state, spiral, and transitory career paths. In your opinion, do these categories adequately represent real-life situations? Can you think of people who fit into the various categories?

12. What questions would you ask about a potential employer who is a private company—as a part of your career planning process?

13. Is it true that there are few differences (except salary) among the various government jobs, since all government agencies are subject to controls? Discuss.

14. What is a source of assistance for self-appraisal during the career planning process?

15

THE FLEXIBLE SUPERVISOR: PROBLEMS AND CASES

CHAPTER OUTLINE

PROBLEMS AND CASES
YOUR RELATIONSHIP WITH THE BOSS
IDEATION PROBLEM SOLVING
USING QUANTITATIVE DATA
ELECTRONIC INFORMATION SYSTEMS

DEALING WITH
EVERYDAY PROBLEMS
CASE STUDY: CODE OF ETHICS
CASE STUDY: THE SPECIALISTS
CASE STUDY: OLD FRIENDS
CASE STUDY: THE CHRISTMAS "PRESENT"
CASE STUDY: ALICE IN COUNSELING LAND
CASE STUDY: THE DISCONTENT OF WINTER
CASE STUDY: BATTLE FATIGUE

CASES IN ARBITRATING
SUPERVISOR/EMPLOYEE CONFLICT
CASE STUDY: DISCRIMINATING EMPLOYER
CASE STUDY: LOST SENIORITY
CASE STUDY: EMERGENCY MANDATORY OVERTIME
CASE STUDY: THE UNQUALIFIED QUALIFIED APPLICANT
CASE STUDY: MISCONSTRUED DIRECTIVE
CASE STUDY: PREVENTIVE ABSENCE
CASE STUDY: HOW WORK-MEASUREMENT CAN CONTROL COSTS
CASE STUDY: GUARDING THE NEST

PROBLEMS AND CASES

Throughout this book we have developed various supervision related topics from the perspective of an idealistic setting or something close to that. You know as well as we do that ideal situations seldom exist in any organization. As you plan for success in your current or potential position, there are at least four specific areas that need to be considered from a realistic, practical point of view. These are factors that will prepare you for promotion to the positions discussed in Chapter Fourteen. The four areas are: a realistic relationship with your superior, an ideas-orientation to problem solving, an appreciation for quantitative data and electronic information systems, and the ability to handle the routine, unpredictable problems that do not fit neatly into previous chapters of this book.

Proficiency in the above areas will make you promotable. The following pages present discussions of the first three categories, and the collection of cases at the end will provide realistic experiences in dealing with the fourth category. No theory or practice or approach, applied individually and separately, will accomplish much. Hopefully, we have provided the foundation for success; however, this final section provides some realistic directions in which you may go to add quality and promotability to your credentials. These suggestions may involve extra study for you; or at least, they may require a different orientation.

Consider them carefully.

YOUR RELATIONSHIP WITH THE BOSS

Each of us must realize that the individual for whom we work is likely to be anything but perfect. In addition, all superiors have styles of management that reflect their own interests, beliefs, expectations, and attitudes. Many of these characteristics may not coincide with your own. This is sure to set the stage for conflict somewhere along the way. Our suggestion is that you be patient and adjust your expectations accordingly. In a survey of 242 companies, researchers found the major problem with 1981 college graduates was their unrealistic expectations about promotion, job content, and salary.[1] They were highly impatient. The next most mentioned problem was "poor communication skills."

---

[1]American Council on Education, "The 1982 Endicott Report," *Higher Education and National Affairs*, December 18, 1981, p. 3.

In today's organizations, you will not make progress with little effort and limited patience. Short term reward systems are a function of the overall system, but most directly they are a function of your immediate superior. If your superior is the hard autocrat or is very conservative, you simply need to bide your time and develop skills to circumvent the obstacles. There are few totally desirable supervisory jobs. You must adjust to the specific situations in which you find yourself, develop skills for advancement, and be patient with the system. Delayed rewards for your efforts may be sweeter than the rewards of immediate advancement, especially advancement while you are still developing appropriate skills. With this orientation in mind, consider the following skill areas that you might develop not only to improve your position with your current boss, but also to prepare for advancement to better positions.

IDEATION PROBLEM SOLVING

There is no doubt that we all arrive at conclusions about reality in the same general way. However, each of us processes the information in ways that are uniquely our own. Some of us think in a quantitative fashion, others only in a verbal fashion, others in terms of concrete objects that are before us, others in terms of pictures, and yet others only in terms that are consistent with our compartmentalized belief systems. What we would suggest to you, the supervisor who is seeking advancement, is that you learn to think in problem-solving terms.

One group of management theorists maintains that the basic underlying function of management is to ask the right questions.[2] That does not suggest that one should ask questions just for the sake of asking. Rather, you need to seek the underlying questions that might make a difference. To do this, you must learn to think in an "if-then" criteria assignment process. If-then requires the creation of hypotheses of possible outcomes which are dependent upon a variety of possible interactions. The "if" conditions must be met before a particular outcome can be expected. This type of speculation with information requires movement from the concrete—what is tangible and before you—to a future orientation which considers outcomes that would result if conditions were changed.

---

[2]Thomas J. Peters, "Management Systems: The Language of Organizational Character and Competence," *Organizational Dynamics* (Summer 1980), pp. 3–26.

Most of us can learn to think in if-then terms; and if you are diligent in efforts to master this style of thinking, the outcome might be surprising. We would label if-then thinking "Evaluation Ideation." This process, as we envision it, is described in Chapter 12, page 259. A verbal representation, such as this one, does not adequately describe the process of thinking about complex situations. At first, you may have difficulty in concluding that outcome *abd* will result in conditions *xyz*. However, attempts to solve problems within the work setting in such a fashion or a similar fashion will improve your skill. Many techniques have been suggested, and many organizations conduct training seminars to develop insight thinking, imagery thinking in the right side of the brain, and problem-solving skills. The final portion of this epilogue contains case studies and problems typical of those encountered by supervisors every day. You might try the evaluation ideation model for the solving of these problems.

USING QUANTITATIVE DATA

There is no question that the educational system in the United States has fallen short of providing adequate classroom experience in science and quantitative education. Science literacy is a major problem area and is a contributor to the lack of communication skills identified in the 1982 Endicott Report. Skills in understanding numbers (quantitative data) are attainable by most of us; and if the supervisor wants to advance, such skills are a must.

A recent article in a major training journal addressed the issue of researching the outcomes of training and development programs. Not only was there a discussion of management's need to know what the data indicated, but also an attempt to explain what constitutes a meaningful difference in accomplishment among groups of trainees. These differences were described in quantitative terms (numbers).[3] Interpretation of that information requires a basic understanding of statistical description and analysis techniques. These techniques should not frighten the novice; rather, they should be viewed as just one more task to be mastered. Supervisors who are bright and capable people are frequently frightened by quantitative analysis, because they have had little exposure to such analysis or their exposure has been unpleasant or frustrating.

---

[3]Kenneth Hargin and John H. Zenger, "Assessing Training Results: It's Time to Take the Plunge," *Training and Development Journal* (January 1982), pp. 11–16.

Data are the backbone for rational decisions, but understanding data relationships requires some basic and formal concepts about how numbers are treated statistically. These formal concepts can be self-taught or learned from formal training programs or in college courses. The accumulation of quantitative data is now easy with the aid of computers, but the data are of little value unless the standard methods for displaying the data are easily understood by those who can benefit from the data. This is the whole point of this discussion; these methods and techniques are easily obtained and are going to be more and more necessary for management at every level.

The promotable supervisor must understand and use data in at least three areas. One is the standard methods used to display quantitative information such as graphics (charts, graphs, tables, etc.), proportional relationships, sample distributions, and basic descriptive statistics. A second area includes standard indicators that imply relationships (correlations) among conditions or factors. Examples of such indicators are correlation coefficients and trend line analyses. The third is the area of statistical analysis that allows you to conclude that there are actual differences between or among groups of items, individuals or samples.

The use of computers to process and analyze the data at our disposal has greatly enhanced the use of statistics in making business decisions. Analysis that would have consumed weeks of manual tabulation and calculation without them can now be processed in minutes (after the data are entered into the system). The ease of application has also created some problems. Batches of irrelevant data dumped into computers will produce misleading results. There is a great need for understanding the process and for exercising judgment in application of statistical analysis results.

All of this may appear to be beyond your ability and/or interest, but take heart; you just might surprise yourself.

ELECTRONIC INFORMATION SYSTEMS

As we have suggested throughout this book, tomorrow's supervisor faces a revolution in the approach to work that has probably been unequaled by past changes. Changes in the working environment, in our energy sources and consumption, and in our society in general are already occurring at dizzying paces. One facet of this revolution is the dependence upon equipment, particularly electronic equipment. Because workers in the future will be freed from highly repetitive tasks, they will spend increasing amounts of

Any person who expects to supervise employees in the future may be required to work with electronic information systems or to supervise employees who work with these systems.

Photograph by Alan Baker, courtesy of FMC Corporation.

their time thinking, planning, and making decisions. The key resource will be information—supplied, processed, and retrieved by electronic means. An understanding of the concept of computerized information handling will be essential. There is no need to fear this trend. While they may frighten the inexperienced, tomorrow's electronic equipment will be "user friendly." A technical education will be helpful, but an appreciation of the equipment, the systems, and their capabilities will also be important.

The pace of recent developments in computers has made possible a comfortable working knowledge of this technology for almost everyone. Any person who expects to supervise employees in the future may be in a position that will require working with electronic information-handling devices or supervising employees who do. An appreciation of the speed at which this equipment works, the almost-unlimited capacity for rearranging and analyzing information, the accuracy which is possible, and the effect of human error on electronically-processed information—these are the essentials. This knowledge can be acquired with relatively little effort and expense. How? Take a course or begin a study in micro computers. Buy a computer. Combined with an ordinary television set and an ordinary cassette tape recorder, a $200–300 micro computer, available right now, has the capacity and capability of equipment that would have cost thousands of dollars just 10 years ago. These are not high-volume systems for business applications, but they work on the same principles as the huge systems—large quantities of information processed and manipulated very rapidly. Even the smallest system (including one available in kit form for less than $100) will provide an appreciation for two very basic concepts: computer speed and computer accuracy. These appreciations come with practical hands-on experience, even though initial efforts to process personal information may be as time consuming as traditional manual methods.

What else can supervisors do? Read. Books and magazines on this technology abound. Even though some of those are not "reader friendly," the following publications are recommended: 1) Alvin Toffler's *Third Wave*, which we have mentioned frequently, will give you a look into the future and the very positive and important effects that electronics will have and 2) Frank Herbert's *Without Me You're Nothing* (Pocket Books, 1980), a guide to home computers and basic computer terminology.

These publications or similar reading and some instruction or self study will permit you to test your wings with electronic equipment and should enable you to interact in tomorrow's environment.

DEALING
WITH
EVERYDAY
PROBLEMS

Our final real-world preparation deals with everyday problem solving. The material throughout this book should help you in a general way to deal with a supervisory job on a day-to-day basis. No quantity of study or training, however, will provide specific solutions to the everyday problems that you will encounter. No book can provide answers to the 101 most-asked questions by supervisors. The frustration—and challenge—of supervision comes from the daily situations which may appear unimportant or insignificant to others. For the supervisor, however, they are real. For the workers who may be involved, they are very significant. The cases which follow describe real world situations of two types. The first group is a collection of problems which have been faced and described by real supervisors. The second is a collection of situations faced by supervisors in working environments where collective bargaining exists. Each is a situation that was submitted for arbitration.

Study the cases carefully and decide how you would handle the described situations. Your instructor has recommendations and comments from practicing supervisors who have commented about the cases in the first group and from the actual arbitrators for each of the collective bargaining cases.

CASE STUDY: CODE OF ETHICS[4]

Jerry Blake and Lisle Schwartz are supervisors at Moonlight Manufacturing's distributing operation in the southwestern United States, near the Mexican border. More than half of the employees at the facility are of Mexican origin. Jerry and Lisle, though, came from northeastern states and can't claim a drop of Spanish blood between them.

The two departments under Jerry and Lisle's supervision work closely together, since Lisle's staff processes the orders that Jerry's group ships out. Jerry and Lisle work well together, though they have never been really friendly.

One day, Lisle and Jerry are standing on the loading dock going over a new order with Don, who works in Lisle's department. Along the dock comes a forklift laden with cartons and driven by Juan Pico, who works for Jerry. Because his vision is obscured by his freight, Juan isn't aware he is bearing steadily down on the two supervisors and Don, who stand with their backs turned to him.

---

[4]From "Let's Get Down to Cases" series, *Supervisory Management* (January 1981), pp. 44–45. Copyright © 1981 by AMACOU, a division of American Management Association. All rights reserved.

318

Suddenly Juan sees them and swerves, pitching the forklift over the side of the dock. The forklift is wrecked, and so are the goods, but by a miracle Juan is only shaken.

Enraged by the damage, Jerry lashes out at Juan, using the foulest ethnic slurs. "You people are a complete waste of my time," he shouts at Juan. "Is it so difficult to drive a forklift from one end of the dock to the other?" Juan tries to defend himself, but Jerry will have none of it. He suspends Juan for his "wrecklessness."

Lisle watches all this, disturbed by her colleague's reaction, which is not unlike him. In conversation Jerry freely vents his bigoted opinions about the Mexican personnel, which is one reason why the two supervisors have never been friendly. Jerry clearly prefers the non-Mexican members of his crew and makes no bones about his feelings.

Lisle knows that the union is certain to demand a grievance hearing, and that she and Don are bound to be called to give their versions of what happened. Lisle is reluctant to raise during the session serious questions about Jerry's handling of his own department, but, on the other hand, she knows Don saw what happened, too, and would feel no such pressure to protect Jerry's reputation. More importantly, she worries that Don's respect for her would be diminished if she permits an obvious injustice to be ignored.

Dismally, she begins rehearsing her answers to the questions she expects the grievance committee to ask.

Consider these questions and ask your own:

1. What questions is the grievance committee likely to ask Lisle and Jerry during the hearing?
2. Where does Lisle's primary obligation lie? To Jerry? To Juan? To the organization?
3. What are Lisle's obligations to Jerry?

CASE STUDY: THE SPECIALISTS[5]

Jackie Poster looked over her production schedules and began to feel the tension building in the pit of her stomach. Popping an antacid pill, she tried to figure out why the marketing department she headed was so far behind in getting out the promotion pieces.

---

[5]From "Let's Get Down to Cases" series, *Supervisory Management* (February 1980) pp. 39–40. Copyright © 1981 by AMACOU, a division of American Management Association. All rights reserved.

The piece promoting the company's newest line had been written in plenty of time to go to the printer. She had reviewed it herself three days before it was scheduled to be sent out. But according to the report she received from the printer, the copy had not been received for another week.

The schedule on the holiday mailing piece read just the opposite. While the copy had come out of the writer's office late, it had been processed so quickly that they were able to make up for a good deal of the lost time.

"If only the problem were consistent," she thought. "But the snarls and latenesses seem to come from everybody at one time or another. The only person I can blame for these mistakes is myself."

Disgusted with her findings, Jackie decided to speak to a few of her staff members informally to try to discover the root of the problem. She interrupted Mel, who was concentrating intently on the sports page of the newspaper. "Hi, Mel, how are things going?" she asked. "Oh, okay I guess, Jackie. Things are a bit slow for me right now as you probably noticed."

"I see. Why do you think that is, Mel? Sometimes I can barely see you under the pile of work you have."

"I guess things just come in spurts. It all balances out in the end, though."

Next, Jackie knocked on Spencer's door. The look on his face told Jackie that he was thankful for the interruption. But the mess on his desk told her that he probably couldn't spare the time. She decided to speak with him briefly anyway.

"Hi Spence, I was just wondering what you're working on now," said Jackie.

"What *aren't* I working on would be a better question, Jackie. I'm trying to write promotions for our spring line, Jensen's new project, our multiorder discount, and a few other things. Why? Is there something you need right away?"

"Not me, but you could use some help. Mel isn't doing anything right now; let me assign him something that can lighten your load."

"Jackie, you can't do that. These assignments are *my* job. Mel has his own work to do," answered Spence, now obviously upset.

"Take it easy, Spence. I only want to help move things out of this office at a better pace. Our production schedule is about as reliable as the weatherman."

"Don't worry about it," said Spencer. "I'll get the assignments done on time. I planned on staying late."

Not wanting to upset him any further, Jackie left him alone. But that evening when she saw Mel leave for the day and Spencer still bent over his typewriter, she knew that something had to be changed. Mel and Spencer weren't the only ones like that either. It always seemed that half of her staff was overloaded while the other half was somewhat idle. The time had come for a reassignment of work, but she knew that such action would be met with opposition.

The trouble with her subordinates was that they all viewed themselves as specialists in their subjects. Jackie felt that her employees had made themselves too narrow in their jobs. She had to find a way to get them to agree to share the workload more evenly.

Consider these questions and ask your own:

1. Jackie now heads a staff of "specialists." Can she change their orientation to work on a more cooperative basis without seriously damaging morale?

2. What are some of the things Jackie can do to make her department meet its deadlines more consistently?

3. Did Jackie handle her discussion with Spencer correctly? What else could she have said?

CASE STUDY: OLD FRIENDS[6]

After 12 years in the payroll office at Belken Jewelry, Margie Woerter was promoted to department supervisor. The move was applauded by her co-workers, who've known Margie for years and have a high regard for her ability.

Her relations with her staff seemed ideal to Margie when she assumed her new role. "What could be better," she figured. "I've got their respect and their good will. What could make a supervisor's job easier?"

As time went on, however, Margie began to have different thoughts. It seemed to her that her close association with her staffers made it difficult for them to take her new authority seriously. "Easy going" for Margie meant friendly and productive, but to the staff it meant lax.

Just the other day, for instance, Margie ran into Deirdre Loos, one of her department employees, in the lobby of the Belken Building at about 3:30. Deirdre was wearing her coat and carrying her briefcase; clearly she was about to leave. "What's up?" Margie

---

[6]From "Let's Get Down to Cases" series, *Supervisory Management* (December 1981), pp. 37–38. Copyright © 1981 by AMACOU, a division of American Management Association. All rights reserved.

asked her. Looking a little embarrassed, Deirdre said, "I'm just burned out this afternoon. I'd be no good to anyone around here, so I thought I might just as well pack it in and start fresh tomorrow."

It was obvious that she had planned to leave without first telling her supervisor, and Margie was more hurt by this than anything else. She felt Deirdre was taking advantage of their friendship. "Everyone feels that way some days," Margie told her. "The thing to do is ride it out until five o'clock." The moment was embarrassing for both of them, but Deirdre went back to her desk.

Most of Margie's authority problems are not so clear cut, but all of them have to do with her staff's image of her as a pal first and a supervisor second.

Naturally Margie values the staff's warm feelings for her, but she understands that, paradoxically, their warm feelings don't add up to good relations. Margie had expected when she took her new job that she might feel uncomfortable at first as she assumed the unfamiliar role of boss, but she had not expected that the others in the department would stubbornly refuse their new role as her employees. Margie wishes that the work in her department could be done in a cooperative manner, and she can't understand why rank has to become an issue at all.

The staff, however, can't adapt to Margie's new role as supervisor. The department's performance is beginning to reflect this feeling, and Margie needs some way to bring the situation under control.

Consider these questions and ask your own.

1. Is Margie's problem a common one for supervisors who have been promoted up through the ranks?

2. How can Margie insist on her authority without damaging her relations with the staff?

3. Did Margie handle Deirdre correctly?

CASE STUDY: THE CHRISTMAS "PRESENT"[7]

Christmas was in the air, and, as always, shoppers were mobbing the stores. While brightly wrapped presents bring a smile to most

---

[7]From "Let's Get Down to Cases" series, *Supervisory Management* (December 1979), pp. 36–37. Copyright © 1981 by AMACON, a division of American Management Association. All rights reserved.

people's faces, to a department store manager, they also bring headaches, complaints, increased shoplifting, and long hours.

So, as usual at this time of year, Sanford Markin, assistant manager of Tracy's department store, was up to his ears with questions to answer and problems to solve. The newest order from "upstairs" was to cut down on the amount of tissue paper used in wrapping presents.

Although he was getting slightly disgusted with all these seemingly petty details that he was forced to get involved in, Sanford realized that the tissue-paper edict was simply another measure that management was taking in trying to keep operating costs low.

Dutifully, Sanford sent down the order to all section managers to see that no more than two pieces of tissue paper were used in wrapping any package. Section managers were then burdened with the responsibility of "rationing" the paper to their cashiers.

Ellen Lane, section manager of lingerie, had been working for eight hours without a break when she received the tissue-paper edict. She took one look at the memo, threw up her hands in exasperation, and quickly made a decision: She would ignore the order. When customers paid as much as $150.00 for designer lingerie, they were certainly entitled to receive the item properly wrapped, she thought.

About an hour before the store was scheduled to close, the lingerie department ran out of tissue paper. Ellen sent one of her cashiers upstairs to get more, but the cashier returned empty-handed. "The stockboy won't give me any more paper," said Arlene. "He said that we had received our night's amount and that we couldn't have any more." Ellen looked over her shoulder to see the line forming at the cash register. "Arlene," she said, "Go over to housewares and tell them I asked you to get some paper—and hurry."

When Arlene returned with the paper, she and the other cashiers began to be more careful about how they used it up, giving only two or three sheets to a customer. Before long, customers began to complain about the "skimpy" wrapping, and the cashiers had to resume wrapping the fine lingerie more thoroughly.

When the store closed, Ellen breathed a heavy sigh of relief and headed towards the employees' exit. On her way out, she bumped into Sanford Markin. The look on his face quickly told her that the meeting was not an accident—Sanford had been waiting for her. She was exhausted, and in no mood for a confrontation.

"Ms. Lane, I'd like a word with you," said Markin. "I heard about the run on tissue paper you had over in lingerie tonight."

Even as he said the words, he felt they sounded slightly ridiculous. Was this really two adults having a serious discussion about tissue paper? Still, his conscience told him, it was his job to enforce the rules set by top management, so he continued, "What makes lingerie so special that you can't abide by the same rules as everybody else?"

Ellen's nerves were on edge, and all self-control was lost. "What makes it so special," she said angrily, "is that people pay $200 bucks for a flimsy nightgown and they deserve, at least, to get it protected adequately!"

Sanford was somewhat taken aback by her outburst, but even through her anger, he could see that she did have a point. "I can see that you're very tired, Ellen. Let's talk about this in my office—first thing in the morning."

As the two parted, Sanford thought about what he should say to Ellen the next day. Should he drop the matter as simply one of those Christmas-rush problems, or should he make something out of her insubordination?

Consider these questions and ask your own:

1. How should Sanford handle his meeting with Ellen tomorrow? Would it be best to drop the matter, or does he have an obligation to speak for top management?

2. What about the problem of wrapping delicate things in the lingerie department? Should Sanford make an exception?

3. Was Ellen wrong in disobeying Sanford's orders? How could she have handled the situation better?

CASE STUDY: ALICE IN COUNSELING LAND[8]

"Well, that does it," said Will Spear, the operations supervisor at Sunset Bank. "Bob Lewis just told me he's leaving. He's too much the gentleman to say so, but I know it's because he can't work alongside Carrie Garber any longer. Between you and me, I wish it was Carrie who was leaving."

[8]From "Let's Get Down to Cases" series, *Supervisory Management* (May 1981), pp. 44–45. Copyright © 1981 by AMACON, a division of American Management Association. All rights reserved.

Listening to Will's vented frustration was Alice McKinley, the branch manager. What Will said concerned Alice deeply since this wasn't the first time he'd reported the friction caused by Carrie's difficult personality. Alice had a vivid memory of a blow-up between Carrie and Will when he criticized a report that Carrie had prepared.

"It's about time," Alice thought to herself, "that I had a counselling session with that woman."

Because this would be her first counselling session with Carrie, Alice did everything she could to prepare for it. She listed every incident she felt was important. She put everything in Carrie's personnel folder, including the disputed report, Will's discussion of Carrie's problems with her co-workers, and Carrie's frequent latenesses in recent weeks.

Alice held the counselling session in a local coffee shop, which she felt would be neutral ground. She gave Carrie a copy of her report to read. Carrie grew quite upset as she read it and defended herself vigorously. "This is the first time you've ever said anything to me about these issues," said Carrie. "To make them a matter of record before I've had a chance to tell my side is unfair." She claimed, for example, that the argument with Will over the report came about because he had failed to provide her with essential information, which made the report worthless. "And the reason I've been late recently is because Will asked me to pick up the mail on my way in," she said, "and you know how punctual the post office is!"

Carrie had a plausible rebuttal for everything. "Bob Lewis," she contended, "left because he got a better job. I get along well with everyone at the bank—ask anyone!"

By the end of the session Carrie had grown hostile. "I sure kicked over a hornet's nest," Alice thought later. "How could I have goofed so badly?"

Consider these questions and ask your own:

1. Did Alice make a mistake in the way she dealt with Carrie, or is she being too hard on herself?

2. Was it unfair not to give Carrie a chance to defend herself before Alice's report was included in her personnel folder?

3. What are your impressions of Carrie? Of Will?

CASE STUDY:
THE DISCONTENT OF WINTER[9]

The employees at Mason Products are resentful about the long hours and little salary they receive. Their resentment is beginning to get on the nerves of at least one of the organization's supervisors, namely Fran Stabler.

Fran recently went through a bitter confrontation with Tal Winter, one of her employees. Tal found out that a new senior assistant that Fran planned to hire was going to start at a salary several thousand dollars higher than he was getting in the same job. Although Tal got a good raise the last time around, he still felt that it was unfair that his seniority and years of service to Mason Products were not valued more highly than a newcomer.

"It's not fair, Fran, and you know it's not," Tal said heatedly. "I've given you my best for years, and now I find there's been no point in it. It'll be at least a year before the new senior assistant will know the job to do it as well as I do, yet in the meantime she'll be taking home *more* that I do every week. I've got a right to be angry, Fran."

Fran could see some justice in Tal's case, but she could not convince him that her hands were tied. The personnel department at Mason was willing to pay the market value for a new employee but it had a rule about the pace with which a current employee's salary could rise. Unless the system changed, there was no way that Fran could bring Tal to even an equivalent level with the newcomer.

Fran considered taking Tal's case to personnel with the argument that the possibility of an injustice to a loyal staffer like Tal merited an exception to the rule. She decided against this, however, when one of her colleagues, Sal Toro, suggested that management might take a dim view of her end-run around her boss. "And on top of that," Sal pointed out, "you'll have everyone on your staff asking for special consideration once the word gets around."

Fran told Tal that she'd see what John Bugner, her boss, could do for him. But Bugner has a dread of antagonizing the front office and made it clear to Tal that there wasn't much he was going to do for him. So after considering his options, Tal quit.

Now Fran has a gap in her department until a replacement for Tal can be found. She's left with the bitter irony that Tal's replace-

[9]From "Let's Get Down to Cases" series, *Supervisory Management* (July 1981), pp. 43–44. Copyright © 1981 by AMACON, a division of American Management Association. All rights reserved.

ment will be brought in at a salary that was about what Tal had been asking for.

"Why is it that organizations establish rules that only get in the way," Fran complained to Sal the week after Tal left the company. "It must be some bookkeeper who thinks up these policies. How can I explain the rationale behind what's happened to members of my staff?"

The two supervisors commiserated.

Consider these questions and ask your own:

1. Were Fran's hands tied?
2. How does a supervisor cope with apparent inequities in the compensation system?
3. Would it be smart for Fran to try an end-run around Bugner next time?

CASE STUDY: BATTLE FATIGUE[10]

Willy Morrison didn't feel like doing anything today. As he sat down, he knew that it was going to be one of those days when every step of his work routine would require an act of will. He wasn't physically tired, he felt fine, and his personal life was going well—couldn't be better. Yet today he felt no enthusiasm for anything.

Rather than tackle the stack of reports waiting on his desk, Willy reached for his newspaper. With its help and that of some unopened advertisements he found in his mail, he was able to waste 45 minutes. Still unable to concentrate on his work, Willy next decided to visit Steve and some other friends in the office. By the time his tour of the office was completed, it was almost lunchtime.

As Willy picked up his coat to go to lunch, he promised himself that he would knuckle down to work after lunch. But by 5 P.M., when Willy left for the day, little more than a dent had been made in the ever growing mess of papers on his desk.

Now and then this mood of indifference settles on Willy like a cloud, usually when deadlines don't press. On those days it can be downright painful to come to work. He finds himself making re-

---

[10]From "Let's Get Down to Cases" series, *Supervisory Management* (October 1981), pp. 45–46. Copyright © 1981 by AMACON, a division of American Management Association. All rights reserved.

peated trips to the water fountain, sharpening pencils, straightening out his files—spending his time on niggling chores, doing anything other than sit down to the work that waits on his desk.

Sometimes his energy can be reignited by a rush assignment that overcomes his inertia and gets him rolling forward again. At other times it takes a day or even two days to get fed up with his nonproductive funk and shake it off. But at their worst the boredom and passivity hang on for days until the logjam of uncompleted work gets so bad that Willy has to work like a demon for a week just to get back to even. Then he laughs at himself to see how much output he is capable of, realizing how much easier he could make his life if he could fight off the periods when he feels burned out and squanders his time.

Willy's indifferent ways are only occasional, and at the bottom line don't hamper his performance or that of his department. Despite them, he still makes his deadlines, though sometimes only barely. Anyway Willy doesn't know what he could do to ward off the onset of lethargy since he doesn't know what brings it on to begin with.

"Maybe it's just as natural as changes in the weather," Willy figures. "Perhaps everyone has to go through it to give their spirits a breather."

Consider these questions and ask your own:

1. If you were a supervisor like Willy, how would you get yourself to snap out of this languor? What if you had an employee like Willy?

2. What brings on these periods of lethargy? Does everyone go through them, or just certain personalities?

3. Is a mood like Willy's as natural as changes in the weather, as he suspects?

CASES IN ARBITRATING SUPERVISOR/ EMPLOYEE CONFLICT

Where a union contract exists, the union becomes the vehicle for the employee when the employee believes that he or she has been treated unfairly. Union contracts usually spell out a grievance procedure. Supervisors are usually given full responsibility for dealing with the grievances of their subordinates. Most grievances are settled internally. Representatives of the union and management discuss (bargain) the issue until an agreement is reached.

When agreement cannot be reached by internal discussion, three options are available: mediation, conciliation, or arbitration.

Each of these involves an outsider (neither affiliated with the union nor the company). In mediation the outsider merely joins the discussion, attempting to direct the settlement to a conclusion that will be acceptable to both parties. In conciliation, the outsider suggests a nonbinding solution which either party may reject.

Arbitration involves a legally binding solution provided by the outsider—after the presentation of evidence and descriptions of the grievance from both sides.

The following cases involve real grievances which were eventually settled by an arbitrator's decision. Although the information provided here is incomplete and much less than what would have been provided for the arbitrator, there is sufficient evidence for you to form an opinion about each case. Your instructor has the actual arbitrator's decision in each case, but we encourage you to attempt to reach a decision on your own before you learn the outcome.

Although contract provisions will vary, some general suggestions for the supervisor who deals with grievances are applicable to most situations. Study the contract carefully and comply with its provisions. These may include time limits and specific procedures. Attempt to deal with employees in a consistent manner. Be sure that you understand what the employee/union wants. This will usually be presented in writing. Refrain from withholding information, discussing grievances away from the work place, or discussing disagreements with employees in the presence of other employees. Verify facts and keep accurate records of what transpires.

Above all, recognize that every issue has two sides and try to remain objective. Although you may resent the methods used, remember that employees who file grievances are people with feelings, emotions, and needs.

CASE STUDY: DISCRIMINATING EMPLOYER[11]

A week after Alison Reed gave birth, she learned that an opening for a job she wanted had been posted at work. Because she was on maternity leave at the time, she asked a friend to sign her name to the bid sheet. But Alison was not contacted by the firm. Later, she learned that she had been the most senior employee to apply and that the position had been filled by an outside person after the

---

[11]From "If You Were the Arbitrator" series, *Supervisory Management* (November 1981), p. 19. Copyright © 1981 by AMACON, a division of American Management Association. All rights reserved.

other applicants had been interviewed. She filed a grievance claiming that she had been discriminated against in violation of both the union contract and state law.

"Alison was the most senior bidder for the posted position," the union's attorney said. "If she had not been on maternity leave, she would have been given the job. Also, if she had been contacted about the job, she could have made arrangements for someone to care for her child and come back to work immediately."

A doctor's certificate was presented showing that Alison could have returned to work at the time that the posted job was filled from the outside. The union also placed into evidence a section of state law that provides that an employee on maternity leave "shall retain any preferential consideration for another position to which she may be entitled as of the date of her leave."

"When the vacancy occurred, there was an urgent need to fill the job on a permanent basis," the company lawyer argued. "It was our busy season. We had been led to believe that Alison planned to take a maternity leave of six months. We couldn't wait until she returned to fill the vacancy. Alison had not told us that she was willing to return to work immediately."

How would you decide this case?

For the union?
For the company?
Compromise? If so, how?

CASE STUDY: LOST SENIORITY[12]

Quantum Services, Inc. was having a problem with employee absenteeism. The employees were reporting to work in the morning as they should, but many did not return in the afternoon after their lunch break.

One day the company posted a notice to the effect that anyone who left the premises during working hours without permission, or who failed to return from lunch without reporting to management, would be considered a voluntary quit with no option of returning to work.

Several months after the notice was posted, Lucy Garfield failed to return to work after lunch. The next day she was told that

---

[12]From "If You Were the Arbitrator" series, *Supervisory Management* (June 1981), p. 15. Copyright © 1981 by AMACON, a division of American Management Association. All rights reserved.

she was considered to have quit but she could return to work as a new employee, without her previously earned seniority. The union immediately grieved the company's action, and the case went before an arbitrator.

"We have the absolute right to discharge any employee who, without notification, decides not to return from lunch," the personnel director said. "All employees were notified as to the consequences of such an act," she continued. "Moreover, we have the right to rehire such individuals as new employees at any time."

"The union contract provides for a warning as initial discipline when an employee leaves work without permission or fails to report back and continue working until quitting time," the union attorney said. He also claimed that the loss of seniority as a form of discipline was extraordinary.

After hearing both sides of the case, the arbitrator retired to make a decision.

How would you decide this case?

For the union?
For the company?
Compromise? If so, how?

CASE STUDY: EMERGENCY MANDATORY OVERTIME[13]

Almont Corporation's production department was operating at full capacity because of a large order from one of the company's best customers. It looked like the company would make delivery as promised until one of the firm's older machines broke down. To get the machine repaired as soon as possible—a process that might take several days—management asked for volunteers from maintenance to work overtime each day for awhile. Only two employees expressed an interest, so four other employees were also assigned to work overtime until the machine was repaired. On the first day of the assignment, however, the four employees punched out at the end of their regular shift and went home rather than work the overtime. When they were issued written reprimands the next day, they filed grievances.

---

[13]From "If You Were the Arbitrator" series, *Supervisory Management* (February 1981), p. 17.

The union's counsel argued that under the terms of the agreement compulsory overtime for repair work was limited to emergencies and that no emergency existed when management assigned the overtime. "The contract defines an emergency as conditions involving danger to personnel, product, or property. In the absence of any of these conditions, overtime is to be voluntary," he said.

Management argued that it had the right to make overtime work assignments if it failed to get sufficient volunteers to accomplish a required task. It quoted the last sentence of the overtime provision in the union contract that stated that "where volunteers are not available, the junior qualified employee may be assigned." The work was necessary, management stressed, since failure to make delivery could have affected the company's position with a major customer and endangered the jobs of 21 production employees.

Having heard both sides, the arbitrator retired to make a decision.

How would you decide this case?

For the union?
For the company?
Compromise? If so, how?

CASE STUDY: THE UNQUALIFIED QUALIFIED APPLICANT[14]

When an opening for a junior accountant was posted, Janet Clark, a clerk-typist, applied. Although her only formal schooling in accounting consisted of several courses taken when she was in high school, Janet felt she was qualified because of her past work experience and her willingness to study accounting while on the job. At her interview, Janet was told that she was not now qualified for the job, but that the company, because of her superior past performance, was willing to give her a chance if she would waive her seniority rights for the first six months in case of a layoff. Janet refused to agree to the waiver. When an outside applicant with formal accounting training was hired, Janet filed a grievance. In time the case went before an arbitrator.

---

[14]From "If You Were the Arbitrator" series, *Supervisory Management* (March 1981), p. 13. Copyright © 1981 by AMACON, a division of American Management Association. All rights reserved.

"Ms. Clark was simply not qualified for the job of junior accountant," the personnel director testified. "All previous employees in the position have had college-level training in accounting. Ms. Clark does have the potential to become qualified, but it was necessary to request a waiver of seniority rights to protect experienced employees in the event of a layoff."

"The mere fact that Ms. Clark was offered the position indicated that the company viewed her as qualified," the union attorney argued. "Ms. Clark was qualified for the vacancy by virtue of her previous experience in working with budgets, payrolls, and bills. The schooling in accounting was necessary for future advancement and was not a necessary condition for selection as a junior accountant."

At the close of the hearing, the arbitrator retired to make a decision.

How would you decide this case?

For the union?
For the company?
Compromise? If so, how?

CASE STUDY: MISCONSTRUED DIRECTIVE[15]

Several hours prior to the start of his workday, Jonathan Howell called his supervisor at Hobart Supply Company to tell him that he was not feeling well and would not be coming in to work. Later that day a problem arose, and Jonathan's supervisor tried to reach him at home. No one answered. The next two days Jonathan was scheduled to be off. His supervisor continued to call Jonathan at home but was unsuccessful in reaching him until late on the second day. He told Jonathan that he would need a doctor's statement about his illness before returning to work the next day. Jonathan complied with this directive but also put in a request for four hours' overtime for the time spent in seeing the doctor. When his request was denied, he filed a grievance.

"Jonathan was following an order from management," the union president asserted, "and he should be paid for the time spent in trying to follow that order."

---

[15]From "If You Were the Arbitrator" series, *Supervisory Management* (April 1980), p. 9. Copyright © 1981 by AMACON, a division of American Management Association. All rights reserved.

The company stated that neither past practice nor the union contract calls for payment when an employee is required to obtain medical verification of illness. Further, the request that Jonathan obtain a doctor's certificate did not constitute authorization to return to work or duty for the time spent in getting that certificate.

The company stated that neither past practice nor the union contract calls for payment when an employee is required to obtain medical verification of illness. Further, the request that Jonathan obtain a doctor's certificate did not constitute authorization to return to work or duty for the time spent in getting that certificate.

When both sides had been given the chance to present their cases, the hearing adjourned, and the arbitrator retired to make a decision.

How would you decide this case?

For the union?
For the company?
Compromise? If so, how?

CASE STUDY: PREVENTIVE ABSENCE[16]

Alice suffered from a chronic asthmatic condition, and she occasionally stayed home from work because of it. Her condition caused her a great deal of discomfort, so she was always reading health magazines and searching for any news of a treatment or cure for it. When her doctor suggested that she might benefit by receiving periodic treatment from an allergist at a local clinic, she jumped at the opportunity.

On the first day of her treatment, Alice missed five hours of work, and she requested and received sick leave payment. Her supervisor told her, however, that in the future any similar requests for sick leave time to see the allergist would not be approved. Alice promptly brought this matter to the attention of her union leader, who decided to file a grievance for her.

The company attorney argued that the sick leave provision clearly required that an employee be ill or incapacitated for payment to be warranted. Since Alice had not been ill, she was not entitled for payment under the sick leave provision.

---

[16]From "If You Were the Arbitrator" series, *Supervisory Management* (March 1980), p. 23. Copyright © 1981 by AMACON, a division of American Management Association. All rights reserved.

The union disputed the company's position, stating that the language referring to "personal illness" in the contract was ambiguous. Further, it contended, the company should have been pleased that Alice, in trying to treat her condition, was working on cutting down on the absences that her illness forced her to take.

The arbitrator listened to both sides of the disagreement and promised to return a verdict the following week.

How would you decide this case?

For the union?
For the company?
Compromise? If so, how?

CASE STUDY: HOW WORK-MEASUREMENT CAN CONTROL COSTS[17]

by Joan B. Glazer, Methods Officer
Union Trust Company; Stamford, Connecticut

America's productivity record is dismal and the outlook gloomy. Upward pressure on salaries and employee benefits will continue. What, then, can a bank do?

It can, as Union Trust Co. of Stamford, Conn., has done, create a methods improvement department to accomplish these purposes: (1) determine staffing requirements through a work-measurement program; (2) standardize procedures; and (3) improve methods by which work is done.

This was among the reasons why Union Trust's net income per share reached a record $4.49 in 1979, as against $2.31 in 1970, a 94% gain. And the bank earned more than 1% on assets last year.

Obviously, steps were taken (and are being taken) to mitigate the negative economic influences and to accentuate the positive. One of these steps was the formation in 1973 of a Methods Improvement Department, generally referred to as MIP within the organization.

---

[17]Joan B. Glazer, "Case Study: How Work-Measurement Can Control Costs," *ABA Banking Journal*, Washington, D.C.: Simmons-Boardman Publishing Corp. (August 1980), pp. 93–95. Reprinted by special permission from the August 1980 issue of *ABA Banking Journal*. Copyright 1980 by the American Bankers Association.

Results. The MIP program has had the following impact on the bank in the last seven years:

Average savings of $700,000 per year in personnel costs;

$3.50 saved in personnel expense for each dollar spent on the program; and

Bankwide productivity up as much as 45% in some departments and at least 10% on average.

The MIP program utilizes a work-measurement approach to analyze the operating efficiency of all bank departments and branches. By making improvements in procedures, personnel staffing, and equipment utilization, the program has significantly improved bankwide productivity.

What it is. Work-measurement is a productivity ratio that divides output by input. The output is the time it should take a trained employee working under normal conditions to complete a unit of work. The input is the actual time spent to produce that work.

The cornerstone of any work-measurement program is a determination of the output. How long *should* it take an average employee to complete a particular procedure or produce a unit of work? What is the standard?

Union Trust's work-measurement program uses a standard time for nearly every bank operation—based upon scientifically pre-determined time standards developed specifically for office work. The time standards provide management with an objective tool for assessing and improving bankwide productivity.

In the seven years of its existence, the MIP department has helped management achieve the following goals: (1) to standardize procedures and improve methods; (2) to determine staff requirements; (3) to schedule and distribute workflow properly; (4) to assess department performance objectively; and (5) to determine costs and help price bank services.

Analysis. Union Trust Company has 54 branches, 24 of which were once independent banks and their branches. Each merger partner approached its work differently. Not incorrectly, necessarily, but differently. *De novo* branches presented another dimension. The work-measurement program analyzed the various methods used by the 54 branches, plus 46 departmental cost centers and other units, and established standard bankwide procedures.

For many of the branches and operating departments, this was a unique opportunity to examine methods and procedures which had developed haphazardly over time. Inefficiencies, duplication of effort, and wasteful steps were spotted immediately.

The work-measurement technique of developing a standard time for all bank operations provides Union Trust the basis for determining staffing requirements for every bank department. By comparing standard times with the actual time taken by a bank unit to process a certain amount of work, the work-measurement analyst calculates the productivity ratio.

For example, if it takes a department 2,000 hours per month to process work that can be completed, according to the time standards in 1,000 hours, the department's productivity ratio is 50%. Proper staffing levels are determined based on the desired level of productivity. The optimum can range anywhere from 75% in a branch to 95% in an operating department.

Understanding workflow and customer traffic is crucial to providing quality customer service. A branch office traditionally has an uneven workflow. Activity peaks and valleys differ from branch to branch depending on location and clientele. Work-measurement analysis determines the proper full-time and part-time staff complement. Union Trust uses part-time employees liberally to "smooth out" peaks and valleys in workflow.

Reporting. Branches and departments chart their progress toward the program recommendations through monthly compliance reports. The resulting productivity index (standard hours divided by available hours) enables management to assess a unit's operating effectiveness, as compared with a dissimilar unit's.

For example, it is difficult to compare a branch's performance with a computer room's performance without some common point of comparison. The number of checks cashed does not equate with the number of programs run. But the work-measurement approach enables management to compare how well each department utilizes its available labor force in relation to each department's standards. The productivity index shows management how long certain work should take a department and how long it actually did take.

Specifics. The analysis of the bank's branches and operating departments was MIP's first task. Once accomplished, maintenance and updating were all that was required. The department then turned to special cost projects as requested by management. The unit time standards developed for the work-measurement studies provided the basis for determining unit costs.

For example, the unit time multiplied by the labor cost of that time yields the unit labor cost. When that is added to other costs involved in producing the service, a comprehensive unit cost can be developed.

Union Trust recently completed a study assessing the cost to supply its branches with cash and currency through outside sources. Working with the branch administration department, originator of the project, MIP analyzed current cash needs, developed projected staffing requirements for an in-bank supply center, and charted potential procedures. The study resulted in the establishment of a money center, currently staffed at the projected levels and using recommended procedures. The new money center saves the bank $300,000 per year.

MIP also conducted a study of the bank's copier system—or non-system, as was really the case. The bank had been functioning with a conglomeration of different equipment, some purchased, others rented, some overutilized, others underutilized. MIP's recommendations resulted in more copiers throughout the bank, but a cumulative savings of almost $300,000 in less than two years.

Steps to take. Response to work measurement is typically negative; the mere words evoke a multitude of fears.

From employees: "Will someone stand over me with a stopwatch? How can a stranger know how long my job should take? You're going to tell *me* how to do my job? Will I be fired?"

From managers: "How can anyone know my department better than I? How can I possibly run my department with *your* recommended staff? What do you mean we're running 70% effective? We work all the time!"

These questions must be answered at the outset, preferably before they are asked. Union Trust's approach to these attitudes, though not unique, was certainly effective.

First—Senior management support was visible from the beginning. It provided much of the initiative in the early studies, and strong encouragement toward carrying out study results. Today, senior management is still involved through monthly performance reports and annual personnel budget reviews.

Second—The program was carefully introduced to all department managers. A series of seminars explained the work-measurement method as a management tool for planning and controlling operating expenses, and as an objective tool for communicating with senior management.

Third—Management pledged that no employee would be terminated as a result of the study. This policy is restated at the outset of any new study. Overstaffing is dealt with through attrition or through absorption of increased workload. Economies are achieved through normal personnel turnover, without affecting employee morale.

Fourth—Management created a department to conduct the studies; this gave the program permanence, and continuity. The Union Trust analyst team was trained by a consulting firm to assure skill and to provide periodic access to additional expertise and materials. However, the consultants were not responsible for conducting the studies. It is very important for the bank department or branch being surveyed to know that, when the study is completed, the analyst does not disappear.

Further, the work-measurement department was staffed initially by the promotion of qualified candidates from within the bank. When first established, the analyst group was comprised of former auditors, tellers, and computer center personnel. Fellow employees were encouraged by this and cooperated with the analysts' first studies. A teller-line study conducted by a former teller is bound to have a high level of credibility, both to the supervisor and to the tellers. In fact, this was the case at Union Trust.

Fifth—Management stressed the importance of employee participation in the work-measurement program through the study method itself. The analyst conducts a study by interviewing the department supervisor away from the work place. Together, they analyze the department's workflow and determine the most efficient procedures for each task. During this process, tasks are often recognized as unnecessary and are eliminated. Often, procedures are streamlined. The result is a series of flow charts which visually depict each department function.

Updating. Finally, monitoring the accomplishments of each department is a key factor in the program's success. All studied departments submit monthly progress reports to the work-measurement department; these outline current conditions as compared to recommended conditions. They are then consolidated into a bankwide report, which is issued to senior management. This summary provides an effective two-way line of communication between first-line managers and senior executives.

339

Updating studies is another important factor in the program's continued success. Each work-measurement study defines the operating efficiency of a department at a point in time. Obviously, departments change. The monthly reports enable the work-measurement analysts to monitor these changes and determine the need for updates.

Union Trust devotes the equivalent of two full-time analysts to revising the 100 bankwide studies, in order to maintain the statistical integrity of the program. More importantly, though, these updates promote goodwill among the managers; they feel the studies reflect accurately the productivity of their departments.

Phases. To summarize, the Union Trust work-measurement program progressed in three phases.

The first phase consisted of surveys of all bank branches and departments. Skepticism prevailed but, because of a positive approach, employee acceptance and cooperation has been excellent.

The second phase came as managers realized two things:

(1) The studies were accurate. When managers carried out the recommendations, they found that employees actually performed each task within the allotted times. In fact, many compared the actual time to the standard time and were surprised to find employees working faster than the standard.

(2) Despite initial fears of losing control of their departments, managers discovered the studies gave them *more* control. The work-measurement process provided them with a clear understanding of their departments' operations, from a broad overview down to the fine details.

The third phase is that the Methods Improvement Department is now inundated with study requests. Department managers consistently ask for updates on or before schedule. Requests emanate from many bank areas for special projects. Before new procedures are adopted, or new bank services offered, MIP is asked to propose the most efficient methods.

Cumulative savings over the seven years of MIP's existence are $2.3 million. In 1979 alone, savings represented almost 5% of all salaries and benefits paid.

Questions:

1. How does the bank in this case define and compute its productivity ratio?

2. What goals have been achieved because of the work-measurement program over the seven-year period of its existence?

3. What did the bank use as "standard time"?

4. Find and cite an example of a productivity ratio calculation in the case.

5. What is the *productivity index* and how is it calculated? What is the value of this index? How is it used?

6. How did this plan for work measurement enable the bank to identify a $300,000 annual saving?

7. What negative employee reactions might be expected when a work measurement program is announced? How did this organization handle these types of reactions?

8. Identify the three phases of the program's implementation at Union Trust.

9. What is the average annual dollar saving as a result of this program?

10. How would you react to this type of program as an employee of a firm using it? as a supervisor? as a corporate official?

CASE STUDY: GUARDING THE NEST[18]

Sandy Miller had been with Interstate Insurance as a programmer for five years. She was well liked and naturally friendly, and people from other departments were always calling or dropping by. In past evaluations, Jack Kramer, her supervisor, had rated her work as satisfactory, but during the past few months he had noticed her output beginning to decline. Jack met with Sandy to discuss the problem. Sandy's subsequent performance improved, but two months later it dropped off again, precipitating another conference.

During this period, Sandy became pregnant. Because she had previously miscarried, she was advised by her doctor to avoid stress or excitement. Although Jack was aware of Sandy's previous medical history, he was concerned that her work was declining while her socializing seemed to be increasing.

One afternoon, several problems with Sandy's work occurred at once, and Jack called Sandy into his office. "I'm disappointed in

---

[18]Reproduced with permission from *Supervisory Management* (February 1981), pp. 44–45.

your work, your lack of improvement, and your continual socializing in spite of our conferences," he told her. "You aren't maintaining the log sheets, I had to bring your programs to the operations area and retrieve your output, you left passwords out in plain view, and you took an unauthorized 30-minute break." Sandy, surprised and upset at these accusations, got up and walked out of Jack's office, saying, "Nobody's going to talk to me that way."

Jack went to see Chuck Hitchcock, his boss. Chuck agreed with Jack's assessment and gave him his full support to begin disciplinary action. Jack held a conference with Sandy and gave her the verbal warning called for in the policy manual. Sandy had no reply. The next week, however, she delivered a six-page response to Chuck contradicting Jack's accusations. "The log sheets were being maintained—the last entry was going to be made later that day," she insisted. "The quality of my work is the same as always. The programs were going to be delivered later, and the output was going to be picked up shortly. The passwords on my desk were left there by someone else, and the 30-minute break was in fact a five-minute break to arrange lunch and 25 minutes in the ladies' room due to problems of my pregnancy."

Sandy further stated that Jack's reaction was causing her tremendous stress and could cause her to lose the baby. Unless the disciplinary action were retracted, she would file a grievance for harassment. She and her husband also threatened to sue the firm if the baby was lost unless the disciplinary action was immediately dropped.

Jack was flabbergasted when he was told of Sandy's stand. If he gave in to Sandy's demands, he know that his authority as a supervisor would be diminished, and the question of Sandy's work and socializing would remain unresolved. But Chuck had told him that top management was concerned because of the company's vulnerability in contesting a case brought by a pregnant woman.

Questions

1. How can Jack maintain his image of authority and do the best thing for Sandy?
2. Should Jack make some exception for Sandy?
3. Can Jack reasonably expect top management to stand behind him on this one?
4. How could "performance management" appraisal techniques have been applied by Jack Kramer?

5. Evaluate the nature of Jack's statements when he identified problems for Sandy. Were his statements behavior-oriented?

6. Rewrite the narrative of the case, changing the wording to reflect what you would have done to prevent this situation if you had been in Jack Kramer's position.

7. How could a performance appraisal system (we don't know whether or not they had a system) have affected this situation?

PART SIX

APPENDIXES

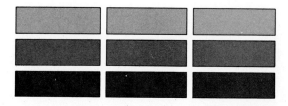

Appendix A

FORMATS FOR WRITTEN MESSAGES

This letter is typed in the *block* style.

(Organization's Letterhead)

November 26, 19--

Mr. James Roberts, Manager
General Sales Company
1432 Nashville Road
Franklin, TN 37064

Dear Mr. Roberts:

Thank you for supplying the remaining details regarding the construction of your supply building in Frankewing. Your Giles County customers will be eager to see that facility completed.

We now need information regarding two other facilities which you plan to open in the future. If you have answers to the following questions, this data would aid our coordination of activities here with the opening of your new facilities.

Will the Lascassas building be the only storage facility in Rutherford County and will you be expecting us to deliver materials to that facilty before the end of the year?

Will the Shelby Central facility replace the East Memphis branch?

We look forward to serving your new facilities.

Sincerely

Mary G. Baker

Mary G. Baker, Manager
Customer Services

lbo

This letter is typed in the modified block style.

(Organization's Letterhead)

May 6, 19--

Ms. Mary G. Baker, Manager
Customer Services
The Kyle Corporation
6390 Lancing Highway
Friendship, TN 38034

Dear Ms. Baker

Although our plans for the Lascassas and Shelby Central branch
warehouses are not complete, construction on both buildings is well
under way. The Lascassas building will be the only one in that county.
We expect to begin deliveries to that building by the first week in
December. If these plans should change, we will let you know.

The Shelby Central branch is an additional warehouse; we will not
be closing the East Memphis branch. However, these warehouses
will be no more than 10 miles apart, so we do not expect any
great increase in delivery time for you.

Gearld Stanford is supervising these construction projects, and
he will be calling or writing to you several weeks before they
are completed. The two of you can work out any last minute changes
in the procedure for your deliveries to us.

Thank you for your patience in this year-long conversion. We hope
that the final result will be smoother operations for all of us.

Sincerely

James Roberts, Manager

lwr

This memorandum format is used for most correspondence within an organization. Some firms use printed forms and refer to the message as an interoffice memo. Extensive reports may also be typed in this format—even though they might fill several pages.

MEMORANDUM

TO   Gearld Stanford

FROM   James Roberts

DATE   May 6, 19--

SUBJECT   General Sales Company Deliveries

Mary Baker, Customer Services Manager for The Kyle Corporation, is working out details for their new delivery schedules once our Frankewing, Lascassas, and Shelby Central buildings are complete.

Please report to her every six to eight weeks regarding the progress of the buildings and expected completion dates. They have made an effort to be ready for us when we change our routines, so I want to be sure that we keep them well informed.

Call me if you have any questions regarding this.

pe

Appendix B

SAMPLE FORMATS
FOR RESUMES

A brief, one-page resume.

Robert E. Ison
1223 South Hadley Hill
San Francisco, CA 94110
(415) 842-1794

CAREER OBJECTIVES

Gain broad experience in all areas of the supervision of administrative support and information systems for a progressive organization. Eventually, assume the position of Director or Vice President of Administrative Services.

MAJOR QUALIFICATIONS

Broad educational background in general education and business administration. Specific educational background in administrative support management and communication.

Extensive part-time experience in office environments. Internship experience with a manual information systems analyst.

EXPERIENCE

Part-time (20 hours per week) during college years:

Department of Administrative Support Management; Western Kentucky University; Bowling Green, KY 42101. Duties: Miscellaneous office tasks, grade examinations, supervise administrative systems laboratory.

Internship (full time, May-September, 19--) Assistant to Manual Information Systems Analyst, Ashland Oil Company, Ashland, Kentucky. Duties: Interviewing, flowcharting, forms analysis, systems documentation.

EDUCATION

Bachelor of Science, College of Business Administration, Western Kentucky University, 19--; Major in Administrative Support Management.

Associate of Arts, College of Business Administration, Western Kentucky Universiry, 19--; Major in Information Systems.

PERSONAL DATA

23 years old
Single
Interests: piano, fishing, organic gardening

REFERENCES

Available from Center for Career Planning and Placement; Western Kentucky University; Bowling Green, KY 42101.

First page of a two-page, detailed resume.

PERSONAL AND EDUCATIONAL RECORDS

FOR

ROBERT E. ISON

Personal Data

Current Address: Permanent Address:

312 East Hall   1223 South Hadley Hill
Western Kentucky University   San Francisco, CA 94110
Bowling Green, KY 42101   (415) 842-1794
(502) 748-0001

Birth Date: March 3, 19--
Marital Status: Single
Health: Excellent
Personal Interests: piano, fishing, organic gardenting

Career Objectives

Initially, to gain broad experience in the supervision of all areas of
administrative support and information systems in a progressive,
information-conscious firm.

Eventually, to assume a position of Director or Vice President of
Administrative Services

Educational Data

Bachelor of Science, Major in Administrative Support Management; College
of Business Administration, Western Kentucky University; Bowling Green,
Kentucky; 19--.

Associate of Arts, Major in Information Systems; College of Business
Administration, Western Kentucky University; Bowling Green, Kentucky; 19--.

Business Administration Courses:
    Accounting   Marketing   Business Policies
    Economics   Finance   Information Systems
    Statistics   Business Communication
    Management   Quantitative Methods

Specialized Courses:
    Programming (BASIC, FORTRAN, RPG, COBOL)   Business Report Writing
    EDP Systems Analysis   Word Processing
    Office Systems Analysis
    Administrative Support Services Management
    Records Management

Grade Point Average: overall--3.4 (A=4); major courses--3.67

**Second page of a
two-page, detailed
resume.**

```
Robert E. Ison
Page 2

                         Work Experience

19-- to 19--    Department of Administrative Support Management
                Western Kentucky University
                Bowling Green, KY  42101
                Supervisor:  Dr. Dorinda Clippinger
                Duties:  Miscellaneous office tasks, assisting professors
                  with grading assignments and examinations, preparation
                  of research questionnaires for mailing and tabulating
                  results, data entry for computer analysis, supervision
                  of administrative systems laboratory.

Summer, 19--    Internship (full-time for three months)
                Management Information Systems Department
                Ashland Oil Company
                Ashland, KY 41101
                Supervisor:  Mr. Patrick Jenny, Manual Information Systems
                  Analyst
                Duties:  Follow-up interviews for systems projects; editing
                  and typing written procedures, flowcharting manual systems,
                  forms analysis, proofing and editing systems documentation.

Summers,        Miscellaneous part-time jobs: fast foods restaurant,
19-- to 19--      construction firm, and newspaper carrier.


                         Honors and Activities

High School     National Honor Society
                Future Business Leaders of America (state officer)

College         Dean's List, Six Semesters
                Phi Beta Lambda (professional organization, business students)
                Representative to Student Government
                Data Processing Management Association
                Phi Beta Lambda Competitive Events Program--Business
                  Administration Event (first in state; third in nation)
                Freshman Poetry Award

                             References

Mr. Patrick Jenny                      Dr. Dorinda Clippinger
Management Information Systems          Department of Administrative
Blazer Building                          Support Management
Ashland Oil Company                    Western Kentucky University
Ashland, KY  41101                     Bowling Green, KY  42101
```

353

Appendix C

REFERENCES FOR ADDITIONAL READING

CHAPTER 1

Baker, H. Kent and Steven R. Holmberg. "Stepping Up to Supervision: Being Popular Isn't Enough." *Supervisory Management*, January, 1982.

Baker, H. Kent and Steven R. Holmberg. "Stepping Up to Supervision: Making the Transition." *Supervisory Management*, September, 1981.

de Grazia, Sebastian. *Of Time, Work, and Leisure*. New York: Twentieth-Century Fund, 1962.

Drake, R. T. "How Good a Supervisor Are You?" *Supervisory Management*, March, 1981.

Katz, Robert L. and Daniel Kahn. *The Social Psychology of Organizations*, 2d ed. New York: John Wiley & Sons, 1978.

Mandt, Edward J. "A Basic Model of Manager Development." *Personnel Journal*, June, 1979.

Rogers, Daniel T. *The Work Ethic in Industrial America*. Chicago: University of Chicago Press, 1974.

Sharinger, Dale H. "Simplifying the Job of Supervision." *Supervisory Management*, January, 1982.

Terry, George R. "The Supervisor of the (Near) Future." *Training and Development Journal*, January, 1977.

Toffler, Alvin. *The Third Wave*. New York: William Morrow and Company, Inc., 1980.

CHAPTER 2

Adizes, Ichak. "Organizational Passages—Diagnosing and Treating Lifecycle Problems of Organizations." *Organizational Dynamics*, Summer, 1979.

Kur, C. Edward. "OD: Perspectives, Processes, and Prospects." *Training and Development Journal*, April, 1981.

McAlindon, Harold R. "Toward a More Creative You: Creating the Ideal Organization." *Supervisory Management*, January, 1980.

Ouchi, William G. *Theory Z: How American Business Can Meet the Japanese Challenge*. New York: Avon Books, 1982.

Rasow, Jerome M. "Quality of Work Life Issues for the 1980s." *Training and Development Journal*, March, 1981.

Rendall, Elaine. "Quality Circles—A 'Third Wave' Introvention." *Training and Development Journal*, March, 1981.

CHAPTER 3

Drucker, Peter F. *An Introductory View of Management*. New York: Harper's College Press, 1977.

Haynes, Marion E. "Delegation: There's More to It Than Letting Someone Else Do It!" *Supervisory Management*, January, 1980.

Miller, George. "Management Guidelines: Building an Effective Organization." *Supervisory Management*, July, 1981.

CHAPTER 4

Ackerman, Leonard. "Let's Put Motivation Where It Belongs within the Individual." *Personnel Journal*, July, 1970.

Blum, M. and J. Russ. "A Study of Employee Attitudes Towards Various Incentives." *Personnel*, 1942.

Broad, Bruce M. "Not by Bread Alone." *Personnel Journal*, November, 1970.

"Hawthorne Revisited: The Legend and the Legacy—A Symposium." *Organizational Dynamics*, Winter, 1975.

Hersey, Paul and Kenneth H. Blanchard. *Management of Organizational Behavior: Utilizing Human Resources*. Englewood Cliffs, New Jersey: Prentice-Hall, 1977.

Herzberg, F., B. Mausner, and B. Synderman. *The Motivation to Work*. New York: Wiley & Sons, 1959.

Herzberg, Frederick. "The New Industrial Psychology." *Industrial and Labor Relations Review*, March, 1965.

Herzberg, Frederick. "One More Time: How Do You Motivate Employees?" *Harvard Business Review*, January-February, 1968.

Karpik, Lucien. "Expectation and Satisfactions in Work." *Human Relations*, April, 1968.

Maslow, A. H. *Motivation and Personality*. New York: Harper & Row, 1970.

McClelland, David C. *Motivational Trends in Society*. New York: General Learning Press, 1971.

Paul, William J., Jr., Keith B. Robertson and Frederick Herzberg. "Job Enrichment Pays Off." *Harvard Business Review*, March-April, 1969.

Roche, William J. and Neil L. Mackinnov. "Motivating People with Meaningful Work." *Harvard Business Review*, May-June, 1970.

Rodney, Thomas C. "Can Money Motivate Better Job Performance?" *Personnel Administration*, March-April, 1967.

Ross, Irwin. "The Booming Benefits of Profit Sharing." *The Reader's Digest*, August, 1969.

Sorcher, Melvin and Herbert H. Meyer. "Motivation and Job Performance." *Personnel Administration*, July-August, 1968.

CHAPTER 5

Aronson, Elliot, ed. "Making Sense of the Nonsensical: An Analysis of Jonestown." *The Social Animal*, 3rd ed. W. H. Freeman and Company, 1981.

Austin, Terence W. "What Can Managers Learn From Leadership Theories?" *Supervisory Management*, July, 1981.

Blake, R. R. and Jane S. Mouton. *The Managerial Grid*. Houston: Gulf, 1964.

Bradford, L. P. and R. Lippit. "Building a Democratic Work Group." *Personnel*, August, 1964.

"How Japan Does It—The World's Toughest Competitor Stirs a U.S. Trade Stone." *Time*, March 30, 1981.

Janis, Irving L. *Victims of Group Thinking—A Psychological Study of Foreign Policy Decisions and Fiascos*. Boston: Houghton Mifflin Company, 1972.

Katz, Daniel, N. Maccoby and N. Morse. *Productivity, Supervision, and Morale in an Office Situation*. Ann Arbor: Survey Research Center, University of Michigan, 1950.

Maccoby, Michael. *The Gamesman*. New York: Simon and Schuster, 1975.

McGregor, Douglas. *The Human Side of Enterprise*. New York: McGraw-Hill, 1960.

CHAPTER 6

Baumhart, Raymond C. "How Ethical Are Businessmen?" *Harvard Business Review*, July-August, 1961.

Brenner, Steven N. and Earl A. Molander. "Is the Ethics of Business Changing?" *Harvard Business Review*, January-February, 1977.

"Ethics in America." *Leadership*, September, 1980.

Kohlberg, Lawrence. "Moral Development and Identification." Edited by H. W. Stevenson. *Yearbook of the National Society for the Study of Education*. Chicago: University of Chicago Press, 1963.

"The Pressure to Compromise Personal Ethics." *Business Week*, January 31, 1977.

Schein, Edgar H. *Process Consultation: Its Role in Organizational Development*. Reading: Addison-Wesley, 1969.

Stone, Marvin. "Ethics—Making a Comeback?" *U.S. News and World Report*, December 8, 1980.

Twedt, Dick Warren. "Society and Management: Where Do We Go From Here?" *Administrative Management*, January, 1975.

CHAPTER 7

Caruth, Don, Debra Davis, and Bill Middlebrook. "How to Communicate to Be Understood." *Supervisory Management*, February, 1982.

Driver, Russell W. "Opening the Channels of Upward Communication." *Supervisory Management*, March, 1980.

Luft, Joseph. *Group Processes*. Palo Alto, California: National Press Books, 1963.

Pearce, W. Barnett. *An Overview of Communication and Interpersonal Relationships*. Chicago: Science Research Associates, 1976.

Pancrazio, Sally Bulkley and James J. Pancrazio. "Better Communication for Managers." *Supervisory Management*, June, 1981.

Timm, Paul R. *Managerial Communication: A Finger on the Pulse*. Englewood Cliffs: Prentice-Hall, Inc., 1980.

Quaglieri, Philip. "Feedback on Feedback." *Supervisory Management*, January, 1980.

CHAPTER 8

DeGrise, Robert F. "A Systems Approach to Business Writing." *Supervisory Management*, October, 1979.

Dunsing, Richard J. "You and I Have Simply Got to Stop Meeting This Way." *Supervisory Management*, September, 1976–February, 1977 (a six-part series).

Harrington, JoAnn C. *Easy Writer*. 3rd ed. Minneapolis: Burgess Press, 1981.

Holcombe, Marya W. and Judith K. Stein. *Writing for Decision Makers*. Belmont, Calif.: Lifetime Learning Publications, 1981.

Nichols, Ralph G. "Listening Is a 10 Part Skill." *Nation's Business*, July, 1957.

Richards, Paul. "Sentence Control: Solving an Old Problem." *Supervisory Management*, May, 1980.

Swenson, Dan H. "Write Clear Reports: A 'Readability' Index." *Supervisory Management*, September, 1980.

CHAPTER 9

Dreyfack, Madeleine. "Five Surefire Ways to Undermine Productivity." *Supervisory Management*, October, 1980.

Ghorpade, Jao and Thomas J. Atchison. "The Concept of Job Analysis: A Review and Some Suggestions." *Public Personnel Management Journal*, August, 1980.

Harvey, Frederick W. "Allowing Productivity to Happen." *Supervisory Management*, June, 1980.

"Job-Restructuring Plan Adds to Satisfaction of Monsanto Employees." *The Office*, March, 1981.

"Productivity in Most Industries Fell in '80." *Washington Report*, January, 1982.

"With Output Off Sharply, Experts Say Worse to Come." *The Courier-Journal*, January 21, 1982.

CHAPTER 10

Association for Systems Management. *Business Systems*, 5th ed. Cleveland: Association for Systems Management, 1979.

Bingham, John E. and Garth W. F. Davies. *A Handbook of Systems Analysis*. New York: Halsted Press, 1972.

Glazer, Joan B. "Case Study: How Work Measurement Can Control Costs." *ABA Banking Journal*, August, 1980.

CHAPTER 11

Dunnette, Marvin D. *Personnel Selection and Placement.* Belmont, California: Brooks/Cole Publishing Company, 1966.

Hyde, Janet Shibley. "How Large Are Cognitive Gender Differences? A Meta-Analysis Using W^2 and d." *American Psychologist*, Volume 36, No. 8.

Newgarten, Dail Ann and Jam M. Shafritz, eds. *Sexuality in Organizations: Romantic and Coercive Behaviors at Work.* Oak Park, Illinois: Moore Publishing Company, 1980.

Nichouse, Oliver L. and Joanne Ross Doades. "Sexual Harassment: An Old Issue—A New Problem." *Supervisory Management*, April, 1980.

Wexley, Kenneth N. and Gary A. Yukl, eds. *Organizational Behavior and Industrial Psychology: Readings With Commentary.* New York: Oxford University Press, 1975.

Wexley, Kenneth N. and Gary A. Yukl. *Organizational Behavior and Personnel Psychology.* Homewood, Illinois: Richard D. Irwin, Inc., 1977.

CHAPTER 12

Bass, Bernard M. and James A. Vaughan. *Training in Industry: The Management of Learning.* Belmont, Ca.: Brooks/Cole Publishing Company, 1966.

Furth, Hans G. *Piaget and Knowledge: Theoretical Foundations.* Englewood Cliffs, N.J.: Prentice-Hall, Inc., 1969.

Wexley, Kenneth N. and Gary A. Yukl, eds. *Readings in Organizational and Industrial Psychology.* New York: Oxford University Press, 1971.

CHAPTER 13

Baroni, Barry J. "The Legal Ramifications of Appraisal Systems." *Supervisory Management*, January, 1982.

Henderson, Richard. *Performance Appraisal: Theory to Practice.* Reston, Virginia: Reston Publishing Company, 1980.

Lazer, I. "Performance Appraisal: What Does the Future Hold?" *Personnel Administration*, July, 1980.

Levine, Edward L. "Let's Talk: Discussing Job Performance." *Supervisory Management*, October, 1980.

Levine, Edward L. "Let's Talk: Effectively Communicating Praise." *Supervisory Management*, September, 1980.

Nix, Dan H. "Getting Ready for the Appraisal Interview." *Supervisory Management*, July, 1980.

Rendero, T. "Performance Appraisal Practices." *Personnel*, November-December, 1980.

Schnake, M. E. "Apples and Oranges: Salary Review and Performance Review." *Supervisory Management*, November, 1980.

Yager, Ed. "A Critique of Performance Appraisal Systems." *Personnel Journal*, February, 1981.

CHAPTER 14

Bell, Robert R. and J. Bernard Keys, "Preparing for a Move to Middle Management." *Supervisory Management*, July, 1980.

Cook, Mary F. "Interviewing for the Next Rung Up." *Supervisory Management*, November, 1980.

Delaney, William A. "Bicycle Management." *Supervisory Management*, April, 1980.

Kaye, Beverly L. "Career Development: The Integrating Force." *Training and Development Journal*, May, 1981.

Kleiner, Brian H. "Managing Your Career." *Supervisory Management*, March, 1980.

Leach, John. "The Career Planning Process." *Personnel Journal*, April, 1981.

Louis, Meryl Reis. "Toward an Understanding of Career Transitions." *Work, Family, and Career*. New York: Praeger Publishers, 1980.

Phare, G. Rowland. "Career Planning: A Do-It-Yourself Approach." *Managerial Planning*, July/August, 1980.

Appendix D

GLOSSARY

active voice sentence structure in which the subject performs the action.

activity evaluation quadrant a matrix of activity types for classifying past experiences into "liked" and "not liked" and "achievement" and "non-achievement" categories.

adaptation within open systems theory, those units which are concerned with research, development, marketing research, and external change factors for the continuation of the organization.

administrative information systems mechanisms for providing the information needed by an organization's management, particularly those who manage administrative or organizationwide activities.

administrative procedures the people processing systems of an organization; the dignity with which employees are treated by the established processing functions.

adversary climate condition where two or more groups are pitted against one another because of lack of trust, fear, and concern that there is not enough wealth to go around; labor-management disputes reflect this condition.

affirmative action action taken by employers to provide jobs for identified minority groups.

apprenticeships training provided for employees who work alongside an experienced worker.

authority in management, the right to act and to require official action of others.

barrier in communication, any interference with the process.

behavioral approach the method of studying people in terms of what is done (behaviors or outcomes) rather than in terms of what the individual is; identifying psychological outcomes.

block diagram flow-chart paper drawing of methods and sequence in a procedure; uses phrases or sentences to describe major steps in a procedure.

bureaucrat the head of a governmental unit called a bureau; in general usage, one who manages for a government.

career development planning one's employment future, based upon job options and personal skills development.

career path the stages in one's employment life or route to ultimate goal.

career transition a significant change in employment status or condition.

change factor those factors of organizational age, company research and development functions, and external needs for the organization's existence.

checklist a list of employee traits against which employees are evaluated.

classical management theory theories developed by Taylor and others stressing functions (general) of manag-

ers, worker's desire for better wages.

closed system organization ruled from the top down; opposite of open system.

code of ethics standards of conduct that are formalized into a list of do's and don'ts; usually adopted by organizations or professional groups.

cognitive differences recognizable differences, particularly between groups or types of people, such as male/female.

cognitive participation level of involvement or a continuum from awareness to changed behavior.

communication common understanding, the process of sharing information, feelings, and understandings among people.

communication climate the intangible conditions surrounding communication situations; affected by rapport, attitudes, and perceived honesty within the organization.

comparative performance measure an attempt to evaluate the performance of trainees, in comparison with those not trained in a particular area.

concern for people as a leader, being employee-centered or giving consideration for peoples' feelings; being relationship oriented.

concern for production as a leader, the interest is focused on getting the job done; setting up the structure for tasks to be accomplished.

concrete reasoning in learning, relating to observable conditions or tangible phenomena.

contingency model a leadership system that takes into consideration the leader's concern for people, concern for production and supervisor power position.

controlling management function; process of evaluating and taking necessary steps to keep organization on target; set of checks and balances.

conventional stage period of moral development when the individual is concerned with law and order or society's norms as reasons for behavior.

creative gamesman description of our imaginative, flexible, and internally motivated manager that is evolving in today's organization; described by Maccoby in the book, *The Gamesman.*

criterion basis against which an employee can be measured to determine accomplishment in his or her work.

critical incidents outstanding or unique experiences as remembered by the individual; incidents may be used in evaluating supervisors.

decoder the person who assigns meaning to symbols used in a communication situation.

delegating in management, passing of authority to another; literally, to give away.

destination organization represented by the decoder in a communication process.

developmental phases concept that organizations mature much as a human does and goes through specific age periods that present unique problems to be solved; if the system does not solve those problems the organization is in trouble.

diagonal promotion movement to a higher level position in another unit.

direct supervision those interactive factors that relate to a climate of trust, task orientation, and people orientation.

directing management function; leading people; ordering processes; coordinating of people and processes.

discrimination an illegal act when race, color, religion, sex, national origin, age, or handicap are used in employment practices.

downward communication refers to the flow of communication from one person in an organization to subordinates.

EEOC Equal Employment Opportunity Commission; created by the Civil Rights Act of 1964 to oversee plans for the prevention of discrimination in employment.

encoder the person who selects symbols to represent a message in a communication situation.

entrepreneur the owners of private enterprise; the risk takers.

ergonomics the study of the effect of one's physical environment in work situation.

ethics the behavior, based on standards of conduct, that enables people to live together in a free society.

external communication communication flows from those inside the organization to those outside the organization and visa versa.

feedback communication: response, reaction by receiver in a communication cycle. learning: evidence of learning; response of the learner.

first-line supervisor first level manager, lowest managerial level in a hierarchy.

flextime plan for flexible work hours; employees report for work at various times; individuals' schedules may be fixed.

flowchart a paper drawing, using symbols and words to depict methods in a procedure; includes documents, people, and departments involved.

formal communication official communication; that done in one's capacity as an employee.

formal organization official designation of positions in an organization; hierarchy of positions.

formal reasoning in learning, an approach to problem solving using abstractions and indirect relationships.

general precepts code guidelines that identify conduct which is to be avoided.

goal setting an approach to employee appraisal and performance planning; involves setting goals for employee.

group think syndrome tendency for members of close-knit groups to think in terms of acceptable inter group norms; members begin to believe anything they say.

growth mapping identification of possible future career changes and the charting of experiences that would be necessary to achieve those goals.

Hawthorne studies productivity studies carried out during the 1920s at a Western Electric Plant to identify effect of various working conditions on performance.

hierarchy of needs an ordering of needs that indicates that humans must satisfy the more basic (primary) needs before satisfying the secondary needs.

homeostasis tendency for organisms to seek a stable state of being; state of limited change; status quo.

horizontal communication refers to the flow of communication in organizations among people on the same level in the organizations' hierarchy.

human relations era period of time during the early to mid 1900s when management took a paternalistic approach toward the worker; personnel managers became the helper for employees.

human relations movement another term for neo classical management theory; the era when this movement was developed.

human resource development label for a group of management specialists that deal in personnel training and development efforts.

informal communication unofficial communication (conversation and other exchanges among employees—not done as a function of their jobs).

informal organization unofficial relationships among employees in an organization.

insightful learning behavior change (learning) that requires perception of various possible outcomes from various conditions; beyond stimulus response behavior.

interference in learning, factors which complicate the process.

internal communication communication among the people associated with a particular organization (firm, institution, agency, professional society).

interpersonal relations era period of time during the middle 1900s when management sought to match the individual's goals with the organization's goals; done on a verbal level in many cases.

interpersonal skill skill in leading, directing, understanding people.

interrole transition employment changes involving major role changes.

intrarole transition changes which affect one's employment but do not require role changes, usually outside the working environment.

JR (job rotation) rotation from one job assignment to another during training; sometimes involves assisting experienced workers in these positions.

job analysis job analysis is the process of examining jobs to determine what is done in these jobs.

job description a document which describes a job—its functions, major responsibilities, duties, and relationships with those who hold other jobs.

job dissatisfiers those environmental conditions that contribute to an individual feeling unhappy about the work life.

job evaluation the process of assigning monetary values (usually in ranges) of specific jobs, as they relate to other jobs in the organization.

job satisfiers task or job content elements that contribute to an individual's feelings of being happy and pleased with the work life.

job specification a document which specifies educational, experience, and physical requirements.

Jo-hari window a model of interpersonal communication situations; identifies bodies of information surrounding interpersonal communication (information known or not known by various participants).

kinesics the analysis of nonverbal messages communicated via body movement, positioning, and gestures.

lateral transfer job change to another unit but at the same level of one's current job.

leadership getting others to do required tasks and believing those tasks are worth doing.

leading management function; activating and carrying out plans that have been made.

learning curve graphic representation of achievement; after multiple attempts accomplishment increases and errors decrease.

line management those in charge of a portion of the work force, receiving authority from next higher level, responsible for subordinates.

linear in describing a career path, one which is followed by employees who are seeking advancements; aggressive, confident employees.

long-term appraisal in training, the long-term evaluation of the effect of training.

maintenance within open systems theory those units concerned with personnel functions, reward systems, and socialization of employees.

management process of leading, directing, organizing, and controlling; group of people who perform this process; within open systems theory, those units that provide overall control, coordinating and direction of other subsystems.

Management by Objective (MBO) system of management requiring formal objectives for each manager, series of conferences to review progress.

management climate employee perceptions of managements standards, job security and managerial style.

management function generalizations about the nature of work performed by managers.

managerial/administrative skill category of managerial skills identified by Mandt; applies to organization as a whole; skills, activities that involve its general direction.

managerial grid a two-dimensional chart used to describe managers in terms of concern for production and concern for people; see Blake and Mouton.

mechanistic approach traditional way of viewing an organization in terms of structure and mechanics of the system; people were set in motion to best serve the system.

medium the means of conveying a message, such as conversation, letter, memo, report, phone call, etc.

message content when used to differentiate between content and intent, the facts or information in a message, the literal message.

message intent the expected outcome of a message, the reason for communicating.

method subdivision of a procedure; one step in a procedure.

methods time measurement (MTM) the process of measuring or quantifying work.

micrographics records or documents on film and the technology related to processing these records.

middle management levels of management between top management and supervisory management.

modern management theory management theory followed in most recent past; combination of systems approach, greater emphasis on behavioral sciences, and theories of past eras.

moral the judgmental basis for making a decision that may influence other individuals in your social order.

motivation individual internal energizer system with directional characteristics.

narrative evaluation in employee evaluation, a textual (sentence) description of employee performance.

need physical or perceived deficit that should be changed or satisfied.

negative reward reinforcement that is punishing in nature; systems that cause people to do things out of fear use negative rewards.

neo classical management theory management theory that emphasized people and their role in the work setting.

noise in communication, any barrier or interference in the process.

nonverbal communication without words.

norms average test results based upon the scores of large numbers of people.

OJT (on-the-job-training) training provided for employees after placement in a job.

open system organization with characteristics of a living organism; fully developed functions, structure to carry out functions; stresses balance of internal and external forces.

operant conditioning responding patterns for reinforcement or reward.

operative another term for worker; the person who performs at the basic level in an organization.

organization chart paper drawing of positions (jobs), particularly management positions in an organization.

organizing management function; establishment of effective relationships among people and with division of activity among sub-units.

orientation activities associated with introducing a new employee to the work environment.

passive voice sentence structure in which subject is acted upon (opposite of active).

performance appraisal any exchange between supervisor and subordinate which provides feedback about current and recent performance.

performance management mutual identification of expectations of employee by supervisor and employee.

performance planning appraising employee's future and identifying alternative directions.

performance review periodic formal review of employees by superiors.

personal satisfaction individual's perceptions of the rewards systems available and work related relationships.

placement situating people in specific jobs.

planning management function; anticipating the future and stipulating necessary arrangements.

policy organizational guideline for decision making; suggests permanent decision for some set of circumstances.

position power supervisor and employee perceptions of the degree of power held by leader with consideration given to the formality within the organization.

positive reward reinforcement that is an incentive for behavior; money is a reward for work performed.

post-conventional stage period of moral development when the individual is concerned with a social contract or universal principles as reasons for ethical behavior.

pre-conventional stage period of moral development when the individual is concerned with punishment and personal gratification as reason for doing what is right or otherwise.

predictors indexes of future behavior that will lead to job success.

primary (motive) motives that originate from a physical or biological basis; e.g. hunger, thirst, physical safety.

principle guide to management action.

procedure subdivisions of systems; the methods or steps involved in a complete process.

product value perceptions of internal and external participants as to the quality worth of those items that are produced by the organization.

production within open systems theory, the organizational units that provide for the primary outputs; assembly line units, constructors, builders and their immediate managements; to describe results of effort: that produced in a job; for organizations, the total value of quantity of output.

productivity a measure of employee output.

professional manager those educated, trained, and paid to manage other people or some facet of an organization's activity.

programmed learning self-directed learning involving printed or computerized instructional materials and self-analysis or progress.

quality circle management and employee sanctioned and supported weekly meeting to solve problems of a work nature; made up of 8–12 participants with orientation toward problem solving.

quality control circle a small (10 or fewer) group of employees, engaged in similar work, who meet regularly to discuss problems, pursue special projects, and suggest action for management.

quota systems in employment, a system which calls for hiring a specific number of people from minority groups; usually determined by the percent of that minority in the total population of an area.

ranking arranging a group of employees in sequence according to performance, best to worst.

rating scale a scaled (usually with five or more quantities) evaluation of employee performance on an instrument which measures multiple characteristics.

reaction survey measuring reaction to training programs by surveying those who participated.

reinforcements another term for rewards; e.g. that which is received for services rendered.

reliable as a test quality, consistency; a worker who is retested would score about the same as in a previous attempt.

reprographics document reproduction; includes printing, duplicating, and copying processes and their related technologies.

responsibility in management, the obligation to act or to be accountable for actions of others.

resume lists of personal qualifications, particularly education and work experience, for submission to prospective employers.

reward stimuli or condition that increases the likelihood that a specific future behavior will occur; a carrot on a stick held in front of a donkey acts as a reward for the animal's movement forward.

scientific management era period of time in the very early 1900s when scientific engineering techniques were used to develop approaches to obtain maximum productivity from the worker; mankind was treated like a machine.

secondary (motives) motives that are thought to be acquired by learning; e.g. need for achievement, affiliation, power.

self-actualize the tendency for individuals to fulfill their potential capabilities if given an opportunity to do so.

semantics a critical analysis of the meaning of words, particularly the changing meanings of words.

sexual harassment generally thought of as continual annoyance of females in a working environment by male peers or superiors; acts, requests, or suggestions which carry sexual overtones.

source the organization represented by the encoder of a message in a communication situation.

spaced learning learning attempts interspaced with rest periods or diversion.

span of control principle

that suggests that there is a limit to the number of people that one supervisor or manager can effectively direct.

specific code identifies specific practices which are to be avoided.

spiral a career path associated with employees who are capable of attending to several disciplines at one time; this type of employee is uncomfortable in organizations with elaborate rules.

staff management serves in an advisory capacity; officially, have little authority; in actual practice, sometimes have considerable authority.

standard a quantity of work that can be produced in some measurable expanse of time; time span is very short (fraction of a second) or expressed in minutes, hours or days.

steady state a career path associated with employees who are interested in a single discipline or employment area; more concerned about security than moving to new jobs.

supervisor the first level manager; the one to whom operatives (workers) report.

supervisory management the field of management comprised of first level managers.

support within open systems theory those units concerned with obtaining organizational

raw-materials, distribution of completed products and providing administrative services.

system a family or group of related work procedures; scope may vary from an entire organization to a collection of related activities within one unit of organization.

systems and procedures analysis analysis of work routines for improvement of efficiency.

targets positions to which one aspires.

technical/professional skill category of managerial skills, as defined by Mandt; techniques and methods used by workers in a particular specialty.

telecommunications voice, data, and image transmission using telephone lines and related technologies.

the third wave that period of transition when industrialized nations will experience the development of multipurpose institutions, emphasis on basic value issues, dominance of the data/information controllers and a new flexibility of work life.

therblig a measured basic time and motion unit that could be combined with other units to define a specific work task; coined by Frank Gilbreth during the Scientific Management Era.

time study another term for *work* measurement; quantifying time required to perform one element of a job.

top management highest level of management; may include one or more "levels" in hierarchy.

transfer ability to apply that learned for one purpose or in one place to another purpose or in another place.

transitory a career path associated with employees who change jobs and/or employers frequently.

turnover rate the percent of a work force which must be replaced in a year's time.

type model system used to classify leaders into specific groups based on personality descriptions.

upward communication refers to the direction of the flow of communication from one person in an organization to superiors.

valid as a quality in employment test, that it tests skills required in the job.

vertical promotion movement to a higher level position within unit where employee is currently employed.

vestibule training that training provided for a worker prior to being placed in a job; usually brief, pre-job training.

word processing electronic processing of written communication.

work measurement a technique for quantifying employee production for the establishment of standards; based on the output of an average, well-trained worker.

written procedure a document which describes how to perform a specified set of routines.

you attitude a conscious effort to involve receivers' interests in communications situations.

INDEX